Writing the Twilight

TRANSCULTURAL MEDIEVAL STUDIES

General Editors

Matthias M. Tischler, *ICREA/Universitat Autònoma de Barcelona, Bellaterra, Spain*
Alexander Fidora, *ICREA/Universitat Autònoma de Barcelona, Bellaterra, Spain*
Kristin Skottki, *Universität Bayreuth, Germany*
Kordula Wolf, *Deutsches Historisches Institut in Rom, Italy*

Editorial Board

Esperanza Alfonso Carro, *Centro de Ciencias Humanas y Sociales, CSIC, Madrid, Spain*
Alexander Beihammer, *University of Notre Dame, South Bend, USA*
Nicola Carpentieri, *Università di Padova, Italy*
Aline Dias da Silveira, *Universidade Federal de Santa Catarina, Florianópolis, Brazil*
Arianna D'Ottone Rambach, *Università La Sapienza di Roma, Italy*
Harvey J. Hames, *Ben Gurion University of the Negev, Be'er Sheva, Israel*
Patrick Henriet, *École Pratique des Hautes Études, Paris, France*
Konrad Hirschler, *Freie Universität Berlin, Germany*
Christian Høgel, *Syddansk Universitet, Odense, Denmark*
Daniel G. König, *Universität Konstanz, Germany*
Nicholas E. Morton, *Nottingham Trent University, United Kingdom*
Klaus Oschema, *Deutsches Historisches Institut, Paris, France*
Helmut Reimitz, *Princeton University, USA*
Joan-Pau Rubiés Mirabet, *ICREA/Universitat Pompeu Fabra, Barcelona, Spain*
Roland Scheel, *Universität Münster, Germany*
Gerrit Jasper Schenk, *Technische Universität Darmstadt, Germany*
Dittmar Schorkowitz, *Max-Planck-Institut für ethnologische Forschung, Halle, Germany*
Angela Schottenhammer, *Paris-Lodron-Universität Salzburg, Austria*
Ryan Szpiech, *University of Michigan, Ann Arbor, USA*
Daniel Ziemann, *Central European University, Vienna, Austria*

VOLUME 2

Writing the Twilight

The Arabic Poetics of Ageing in Medieval Sicily and al-Andalus

by

Nicola Carpentieri

BREPOLS

British Library Cataloguing in Publication Data

A catalogue record for this book is available from the British Library.

D/2023/0095/43
ISBN: 978-2-503-60053-6
e-ISBN: 978-2-503-60055-0
DOI: 10.1484/M.TMS-EB.5.129708
ISSN: 2983-5461
e-ISSN: 2983-547X
Printed in the EU on acid-free paper

In loving memory
of my parents,
Luisa and Giacomo

Contents

Acknowledgements ix

Introduction. A Poetics of Ageing 1

Chapter One. The Twilight of Arabo-Muslim Hegemony in the West: The Rise of Abū Isḥāq and Ibn Ḥamdīs as Political Poets 9

Chapter Two. The Poetics of Ageing: *Al-Shayb wa-l-shabāb* as a Poetic Motif 71

Chapter Three. A Poetics of Loss: The Elegies 119

Chapter Four. The Poetics of Withdrawal: Ascetic Verse 147

Conclusion 169

Bibliography 175

Indices 185

Acknowledgements

Heartfelt thanks go to my beloved wife Sarah, for her generous proofreading of this text, and for being such a star, always. Also thanks to my mentors: Bill Granara at Harvard, James Monroe at UC Berkeley, Giuliano Pisani at the Liceo 'Tito Livio'. To the late Wolfhart Heinrichs. To the many colleagues and friends, too many to mention, who helped me survive my doctoral years and the drudgery of the writing process. To the anonymous reviewers of my manuscript, who attempted to rescue me from the brink of disaster. Thanks also to Maria Whelan, for her thorough proofreading of my manuscript, and to all the editorial staff at Brepols.

Introduction: A Poetics of Ageing

From back aches to impotence, myopia to mid-life crises, hair dyes to walking sticks, nostalgia to dementia, scarcely has any aspect of getting old been left untouched by medieval Arabic poets. If verse on old age is hardly an unknown in world literature, and one may conjure up Mimnermus's sombre reflections on 'grim old age', the Arabic poetic canon is unique in its almost obsessive concern with the quest of ageing. Leafing through the *dīwāns* (poetic collections) of great Arabic poets, one finds entire poems, scattered verses, and snippets of odes that indulge in graphic descriptions of the many challenges that leaving youth behind poses. In a day and age that all but rejects senility, in which we are constantly offered remedies, disguises, and miraculous aids to avoid its inevitable onset, it seemed a good idea to devote a book to the 'poetics of ageing'.

This book is an attempt to read the late verse penned by two medieval Arabic poets as a testament to a personal and collective twilight. I will argue that, in old age, these two poets fashioned a similar poetics specific to the time and place in which they lived, that is to say, at the periphery of the Islamic world, at a time when its political unity and cohesion were dissipating, and when the peak of its cultural and intellectual florescence was on the decline. This poetics encapsulated, at once, the two poets' intimate worlds as ageing men, and their public voice as members of a politically ageing society.

The first poet, chronologically speaking, is Abū Isḥāq al-Ilbīrī, a native of al-Andalus (Muslim Spain) who was born in Elvira, nearby modern-day Granada, around 995 and died in Granada in 1067. The second is Muslim Sicily's best known Arabic poet, Ibn Ḥamdīs, who was born in Syracuse around 1055 and died in North Africa around 1133. During their long lives, the two poets were witnesses to the political disintegration of their homelands: both the Caliphate of al-Andalus and the Emirate of Sicily fell to internal squabbles for power, were fragmented into precarious statelets, and these, in turn, were to be eventually swept away by foreign powers. As the bodies and minds of the ageing poets enfeebled, so did the social cohesion around them: establishments were overturned, former allies turned into enemies, loyalties shifted, and both Sicily and al-Andalus were plagued by fratricidal civil wars in which the sword of the Muslim was more often directed against his co-religionists than against the Christian 'enemy'. While adopting different poetic personae, these two poets resorted to similar strategies to make sense of the dramatic changes they observed in themselves and in their own societies as they aged. On the one hand, they tapped into the codified themes, tropes, and motifs of the Arabic ode (*qaṣīda*) to convey their late-life reflections, their apprehension over death and the afterlife, their sorrow over the loss of their beloved ones and of their homelands. On the other hand, they reworked these codified themes adapting them to their expressive needs and bending them to carve their own poetic personae within the revered tradition of the *qaṣīda*. In so doing, I argue, they crafted a personal 'poetics of ageing' that includes, but is not limited to, three main 'poetic thoughts' (I will return to this definition in Chapter Two): the motif of ageing (*al-shayb wa-l-shabāb*), the elegy (*al-rithā'*), the ascetic poem (*zuhdiyya*). To these three main pillars of their poetics of ageing, I add a fourth, represented by the two poets' 'public poems': panegyrics and invectives through which they participated in the public life of their times. By combining these four elements, we obtain a late poetics that encapsulates, at once, the challenges of growing old: physical and mental decline, the loss of near and dear ones, apprehension over the afterlife while facing, at the same time, the deterioration of a political and social status quo. All these elements, I argue, inform a 'poetics of ageing' for Abū Isḥāq and Ibn Ḥamdīs. Emerging from these verses is a fascinating combination of a political documentation of Maghribī history and a quasi-autobiographical voicing of the anxieties these two poets experienced living at both the temporal and spatial margins.

I. Arabic Poetry of Old Age: Sources and State-of-the-Art

As they wrote about their own ageing, Abū Isḥāq and Ibn Ḥamdīs were tapping into a well established poetic motif in the Arabic poetic tradition, the so-called *al-shayb wa-l-shabāb* (translated literally: 'white hair and youth', more idiomatically youth vs. old age). The motif of *al-shayb wa-l-shabāb* gained a position of prominence after the ʿAbbāsid era (eighth–thirteenth century AD), when it became practically ubiquitous in Arabic poetry. Prior to that, Arabic poets touched upon old age occasionally, producing lines on images such as white hair which were scattered here and there but which did not form discrete parts within a poem. It was only in the ʿAbbāsid period that 'modernist poets' (*al-muḥdathūn*) began to cultivate a new taste for writing on old age, consecrating the new poetic of *al-shayb wa-l-shabāb*. In specific sections of their poems,

ʿAbbāsid poets examined their own ageing and its physical and psychological effects: bodily fatigue, a failing mind, a nostalgia for youth, or a renewed relationship with God. Such themes slowly replaced some of the quaint desert conventions that had begun to ring hollow with urban audiences. Medieval critics also testified to the appeal of the new motif, composing thematic anthologies on old age. One such anthology, *al-Shihāb fī al-Shayb wa-l-Shabāb* by al-Sharīf al-Murtaḍā (966–1044) described old age poetry as being able to 'reach the heart without a veil', ostensibly, for its capacity to forge bonds of intimacy between poets and their audience. *Al-Shihāb fī al-Shayb wa-l-Shabāb* comprises verses on old age by four poets only: Abū Tammām (805–845), al-Buḥturī (821–897), al-Sharīf al-Murtaḍā himself, as well as his brother al-Sharīf al-Rāḍī (970–1015), but still contains a vast amount of verses, over fifteen hundred, a fact which testifies to the popularity of this motif. A second work, Abū Ḥātim al-Sijistānī's (d. 869) *al-Muʿammarūn*, focused on pre-Islamic poets who lived to a grand old age. Ageing as a poetic motif was also addressed in Arabic critical works, for example in al-Mubarrad's (826–898) *al-Fāḍil* and others;[1] these will be covered in further detail in Chapter Two of this book. Outside the realm of poetry, Arabic literature provides a multiplicity of works in praise or blame of old age.[2] Perhaps one of the more singular among these works is al-Jāḥiẓ's (781–868) *Salwa al-Kharīf* (*Autumnal Comfort*), a book in the *munāẓara* (debate) style in which autumn and spring argue about their own respective merits and advantages.

Arabic poets took sides, either disparaging or praising old age, in particular when it came to its most apparent sign: white hair. Some poets lament their white hair, the harbinger of decline, while others praise it as a sign of dignity, experience, and wisdom, a warning of the transience of life and the ultimate reformer of the profligate. At times, poets voiced complaints that their white hair came before its due time because of hardships they had to endure (the vicissitudes of time — *al-dahr*). Hair dye and its uses are also ubiquitous, and they also receive mixed appraisals. Some poets considered dye a blessing (the second youth!). Others rejected it as foppish and a poor remedy against the inevitable resurfacing of the detested whiteness. In sum, the thematic panoply of classical Arabic poetry on old age is extensive. Yet, despite its importance within the Arabic literary canon, studies devoted to the theme of ageing in Arabic poetry are remarkably scant, and have focused mainly on Eastern poets. The most

[1] Orfali, 'A Sketch Map'.

[2] For a thorough survey of the theme see: Shuraydi, *The Raven and the Falcon*, in particular pp. 95–171.

comprehensive English book on the subject is Hasan Shuraydi's *The Raven and the Falcon: Youth Versus Old Age in Medieval Arabic Literature*. Shuraydi's book's scope is vast: its nine chapters cover not only literature but also aspects of sociology and cultural history. Given the prominence of the motif of youth vs. old age in Arabic poetry and poetics, and given also the prominence of poetry within the Arabic literary canon, it is not surprising that Shuraydi paid particular attention to verse. Especially useful in this domain is his treatment of figures of speech, which are a dominant trait in the usage of *al-shayb wa-l-shabāb* — a likely consequence of the development of the motif of white hair in the time of *badīʿ*'s apogee.[3] This is an important asset of Shuraydi's book, since it gives the non-specialist easy access to the intricacies of Arabic rhetoric (*balāgha*). Lamentably, however, while Shuraydi's book is exhaustive in its use of Eastern sources, Maghribī (Western) authors are almost entirely absent. With the exception of a few Andalusian poets and North African Mālikī scholars, the West remains much at the periphery of this work.

Arabic old age poetry has been the subject of two books in Arabic: Muḥammad al-ʿĪd Khaṭrāwī's *Kitāb al-shayb fī al-shiʿr al-ʿArabī al-qadīm* which examines the old age poetry of pre-Islamic Arabia, and Thāʾir Samīr Ḥasan Shammarī's *al-Shayb fī al-shiʿr al-ʿAbbāsī ḥattā nihāyat al-qarn al-rābiʿ al-Hijrī*, which focuses on ʿAbbāsid verse. Yet, no monograph to date has covered medieval Maghribī old age poetry. Academic articles on the topic are also scarce, with the notable exception of Raymond Scheindlin's study of old age in Hebrew and Arabic ascetic poetry (*zuhd*), which focuses on al-Andalus in the persons of Abū Isḥāq of Elvira and Moses Ibn Ezra (1055–1138).[4]

While, therefore, Eastern Arabic old age poetry has received some attention in contemporary and classical scholarship, Andalusian and Sicilian Arabic verse on ageing remains largely neglected. This book aims to rectify the imbalance by exploring the late verses of two medieval Maghribī poets. I will argue that much of the turmoil that shook the Maghrib in the eleventh and twelfth centuries pervades the late poetry of both Abū Isḥāq and Ibn Ḥamdīs who, as they aged, became more and more preoccupied with the political decline of Arabo-Muslim sovereignty in al-Andalus and Sicily. As they faced the outer turmoil, their inner selves emerged from these verses equally shaken: we see the poets engaging in the political lives of their communities while confront-

[3] *badīʿ* is an Arabic poetic style which flourished in the Abbasid period, characterized by innovative use of figurative language. Badīʿ is most commonly associated with the style of the 'modernist' poets (*al-muḥdathūn*).

[4] Scheindlin, 'Old Age in Hebrew and Arabic "Zuhd" Poetry'.

ing defeats and disappointments, losses of relatives, friends and lovers, and the inevitable decline of old age. All these factors converge to shape a poetics of non-resolution, contrast, and unrest. As they wrote about their own ageing, Abū Isḥāq and Ibn Ḥamdīs used the Arabic ode to encapsulate a time of collective ageing: of political and cultural fatigue whose most apparent symptom was the disintegration of social cohesion. This reading of Arabic old age poetry, albeit a simple one perhaps, has thus far never been attempted. I hope it will help to shed light on the many ways in which Arabic poetry remained a living and effective channel, by which, even at the fringes of the Islamic polity, at a time of political turmoil, Arabic writers could confront at once collective and private challenges and (as al-Sharīf al-Murtaḍā has it) 'reach the heart without a veil'.

II. Structure of the Book

This book comprises four chapters and a conclusion. Chapter One focuses on Abū Isḥāq's and Ibn Ḥamdīs's biographies, exploring, through their public verse, their active engagement in the politics of their times. This engagement takes its shape mainly in their attachment to powerful men, whom the two poets eulogized in panegyrics and public elegies. These laudatory poems provide us with precious information on the chronology of the two poets' lives, the momentous events in their political careers, and insights into their political vision and stances. Abū Isḥāq addressed the new rulers of the new urban centre of Granada, the Sanhaja Berbers, using his authority as a *faqīh* (Islamic jurist) and a respected pious man to confront the rising power of their Jewish minister Yūsuf Ibn Naghrīla (1035–1066). Ibn Ḥamdīs worked his way through the difficult terrain of professional praise, finding work outside his homeland of Sicily, first in al-Andalus and later in North Africa. The first chapter brings to the surface a major difference between the two poets: Abū Isḥāq was able to turn to his advantage both the social upheavals in his hometown and the increasing rivalry between Bādīs b. Habbūs (r. 1038–1073) and Yūsuf b. Naghrīlā. After being exiled from Granada, Abū Isḥāq eventually made his way back home and died in his hometown, as a respected member of the religious hierarchy. Ibn Ḥamdīs, on the contrary, would never return to Sicily. Regardless of his appeals to the Zirids of North Africa to restore Islam to Sicily, he had to face the reality that Sicily was forever lost for the Muslims. This disappointment made its way into his poems, to such an extent that his praises to the Zirids rang repetitive, tired, and hollow.

Chapter Two examines the development of old age poetry in the Arabic tradition, surveying the classifications of critics such as Thaʿlab (815–904), Qudāma ibn Jaʿfar (873–932), Ibn Wahb (743–813), Ḥāzim al-Qarṭajānnī (1211–1285), and Ibn Rashīq (1000–1064). The chapter sketches the origins of the theme of the motif of *al-Shayb wa-l-Shabāb* and its development at the hands of *muḥdath* poets. This chapter also includes a concise discussion of al-Sharīf al-Murtaḍā's introduction to his *al-Shihāb fī-l-Shayb wa-l-Shabāb*, which best illustrates the appeal of the motif to medieval audiences. Further, the chapter examines how Abū Isḥāq and Ibn Ḥamdīs fit in this tradition of old age poetry, examining how the two poets adopted, adapted, and reworked the tropes of old age. I interrogate how, where, and for which purpose these tropes are strategically placed within the wider structure of a selection of their poems. From this point on, my analysis focuses particularly on Ibn Ḥamdīs, since he, unlike Abū Isḥāq, who used verses on old age mainly within the restricted boundaries of his ascetic poems, reworked the tropes in more varied and creative ways. Ultimately, the chapter shows how both Abū Isḥāq's and Ibn Ḥamdīs's usage of old age poetry was instrumental to their literary and political agenda to create a mythopoeia of their homelands: Elvira and Caliphal al-Andalus for the former, Muslim Sicily for the latter.

Chapter Three focuses on Abū Isḥāq's and Ibn Ḥamdīs's dirges (*marthiyyāt*), which take up a large portion of the two poets' late production. In their old age, both poets had to confront the death of friends, partner(s), and relatives; in the elegies they devoted to their beloved ones, the poets would often reflect also on their own physical decline and their fears in the face of approaching of death. These elegies are also a testimony to the marriage of the public and the personal poetic personae that Ibn Ḥamdīs and Abū Isḥāq shaped in their twilight years: when read against the rest of the poetry examined in this book, they convey a wider reflection on personal and collective demise and in particular the demise of the world of their youths.

Chapter Four examines the ascetic poems (*zuhdiyyāt*) of Abū Isḥāq and Ibn Ḥamdīs, poems that most vividly capture the psychological and emotional states in which each of these men were plunged as they approached death. The Arabic ascetic poem, which is presented and introduced for the reader at the beginning of the chapter, provided a venue for these poets to reflect on the transience of political success, on the precariousness of life and to voice their own apprehensions about death and the afterlife. Much of the political turmoil that had altered their societies informed these late-life reflections, and the fatigue of ageing, in return, pervaded the two poets's disillusionment in the face of political defeat. Hence, the ascetic verse analysed in this final chapter emerges as a compelling combination of spiritual, physical, and political concerns that surface abruptly as these two poets approach their demise. Ultimately, this chapter problematizes the prevalent reading of *zuhd* poetry as being a form of religious fervour, or as advocating a withdrawal from the world.[5] These two poets, as public figures, were witnesses to crucial times in western Islamic history, and as such continued to be involved publicly. Their ascetic verses were in fact another facet of their relationship with their times and societies: these verses encapsulate the end of the era of political grandeur of Maghribī Islam, in the intimate tone of a confession.

The book's conclusion wraps up the four chapters to provide an overall appreciation of Abū Isḥāq's and Ibn Ḥamdīs's own poetics of ageing. The wider implications of this book extend to a re-examination of the relationship between poetry and politics in the twilight years of Maghribī Islam: even in a time of chaos and uncertainty, classical Arabic poetry was capable of remaining an effective medium to express, creatively, contemporary worldly and universal issues.

[5] Such a reading has been proffered, for instance by Francesco Gabrieli — as discussed in Chapter Four. See Gabrieli, *Ibn Ḥamdīs*, pp. 284–85.

Chapter One

The Twilight of Arabo-Muslim Hegemony in the West: The Rise of Abū Isḥāq and Ibn Ḥamdīs as Political Poets

Since medieval times, historians have been fascinated by the political, cultural, and geographical affinities between the Muslim periods of Spain and Sicily.[1] Ibn Jubayr, the twelfth-century Andalusian traveller, articulated this fascination when he wrote about Sicily after his shipwreck in Messina in 1184:[2]

> The prosperity of the island surpasses description. It is enough to say that it is a daughter of Spain in the extent of its cultivation, in the luxuriance of its harvests, and in its well-being, having an abundance of varied produce, and fruits of every kind and species.[3]

The comparisons between Muslim Sicily and al-Andalus were made in terms of environment, architecture, various aspects of culture, demographics, history, and politics.[4] Sicily shared with al-Andalus its position of being a frontier-state (*thaghr*): the westernmost stronghold of Islam against Christendom.[5] The cultural history of Muslim Sicily was also similar to that of al-Andalus in that both lands, though at the periphery of the Islamic empire, embraced mainstream aspects of Arabo-Islamic culture: literature, science, and art.[6] Iberian and Sicilian courts attracted and patronized scholars and poets, who composed treatises and verses along the same models of those of the great authors from the

[1] On the comparisons between al-Andalus and Sicily see Mandalà, 'Figlia d'al-Andalus!'.

[2] For the most recent translation of Ibn Jubayr's account of his journey to Sicily see: Ibn Jubayr, *Viaggio in Sicilia*.

[3] Ibn Jubayr, *The Travels*, pp. 335–63.

[4] Some of these aspects have been recently underscored by Granara in his *Narrating Muslim Sicily*, see, in particular, pp. 55–67.

[5] See Arcifa, Nef, and Prigent, 'Sicily in a Mediterranean Context', pp. 339–74.

[6] See Granara, *Narrating Muslim Sicily*, particularly pp. 67 and 118–29. See also Mandalà, 'Figlia d'al-Andalus', pp. 43–54.

East. They were loyal to the classical forms as much as they innovated them. It is remarkable that the main pages of the history of Muslim Iberia often find a counterpart in those of Muslim Sicily: the Muslim invasion of Visigoth Iberia at the invitation of the turncoat Count Julian rhymes with the Aghlabid invasion of Sicily, at the invitation of the renegade Byzantine general Euphemius. A 'golden age' of political stability and cultural flourishing was achieved in Spain in the tenth century, with the Umayyad caliphate of Córdoba, and in Sicily, roughly in the same period, albeit much more briefly, with the Kalbid emirate of Palermo. The eventual dismemberment of the centralized governments in both Sicily and Spain led to extended periods of civil strife during which local warlords founded their own independent kingdoms, the *taifas* (from the Arabic *ṭā'ifa*, faction). The Iberian age of the *taifas* and the stages of the Christian conquest of al-Andalus are replicated in Sicily, albeit with different protagonists and varying circumstances, with analogous results. Both Muslim Spain and Muslim Sicily had close but difficult and complex relations with their North African neighbours. The close relations were the result of geographical proximity, and of a shared population in the vast numbers of Arabs and Berbers who, after the conquest, settled in these lands. More often than not, the North Africans, and particularly the Berbers, were an indispensable resource for military service.[7] Trading routes connecting the two shores of the Mediterranean reinforced cultural contacts and ethnic mixes. These contacts are most evident in the realm of art and architecture,[8] as well as literature.[9] But in spite of the shared ethnicities, culture and population, the political interests of both al-Andalus and Sicily came to diverge greatly from those of North Africa. Confrontations between the two sides were frequent, causing dramatic upheavals and lasting repercussions in the political and social landscape of both Iberia and Sicily. Finally, in their political twilight, both Iberia and Sicily had to resort to North Africa for aid and support against the looming Christian threat.

While the tenth century saw the peak of power and prestige in al-Andalus and Sicily, the eleventh saw the collapse of centralized political structures in both lands. The collapse happened in analogous circumstances, that included internecine struggles for power, external military pressure, and ethnic and confessional infighting. These upheavals would change the face of western Islam

7 See, for instance, Fletcher, *Moorish Spain*, pp. 76–77.

8 See Carrillo, 'Architectural Exchanges' and also Dokmak, 'The use of Groin Vault Sections'.

9 See Carpentieri and Symes, *Medieval Sicily, al-Andalus, and the Maghrib*, particularly pp. 59–104.

permanently. As the familiar cast of heroes and villains of medieval Maghribī history left the stage, new figures rose to positions of prominence and contributed to the ongoing processes of political and cultural history.

Abū Isḥāq al-Ilbīrī and 'Abd al-Jabbār Ibn Ḥamdīs, the two protagonists of this book, were first-hand witnesses to the turmoil that shook the Muslim West in the eleventh and twelfth centuries. This turmoil emerges most clearly in their public poems: panegyrics, invectives, instigations, and poems of public mourning. In this first chapter, I analyse some of these public poems, which allow us to sketch their biographies and understand how both poets participated, as public personae, in the politics of their times. As I read these verses chronologically, I show how both Abū Isḥāq and Ibn Ḥamdīs developed, as they aged, a quixotic attachment to the idealized vision of the worlds of their youth. These worlds, however fictional, were rapidly dissipating around them, and the 'old' social system — caliphal al-Andalus, Muslim Sicily — was falling apart and being replaced by an uncomfortable, unfamiliar 'new world order'. Both poets celebrated, mourned, and defended their idealized visions of al-Andalus and Sicily (the al-Andalus and Sicily of their youths, that is) in their public verse, adopting similar strategies, as we will see in what follows.

Abū Isḥāq was a member of the religious establishment whose verse was centred on the ascetic poem (*zuhdiyya*), a poetic genre dominated by the themes of old age, sin, and repentance.[10] In his *dīwān*, his name is followed by the titles of 'jurist and ascetic' (*al-faqīh al-zāhid*). While the fame of Abū Isḥāq in his own time rested mainly on his religious and ascetic verses, his *dīwān* is not devoid of political poems; poems that reveal an altogether different facet of his poetic persona. They reveal how Abū Isḥāq was an active political agent in the *taifa* of Granada until the last days of his life. Especially in his old age, he participated, with harangues, invectives, and panegyrics, in the turbulent events that affected Granada in the mid-eleventh century.

Contrary to Abū Isḥāq, who wrote verses as a complement to his main occupation as an Islamic jurist, Ibn Ḥamdīs was a court poet for much of his long life. As he worked at various Islamic courts of the medieval Mediterranean (notably Spain and Tunisia), he immortalized with his verses the political life of his time, as he praised the powerful figures that gave him shelter and patronage — congratulating them in their victories, and providing consolation for their defeats. Ibn Ḥamdīs is best known for his verses of nostalgia for his homeland, Sicily. Much has been written on this topic but, in this book, I intend to present

[10] See García Gómez, *Un alfaquí Español, Abū Isḥāq de Elvira*, pp. 122–38.

a different facet of Ibn Ḥamdīs: that of an ageing man who crafted, in his late verse, a space for a personal 'poetics of ageing'.[11] The picture that emerges from these verses is that of a poetic persona seeking reconcilement with his turbulent life, a life marked by ambition, exile, personal losses, frustrated hopes, and regrets, and alternating between appeals to withdrawal and repentance, and an almost quixotic engagement with the local politics of Sicily and North Africa.

This chapter reveals important similarities in the lives of Abū Isḥāq and Ibn Ḥamdīs, who crafted their public personae in similar historical circumstances. Both were uprooted from their hometowns in their early youth and sought their fortune elsewhere: although their journeys differed in distance, the changes in social landscapes were similarly profound. Abū Isḥāq left his hometown of Elvira after Zāwī b. Zīrī's takeover, and he obtained the patronage of the chief judge Ibn Tawba in the nearby and newly-founded city of Granada. Ibn Ḥamdīs left Sicily during the Norman conquest and later found a generous patron in al-Muʿtamid of Seville, at whose court he became a renowned poet. In their maturity both poets were forced to a second exile. Ibn Ḥamdīs left al-Andalus after the Almoravids deposed al-Muʿtamid, while Abū Isḥāq seems to have fled Granada due to the dangerous enemies that his polemic verses had earned him (*c.* 1050?), retreating to the monastery of al-ʿUqāb. Both men lived to an old age. Then, they resorted to composing ascetic verses in which they advocated a renunciation from worldly pursuits, while at the same time they maintained an active involvement into the local politics of their times. This chapter will delve into the roots of this involvement, situating the lives of both poets within the political events that affected both them and their poetics.

I. Abū Isḥāq: From the Collapse of the Umayyad Caliphate to the Rise of the Taifas

Abū Isḥāq Ibrāhīm ibn Masʿūd ibn Saʿīd Abū Isḥāq al-Tujībī was born in Elvira, on the outskirts of present-day Granada, sometime in the 990s.[12] Although his biographers do not give the date of his birth, we know that he died in 1067

[11] On this topic, see the recent: Granara, *Ibn Hamdis the Sicilian* — the most up-to-date study of the Ibn Ḥamdīs's life and oeuvre. See also: Amari, *Storia dei Musulmani in Sicilia* (hereafter *SMS*), vol. 2; Gabrieli, *Ibn Hamdis*; Rizzitano, *Ibn Hamdis* in *Encyclopaedia of Islam*, 2nd edition; Sanūsī *Al-Waṭanīya fī shʿiʿr Ibn Ḥamdīs*; Shalabi, *Ibn Ḥamdīs al-Ṣiqillī*; Borruso, 'Poésie arabe en sicile'.

[12] Al-Dāya has Abū Isḥāq born in the neighbouring village of al-ʿUqāb. See Abū Isḥāq, *Dīwān*, ed. by Muḥammad Riḍwān al-Dāya, pp. 51–52.

when, based on evidence from his *dīwān*, he must have been past his seventies. I would place his birth sometime around 995. Abū Isḥāq grew up during a time of immense turmoil for Muslim Iberia:[13] in the early eleventh century, al-Andalus was plunged into a devastating civil war that ravaged the country and undermined its political unity.

The premise to this conflict can be traced back at least to the death of the Umayyad caliph al-Ḥakam II (976), when court officers took advantage of his successor's young age (caliph Hishām, r. 976–1009), and initiated a power struggle for the control of al-Andalus.[14] From this power struggle, a dynasty of chamberlains, the Amirids, emerged as the *de facto* rulers the country, while caliph Hishām was reduced to a figurehead. These Amirid 'regents' tightened their grip on al-Andalus by recruiting large tribal Berber confederations from the North African inland and by capitalizing on successful military campaigns against the Christian principalities of Northern Spain.[15] Among the Amirids' new recruits was a group of the Sanhaja tribe from central Morocco, led by the veteran leader Zāwī b. Zīrī (d. 1019).[16] Zāwī had led an unsuccessful rebellion against his brother Bulukkīn (d. 984) for the control of North Africa but, having been defeated, he had been trying for some time to obtain a safe passage to al-Andalus. He managed to cross the strait in 1002.[17] However, as noted by Richard Fletcher, the Berbers were entering a land where ethnic rivalry between Arab and Berbers was fierce, and where they were distrusted and disliked by the Andalusians.[18] Their resentment against the Berbers would eventually explode in 1009. This year initiated a period of clashes between the Berber soldiery and the citizens of Cordoba, that passed down in history as *al-fitna al-barbarīya*, the Berber insurrection (I will return to this key word, *fitna*, later in this chapter). The Andalusian faction and the Berber faction,

[13] The political history of al-Andalus has been the subject of a vast body of literature, spear-headed by such scholars as Maribel Fierro, Mercedes García Arenal, Janina Safran, Emmanuelle Le Tixier Du Mesnil, Iḥsān ʿAbbās, Alejandro García Sanjuán, Eduardo Manzano Moreno, Maria Rosa Menocal, Anna Akasoy, Hugh Kennedy, and many others. Here, I have limited myself to providing the reader with the bare facts needed to understand how the political turmoil of eleventh-century al-Andalus found a way into the late poetry of Abū Isḥāq and Ibn Ḥamdīs. Historians of al-Andalus will find that the facts summarized in what follows are well known, and can thus move directly to Section ii of this chapter.

[14] Fletcher, *Moorish Spain*, p. 74.

[15] See Fletcher, *Moorish Spain*, pp. 75–76; Ibn Bulukkīn, *Kitāb al-Tibyān*, pp. 31–32.

[16] Ibn Bulukkīn, *Kitāb al-Tibyān*, pp. 31–32.

[17] Ibn Bulukkīn, *Kitāb al-Tibyān*, pp. 31–32.

[18] Fletcher, *Moorish Spain*, p. 76.

each represented by a puppet-caliph, began fighting each other for control of Cordoba. The city was taken and lost by rival factions in turn; throughout this period, roving Berber armies rampaged across the southern provinces of Iberia, sacking the cities and the countryside.[19] Eventually, the Berber faction, strong because of the support of the figurehead Umayyad Sulaymān, managed to wrest Cordoba from the Andalusian faction. Even this puppet-caliph Sulaymān, however, was short lived: in 1016 he was deposed and executed by one of his Berber generals.[20] Throughout this period, the Berbers 'treated Cordoba as a city under enemy occupation, and instituted a reign of terror, killing and looting as they pleased'.[21] As the struggle among warring factions carried on, no one would prove capable of seizing the whole of al-Andalus, and independent city-states were proclaimed across the county:[22] the once-cohesive al-Andalus was split into smaller political entities, the *taifas*. The *taifas* kinglets, also referred to as party kings or petty kings of al-Andalus, (in some instances, they controlled little more than a city and the surrounding countryside), would initiate a period of intense turmoil in al-Andalus, as they fought for supremacy in the region, waging war against each other and swallowing one another's fiefdoms in a back-and-forth of raids and military campaigns.[23]

II. From Elvira to Granada: Abū Isḥāq's Rise as a Public Persona

Leading their people away from the rubble of Cordoba, the Berbers thus sought permanent and secure places to settle. Zāwī b. Zīrī and his Sanhaja headed to the province of Elvira, eighty miles south of Cordoba, and birthplace of Abū Isḥāq.[24] The city of Elvira, the Roman *Illiberis*, lay on the alluvial plain (*vega*) that extends at the feet of the Sierra Nevada. This region, irrigated by the two rivers Darro and Genil, is still among the most fertile lands of southern Spain. By the eleventh century, Elvira had become a thriving capital due also to its position as a crossroads between important urban centres (Málaga, Jaen, and Almeria). During the *fitna* of 1009–1013, the city had been overridden and sacked by Berber armies. Unprotected, crops were destroyed and families deci-

[19] Fletcher, *Moorish Spain*, p. 80.

[20] Fletcher, *Moorish Spain*, p. 81.

[21] Fletcher, *Moorish Spain*, p. 80.

[22] See, for instance, Hodgson, *The Venture of Islam*, vol. 2, p. 29; Ibn Bulukkīn, *Kitāb al-Tibyān*, p. 32; Fletcher, *Moorish Spain* p. 81.

[23] Hodgson, *Venture of Islam*, vol. 2, p. 30.

[24] Ibn Bulukkīn, *Kitāb al-Tibyān*, pp. 33–34.

mated, and the people of Elvira faced the uncertain times of the post-Umayyad era with increasing apprehension for their own survival.[25]

It was in this climate of uncertainty and violence that Abū Isḥāq spent the early years of his life. Abū Isḥāq was not a poet by trade: he earned his living as an Islamic jurist (*faqīh*) and worked as a clerk for at least two prominent religious figures of his time. As a scribe and secretary, Abū Isḥāq had to display a mastery of Arabic and of polite correspondence, both enshrined in the lore and language of the Arabic *qaṣīda*. In keeping with his professional persona, Abū Isḥāq's poetic persona is bound to one type of poetry, namely the ascetic poem, in Arabic *zuhdiyya*. This type of poetry, arguably the only type of Arabic poetry that we can define as properly 'Islamic' (I will discuss this in detail in Chapter Four), is centred on religious themes, on the transience of worldly glory, old age, mortality, and the afterlife. The singular thing about Abū Isḥāq, however, is that while most of his poems sound like heartfelt appeals to abandon all worldly pursuits in view of the afterlife, a small number of poems (his overtly political ones) demonstrate the opposite attitude: a fierce and almost quixotic engagement with the local politics of his time. These poems, as we will see in this chapter, were to play a major role in his professional and personal life, and in the life of his community.

A succinct collection of Abū Isḥāq's poems (*dīwān*) has come down to us. It was edited and published for the first time in 1944 by Emilio García Gómez.[26] García Gómez's edition is based on the only known manuscript of the *dīwān* (El Escorial, Real Biblioteca, MS 404). Drawing largely on biographical dictionaries, García Gómez also assembled a biography of Abū Isḥāq, discussing his oeuvre in the introduction to his book.[27] García Gómez's judgement of Abū Isḥāq's poetry seems heavily marred by the poet's infamous invective against the Jews of Granada, to be discussed later on. Thus writes García Gómez:

> this *dīwān*, of which a manuscript has been preserved in the Escorial (no. 404),[28] has been published by the author of this article, with an introduction. It is very characteristic of the limited poetical faculties of an Andalusian faḳīh of medium culture, who rises to eloquence only when expressing his intolerant fanaticism.[29]

[25] Ibn Bulukkīn, *Kitāb al-Tibyān*, pp. 32–33.

[26] García Gomez, *Un alfaquí Español, Abū Isḥāq de Elvira.*

[27] García Gomez, *Un alfaquí Español, Abū Isḥāq de Elvira*, pp. 102–13.

[28] For a comprehensive discussion of this MS, see García Gomez, *Un alfaquí Español, Abū Isḥāq de Elvira*, pp. 114–18.

[29] Encyclopaedia of Islam, 2nd edition: 'Abū Isḥāq al-Ilbīrī'.

In gauging the quality of Abū Isḥāq's ascetic verse, Dozy had proffered a similar judgement of Abū Isḥāq, when he wrote:

> Je ne sais si je me trompe, mais je crois que l'auteur du poème contre les juifs était plutôt un ambitieux désappointé qu'un fanatique sincère.[30]
>
> (I may be mistaken, but I believe that the author of the poem against the Jews was more a frustrated ambitious man than a sincere fanatic.)

We will see, later in this chapter, how some biographical details extracted from the *dīwān* may point to a series of personal and professional frustrations, which may have led Dozy to his judgment.

Yet, in his 1946 Hispano-Arabic Poetry, Nykl criticized the description of Abū Isḥāq given by Dozy. Addressing the latter, he wrote: 'it shows a great lack of understanding of the Western Muslim psychology'.[31] Nykl was, however, only able to support his attack on Dozy with the fantastical definition of Abū Isḥāq as an Arab mystic poet.

A second edition of the *dīwān* was published in 1991 by al-Dāya.[32] It contains previously unpublished poems drawn from various sources other than the Escorial manuscript.[33] Al-Dāya offers a reconstruction of Abū Isḥāq's biography which differs slightly from García Gómez's; he also provides an overview of Andalusian intellectual life in the tenth– eleventh centuries. Al-Dāya disapproves of Dozy's and García Gómez's negative judgements on Abū Isḥāq. He fashions the poet as a critic of the luxury, ostentation, and decadence which, according to Al-Dāya, prevailed in al-Andalus in the eleventh century. Regrettably, however, al-Dāya does not proffer a literary analysis of any of Abū Isḥāq's poems (they are, however, summarized at the beginning of each poem).

More recently, Raymond Scheindlin explored original traits of Abū Isḥāq's verse in his study of old age in Jewish and Arabic *zuhd* poetry.[34] Scheindlin called attention to the use of poetic dialogue and to Abū Isḥāq's personal reworking of ascetic themes and imagery, using Abū Isḥāq's verse for a study of the *zuhdiyya* as a poetic genre in the Arabic and Hebrew tradition. His discussion of Abū Isḥāq's *zuhd* poetry will be addressed in detail in the fourth chapter of this book.

[30] Dozy, *Recherches*, p. 293.

[31] Nykl, *Hispano-Arabic Poetry*, p. 197.

[32] Abū Isḥāq, *Dīwān*, ed. by Muḥammad Riḍwān al-Dāya.

[33] See Abū Isḥāq, *Dīwān*, ed. Muḥammad Riḍwān al-Dāya, pp. 144–51.

[34] Scheindlin, 'Old Age in Hebrew and Arabic "Zuhd" Poetry', pp. 85–104.

While scholarship has thus attempted to piece together a biography of Abū Isḥāq, and has investigated his work and poetics to some extent, no study to date has attempted to read his verse of old age against his own biography, and in the context of his public poems and public persona. In what follows, I intend to do just that, and thus hope to cast light on the interactions between Abū Isḥāq's public poems and his development of the poetic persona that would emerge most clearly in his twilight years.

But let us proceed in order, and inspect Abū Isḥāq's rise as a poet and a public figure. In his early youth, Abū Isḥāq must have devoted himself to the study of religion and jurisprudence (*fiqh*): what little information we have about his education points to studies in *Qur'ān* and *Ḥadīth*, Islamic law and jurisprudence, and most likely an extensive curriculum of Arabic language and grammar, all the prerequisites of the professional scribe which he was to become. He devoted his literary endeavours almost exclusively to religious poetry,[35] composing, beside that, a very small number of invectives (the one against the Jews of Granada being his most famous), praises, and elegies. Abū Isḥāq emerges from his verses as an austere and conservative figure who, throughout his life, remained close and loyal to the religious establishments and institutions of Elvira and Granada. Of his teachers, the one reported in his biographies is the chief judge (*qāḍī*) of Elvira, Ibn Abī Zamanīn (d. 1008–1009), whose works Abū Isḥāq was licensed to teach. As well as being a powerful public figure, Ibn Abī Zamanīn himself wrote poetry, also primarily ascetic in content. It is clear how the figure of the *qāḍī* exerted a strong influence on Abū Isḥāq, who, like his patron, combined his profession of *faqīh* with writing poetry. Abū Isḥāq built his career as a professional scribe and a *faqīh* by remaining close to prominent religious figures, whom he eulogized in his verses, and whose favour and protection he enjoyed both in Elvira, his birthplace, and in Granada, the city in which he flourished professionally. Moreover, Abū Isḥāq could boost his professional ascent by capitalizing on the fame that his poems earned him in Elvira. This is readily explained by the following point made by Benaboud:

> los ʿulamā' disfrutaron de una privilegiada posición social conseguida sobre todo gracias a su conducta y su saber, así como sus actividades y a su producción literaria[36]
>
> (the *ulama* enjoyed a privileged social position, which they obtained through their behaviour and knowledge, as well as through their activities and literary production.)

[35] See Scheindlin, 'Old Age in Hebrew and Arabic "Zuhd" Poetry'.

[36] Benaboud, 'El papel político y social', p. 26.

Abū Isḥāq's closeness to influential political figures in Granada is testified to in one of his early poems, dedicated precisely to Ibn Abī Zamanīn. The occasion for this praise/invective was an uprising of the people of Elvira against Ibn Abī Zamanīn. In the poem, Abū Isḥāq passionately defends the *qāḍī*, casting invectives against his rebellious fellow citizens.

Abū Isḥāq, no. 29[37]

١. رفعتُمْ على قاضيكُمُ فَخَفَضتُمُ   وحاولتمُ خزياً له ُ فخزيتمُ
٢. وطال، لعمري، ما سعدتمُ بسَعدهِ   ولو أنه يشقى إذن لَشقيتم
٣. وما كانَ إلا سِترَكُم لو عقلتُمُ   ولكنّكم عن رشدكمُ قد عمي
٤. فها هوَ ذا يقضي على رغمِ منكُمُ   فماتوا بغيظٍ واصنعوا كيف شيتم
٥. وحكّوا على ظهر الصعيدِ ستاهَكُمْ   فلن تعشُروه في العُلى لو خريتُمُ

1. You rose up against your *qāḍī*, and you've been put down; you attempted to dishonour him, and you were dishonoured
2. By my life! You prospered from his good fortune for a long time! Were he to have suffered, you too would have suffered!
3. He is but your protection, if you only had intellect! But you have been guided astray!
4. So Lo and behold! He is the judge in spite of you! Now die with your wrath and plot what you will!
5. And scrape your arses on the ground, you will not reach a tenth of his height, no matter how much shit you amass!

Abū Isḥāq delivers his attack against the people of Elvira by casting their rebellion as a brazen trespass against the benevolent rule of Ibn Abī Zamanīn. The opposition between the unruly citizens and the magnanimous *qāḍī* is emphasized by way of figures of speech such as puns (*muṭābaqa*) and paronomasia (*tajnīs*), which Abū Isḥāq deploys in quick succession, creating a closely-knitted architecture of contrasts and parallels within his short poem. In line one, opposition is obtained by juxtaposing the verb *rafaʿa*, 'to raise' and 'to rise in insurrection' with the verb *khafaḍa,* 'to lower' and 'to be subdued', in line five.

[37] The numbering of Abū Isḥāq's poems is based on *Dīwān*, ed. by Muḥammad Riḍwān al-Dāya: Abū Isḥāq, *Dīwān*, pp. 121–22.

In line two, parallels are drawn between the success of the *qāḍī* (*saʿd*) and the prosperity of the citizenry (*saʿadtum*): were he to be harmed (*yashqā*), they would also be harmed (*la-shaqītum*). Similarly, line three creates an opposition between the *qāḍī*'s virtues and the people's lack thereof (*law ʿaqaltum — ʿan rushdikum*). The use of derogatory language in lines four and five sharpens Abū Isḥāq's arrows; it also enhances the metaphorical distance between the lowly citizenry and a lofty elite of religious scholars.

Abū Isḥāq's rebuke to his fellow citizens at a moment when their insurgence was tamed indicates that this poem was not only an invective, but also a praise to Ibn Abī Zamanīn on his triumph, much in the tradition of the classical Arabic panegyric. Given what we know about the co-dependence of the poet and the patron,[38] we can understand how Abū Isḥāq was positioning himself as public defender of Ibn Abī Zamanīn, his cause, and his supporters. In praising Ibn Abī Zamanīn in this place and at this time Abū Isḥāq not only demonstrated his reverence towards his teacher, but also renewed his allegiance to the triumphant religious establishment of al-Andalus's *mālikī fuqahāʾ*. The complex give-and-take relationship of courtly praise, as it is replicated in this poem in the context of Granada's religious hierarchies, gives us a preliminary idea of how the Andalusian *fuqahāʾ* could and would on occasion act as political movers and shakers, in spite of, and even in contrast with, the local rulers.

The poem is also revealing of the intense turmoil that affected Andalusian society after the collapse of the Umayyad caliphate. As Abū Isḥāq was writing this poem, Umayyad authority in Iberia had dissipated and a period of anarchy had ensued: the events described in the poem indicate how large segments of the urban population were now quick to confront the traditional ruling classes. In Elvira, they revolted against their chief judge, ultimate representative of the *mālikī fuqahāʾ*: the old guard of religious elites. We can only speculate about the causes behind this mutiny, based on the findings on the importance of the *fuqahāʾ* as an urban class by Benaboud[39] and Fierro.[40] Fierro, in particular, has documented the delicate balance of power between Andalusian rulers, citizens, and *fuqahāʾ* in eleventh-century al-Andalus, and provided some valuable insights as to the possible reasons behind popular discontent against the *fuqahāʾ*:

[38] See Stetkevych, *The Poetics of Islamic Legitimacy*.

[39] Benaboud, 'El papel político y social', p. 29.

[40] Fierro, 'Ulemas en las ciudades andalusíes', pp. 145–53.

> el radicalismo de los ulemas podía, pues, despertar la animadversión de la población y enajenarles su apoyo. Había otros motivos que podían también llevar a lo mismo. Entre las criticas mas frecuentes a los ulemas se contaba la acusación de codicia y la de hipocresía, críticas dirigidas especialmente contra los alfaquíes.[41]
>
> (the radicalism of the *ulama* would, at times, awaken the resentment of the population and alienate them. There were other factors that had the same results. Among the most common types of criticism against the *ulama* there were accusations of greed and hypocrisy. These criticisms were directed particularly agains the *fuqahāʾ*.)

The insurrection against Ibn Abī Zamanīn may be read as symptomatic of the radical demographic changes Muslim Iberia had begun to undergo in the tenth and eleventh centuries, which Fierro illustrates in her essay on the subject.[42] Fierro's points reinforce the picture that emerges from Abū Isḥāq's poem: the delicate balance of power and co-dependence between rulers, religious elites, and urban population. Another facet which emerges most clearly from this poem is the role of public censorship which the *fuqahāʾ* (such as Ibn Abī Zamanīn and his clerk Abū Isḥāq) had carved out for themselves.[43] This role has been already underscored by Monès:

> Muslim Spain was marked out by a rigid religious consciousness that did not leave the observance of sacred law up to the individual, and insisted on setting in place what could be almost called a religious censorship of all decisions made by the state or his citizens...It is not strange, due to this, that Muslim Spain was the only Islamic land where the fuqahāʾ participated openly in the tasks of government and stood beside the monarchs to make sure that they were legitimate and that they governed according to divine law.[44]

This form of 'religious censorship', as Monès has it, carried out by the *fuqahāʾ* in Muslim Spain is most apparent in Abū Isḥāq's public poems: invectives, praises, and congratulatory odes. Let us look at further examples, the poems for Ibn Tawba.

As seen above, when the Berber warlord Zāwī b. Zīrī, leaving behind the ruins of Cordoba, sought to establish his own fiefdom, he managed to seize the city of Elvira, a once-thriving city near modern-day Granada. According to the *Kitāb al-Tibyān,* a history of the Andalusian Zirids written by a descend-

[41] Fierro, 'Ulemas en las ciudades andalusíes', p. 152.

[42] Fierro, 'Ulemas en las ciudades andalusíes', pp. 153–67.

[43] Fierro, 'Ulemas en las ciudades andalusíes', pp. 143–45.

[44] Monès, 'The Role of Men of Religion', p. 289.

ant of Zāwī, it was the people of Elvira who asked Zāwī and his Sanhaja warriors for protection.[45] In return, the Berbers were offered a generous sum and the shelter of the Elvirans' homes for their families. Although the source of this account is far from impartial, and it may well be that Zāwī simply seized Elvira for himself, it is likely that necessity created an unexpected interdependence, and that the citizens of Elvira had no better option than resorting to the Sanhaja for their own survival. But the city was strategically unsafe, as it offered no natural defences, and major roads crossed right through it. It was clear to Zāwī that the city had to be abandoned if a resistance against other belligerent *taifa* rulers was to be organized. The Berber chief laid his eyes on a small village that overlooked Elvira from the foothills of the Sierra Nevada, on the banks of the river Darro. It was called Granada. The village was settled mainly by Jewish families, and was therefore known as *Gharnāṭa al-Yahūd* (Granada of the Jews). It offered an excellent strategic location. It was positioned on a hill and had a fortress which overlooked the plain of the *vega*. Although the sides of the hill were steep, they were constituted of limestone rock, which was easy to quarry and to use in building. Zāwī addressed the Elvirans with skilful rhetoric and convinced them that their safety depended on their immediate evacuation of Elvira and subsequent relocation to Granada. The resettlement began without delay.[46]

Abū Isḥāq had no choice but to follow, but he would never forsake, emotionally, his hometown of Elvira. In the new city, he sought the protection of the religious hierarchy that he had laboured to become a member of, and attained the post of personal scribe to the chief judge (*qāḍī*) Ibn Tawba (d. after 1058). The latter was an influential figure in the newly established *taifa*. In 1055 he had the *minbar* of the Friday mosque of Granada erected and he had the bridge over the Darro river built (a portion of this bridge can be still seen today, its name referring to Ibn Tawba as Puente del Cadí).

Abū Isḥāq wrote two poems which make reference to Ibn Tawba. In one of these, he applauds the punishment of a licentious peot, Abū Bakr ibn al-Ḥājj (dates of life uncertain), who had satirized Ibn Tawba along with other *fuqahāʾ*. Ibn Tawba, a man obviously endowed with a limited sense humour, had the poet arrested and whipped. Abū Isḥāq described the ordeal in verse, praising the triumphant *qāḍī*, and reviling the poor satirist:

[45] Ibn Bulukkīn, *Kitāb al-Tibyān*, pp. 31–35.

[46] Ibn Bulukkīn, *Kitāb al-Tibyān*, pp. 34–36.

Abū Isḥāq, no. 31[47]

وكان أبو بكرٍ بن الحاجّ قد هجا أبا الحسن أبن توبة وجماعة من الفقهاء معه، فضربه ضربا وجيعاً، وطِيفَ به على الأسواق، فقال ابن مسعود -رضي الله عنه - في ذلك:

١. السّوط أبلغُ مِن قالٍ ومن قِيل	ومن نباحِ سقيهِ بالأباطيل
٢. مُرُّ المَذاقِ كحرِّ النار أبرده	يُعقّلُ المُتَعاطي أيَّ تَعقيلِ
٣. رأى مِنَ الطِّبِّ ما بُقراطُ لم يرهُ	في بُرء كلِّ سخيفِ العقلِ مخذولِ
٤. ضئيلُ جسمٍ تخافُ الخَيلُ سَطْوَتَهُ	أعْدَى وأطغَى مِنَ التِّمساحِ في النِّيلِ
٥. يُرَقِّصُ المَرءَ ترقيصاً بلا طَربٍ	لو كانَ أثقلَ أو أجسَى مِنَ الفيل
٦. عِند السخيفِ به خبرٌ وتَجربةٌ	فقَد رمى تحتهُ ماعُدَّ بالفُولِ
٧. وقد حسا منهُ أمرَقاً مُفلْفَلَةً	جشَّتْهُ شرَّ الجشَا مِنْ شَرِّ مأْكُلِ
٨. وقَد هجاهُ بهَجوٍ مُؤلِمٍ وجعٌ	لا يُشبِهُ الشّعْرَ في نَظْمٍ وتفْصيلِ

Abū Bakr ibn al-Ḥājj had satirized the *qāḍī* Abū al-Ḥasan ibn Tawba and a group of fuqahāʾ along with him. He had him beaten up, flogged and then paraded in the city markets. Ibn Masʿūd [i.e. Abū Isḥāq] wrote about this [event]:

1. The whip is more eloquent than words, and [more eloquent] than the lies of a shameless man!
2. Its taste is bitter and its coldest part burns like fire, it brings to his senses — in what a way! — the one who receives it.
3. It knows more medicine than Hippocrates when curing a dim-witted man.
4. Although it is thin-bodied, even horses fear its strength, and it is more ferocious and terrifying than a caiman from the Nile
5. It makes a man dance without music, even if he were heavier or more thick-skinned than an elephant.
6. A silly man will find knowledge and experience in it, as under it he spills [blood drops as thick as] beans
7. From it, he sipped a spicy broth, he has had bad burps from bad food!

[47] Abū Isḥāq, *Dīwān*, ed. by Muḥammad Riḍwān al-Dāya, pp. 124–27.

8. Pain lampooned him with a painful invective, equal to no poem in metre or imagery

The poem stands out immediately for its vividly graphic account of the satirist's ordeal. Notably, the opening line borrows from the famous panegyric by Abū Tammām to the caliph al-Muʿtasim (r. 833–842):

السيفُ أصدقُ إنباءً منَ الكُتُبِ   في حدهِ الحدُّ بينَ الجدِّ واللعبِ[48]

> The sword is more truthful than books; on its edge is the limit between what's serious and what's idle.

The reference to Abū Tammām's famous line enhances Abū Isḥāq's message: to dignify his patron Ibn Tawba by associating him with the figure of the caliph (and, in passing, to associate himself with none other than Abū Tammām!). Such intertextuality would not be lost on Ibn Tawba, a learned scholar himself, nor on a highly literate public well-versed in poetry. In the poem's next section (lines nine to eleven), Abū Isḥāq revels in the description of the poet's public chastisement, and sends out an implicit warning to anyone who would dare to defy the religious elite: Ibn al-Ḥājj's whipping is fashioned into a cautionary tale for those who would dare attacking the privileges of the religious caste.

٩. فقل لَه إنْ جرى هجوٌ بخاطرِهِ   اذكُرْ قِيامَكَ مَحْلولَ الّسّراويلِ
١٠. واذْكُرْ طَوافَكَ في الأسواقِ مُفْتَضِحا   مُجَرَّداً خاشعاً في ذُلِّ مَعْزُولِ
١١. واذكُرْ عقوبةَ ما زَوَّرتَهُ سَفهاً   في السَّادَةِ القادةِ الشُّمَّ البَهاليلِ
١٢. عصاذَةٌ عظَّمَ الرَّحْمنُ حُرمَتَها   وخصَّها مِنهُ إكراماً بِتبْجيلِ
١٣. هُمُ لوبَابُ الوَرَى حقاً وغَيْرُهُم   عندَ الحَقيقَةِ أبْقالُ الغَرابيلِ
١٤. إنَّ ابنَ توبةَ فيهم رافعٌ علماً   منَ القضاء ومُمْتازٌ بإكليل
١٥. قضى بِتَنْكِيل من لم يَرْعَ حَقَّهُمُ   وحصَّنَ الحُكْمَ في هذا بتَسجيلِ
١٦. الظَّهْرُ قِرطاسُهُ والسّوطُ يطْلُبهُ   بِئسَ الكتابُ بعَقْدٍ غيرِ مَحْلُولِ

9. Tell him, if ever a satire crosses his mind: remember when you stood with your trousers lowered!

10. Remember walking through the market, shamed, naked, head bowed, scorned like a leper!

[48] Abū Tammām, *Dīwān* I, p. 47–79.

11. Remember your punishment for having foolishly insulted the lord judges and great leaders!
12. Men on whom the Merciful has bestowed the greatest stature, granting them a reverence with which they are honoured
13. Verily, they are of the finest grain of humankind, and the rest, in truth, are but the bran left in the sieve
14. Among them, Ibn Tawba is the flag of command, raised high, and their crown, magnificent!
15. He ordered punishment for those who did not care for their right, and has fortified this order with his seal
16. The man's back is his paper, the whip is yearning for it; a miserable book in return for a permanent inscription.

Abū Isḥāq uses the occasion of Ibn al-Ḥājj's chastisement to deliver a praise (*madīḥ*), cast an invective (*hijā'*), and issue a warning (*taḥdhīr*) at at the same time. In line nine the poet admonishes the sharp-tongued satirist, and, with him, all those who would dare speak out against Ibn Tawba's position. As a member of the Andalusian religious establishment, the poet stands up to defend the caste. Much in keeping with the tradition of the Arabic panegyric, he uses his verse to praise and defend his patron, and, with him, the rarefied society to which he himself belongs. We see Abū Isḥāq exerting a function that had been a privilege of the Iberian *fuqahā'* for over two centuries, according to Monès's statement quoted above. However, it seems, these privileges did not go unchallenged. Elaborating on Fierro's argumentations, we can imagine that the subordinate classes in Granada, once delivered of the yoke of the old rule represented by the Umayyad authority (an authority which went hand in hand with that of the religious hierarchy of the Andalusian *mālikī fuqahā'*) felt emboldened to confront these directly. The case of Ibn al-Ḥājj may be read as one example. We can also read more into into Abū Isḥāq's staunch invective against the poet. In his warning against those who dare taking lightly the authority of Ibn Tawba and his peers, we see the poet/*faqīh* exerting efforts to win over the population, rallying the Arab-Andalusians around the religious caste in a new city where the traditional roles of authority had been overturned by Zāwī's bold move. The situation in Granada after the dismantling of Elvira was thus one of political adjustment, a transitional moment that facilitated power struggles for the control of the high posts in administration. While satires and invective against the powerful were surely not an exception in Umayyad al-Andalus, the jokes of Ibn al-Ḥājj in this place and time may be read as a symptom of something bigger: a growing resentment against the traditional ruling elites, who, at this time, used repression and the voice of propaganda (poetry, in this case) to reaffirm their station and privileges.

Abū Isḥāq's poem above may be read as a testament to this period of political uncertainty, which would bring about new challenges for him and his immediate entourage — the *fuqahāʾ* of Granada-. This transitional moment is encapsulated in yet another ode by Abū Isḥāq: his elegy to the city of Elvira. This is virtually the only direct poetic testament by Abū Isḥāq of the turmoil experienced by al-Andalus in the immediate aftermath of the Berber fitna. We can speculate that Abū Isḥāq used the occasion of Zāwī's forcible displacement of the the citizens of Elvira to Granada to write this ode to his hometown.

Borrowing imagery from the pre-Islamic *qaṣīda* and loyal to the Andalusian tradition of *rithāʾ al-mudun*, Abū Isḥāq crafted an elaborate praise for the city. Subtly, he also hinted at the Umayyad Caliphate as the ultimate and lost symbol of the glory of Islam in Iberia. The ode, consisting of twenty-three lines, opens with an accusation against the citizens of Elvira for too readily forsaking their hometown.

Abū Isḥāq, no. 20[49]

١. يصنَّــعُ مَفــروضٌ ويُغفَــلُ واجــبُ   وإنِّــي علــى أهــلِ الزَّمــانِ لَعاتــبُ
٢. أتُنْــدبُ أطــلالُ البــلادِ ولا يُــرى   لإلبيــرَةٍ منهُــمْ علــى الأرضِ نــادِبُ
٣. علــى أنهــا شــمسُ البــلادِ وأُنسُــها   وكلُّ سِــواها وَحشَــةٌ وَغياهِــبُ

1. A [religious] obligation has been breached and a [moral] duty has been neglected, and I stand pointing an accusing finger at those who live in my time
2. Will the ruins of the country be mourned, while not a single man among them is seen mourning Elvira?
3. But she was the sun of the land and its comfort, while all other [places] are desolation and darkness!

With his elegy to his lost hometown, Abū Isḥāq adds his name to the authors of elegies to fallen cities that, particularly in al-Andalus, multiplied from the end of the tenth century onwards, as the pressure of the Christian offensive became more tangible. It is compelling to read Abū Isḥāq's 'Elegy to Elvira' in

[49] Abū Isḥāq, *Dīwān*, ed. by Muḥammad Riḍwān al-Dāya, pp. 85–88.

juxtaposition with another, famous elegy to an Andalusian city, namely Ibn Shuhayd's (d. *c.* 1035)'Elegy to Cordoba', in order to flesh out some of its formal and semantic cornerstones. In his study of Ibn Shuhayd's famous elegy, Alexander Elinson perceptively underscored how Ibn Shuhayd used the first person almost 'reluctantly' and 'cautiously', giving prominence to Cordoba and to the communal mourning of its demise, rather than to the poetic voice. Elinson underscores how the distinctive feature of the elegy is its focus on the deceased or, in this case, on the fallen city; the poetic persona, in the elegy, must remain in the background. In Elinson's words:

> The focus of the rithā' is of course the destroyed Cordoba. Therefore it is natural for the poet to cede attention to the city. Nonetheless, the poet's importance as a spokesperson and elegist is undeniable. Without the poet, there is no poem, and without the poem, Cordoba ceases to exist. So it is from this verse on that Ibn Shuhayd cautiously shares a little space with Cordoba. I say cautiously because the verbal agency of the poet fades as quickly as it came...[50]

Only at the very end of his elegy Ibn Shuhayd does use the first person in order to metaphorically step into the poem. The architecture of the poem starts with the city and closes in on the lone voice of the poet, which fades as quickly as it came. Abū Isḥāq's poem reverses this architecture entirely, calling attention on himself in the poem's very opening. The particle '*inna*' coupled with the first person pronoun foregrounds his poetic persona: Abū Isḥāq is the sole mourner of the otherwise forgotten Elvira. Loyal to his moralizing poetic persona, the poet posits himself as the censor (*ʿātib*) of his contemporaries (*ahl al-zamān*) who have failed to keep alive the memory of Elvira; he posits himself as the lone mourner for the fallen city.

The poem opens with a striking juxtaposition of Islamic lexicon with pre-Islamic lore. Line one evokes an unequivocally Islamic milieu, associating memory with a religious obligation (*farḍ*), as if Abū Isḥāq was capitalizing on his position of *faqīh* to reinforce his accusations against his forgetful fellow citizens. Line two reiterates such accusations, this time by tapping into the pre-Islamic *aṭlāl* motif. The poet is metaphorically standing alone over the ruins of his hometown, which he addresses using the highly evocative term *aṭlāl* — the vestiges of an abandoned encampment whose contemplation customarily opens the Arabian ode. Abū Isḥāq's choice of lexicon in this line is aimed to enshrine his lost hometown within the revered lore of the *qaṣīda*, building a literary memorial that sacralizes the city through both religious and poetic lan-

[50] Elinson, 'Loss Written in Stone', p. 106.

guage. The poet's emotional isolation, which pervades the pre-Islamic *nasīb*, is reinforced through the passive verbs of line two (*yurā*, *tundab*): other cities are mourned, and yet no-one will commemorate Elvira. We find in these initial lines a double-edged invective against the *ahl al-zamān*, the poet's contemporaries, who chose to forget and fail to commemorate Elvira. By deploying the Islamic lexicon on the one hand and pre-Islamic tropes on the other, Abū Isḥāq attacks his fellow-countrymen by aiming at their core values: Islam and 'arabness'. Forgetting Elvira is at once a breach in the shared values of Islam and of tribal coherence: a symptom of the decadence which Abū Isḥāq, as we will see, associated with the new world order of the *taifas*. The word *al-balad* (line two), is particularly telling in this sense. It implies a meaning larger than Elvira itself: namely, al-Andalus in its entirety. Al-Andalus is effaced, and poets left weeping (*tundab*) over its vestiges (*aṭlāl*). This line conveys Abū Isḥāq's outrage in witnessing the downfall of a cohesive, united, highly accomplished world at the onslaught of a new political order, an outrage that is only increased by the cowardice and complacency he sees in his fellow citizens. These two opening lines also project the poetic persona of Abū Isḥāq most concisely and powerfully. The poet stands as censor (*ʿātib*) of his time: in his mourning, as in his victories, he is standing alone.

In the second part of the elegy to Elvira, Abū Isḥāq complies with his role of public mourner: from a focus on his poetic individuality, he shifts attention to the city of Elvira. In this section, the poet deploys a rhetorical arrangement that facilitates bonding with his audience: the effect is obtained through repetition and rhetorical questions. Elinson has examined the use of repetition in Ibn Shuhayd's poem as a rhetorical device that:

> creates a rhythm and a continuity that allow for a certain comfort and expectation that can act as a counterbalance to the unpredictability and severe rupture that occur with a traumatic loss. As well, this expectation can serve to shorten the distance between the poet and the audience: after a rhythm is established, the audience comes to sense what comes next. The line between the poet and the audience is blurred to the point where all the mourners are standing together, listening and reciting at the same time.[51]

Elinson points out how the rhythm created by the repetition of particles such as the vocative *yā* and the enumerative *kam* was registered by Ibn Rashīq in his *ʿUmda* as a customary device of expressing sorrow and grief. Such repetition, Elinson states, is not unlike 'the ritual movements associated with prayer, or

[51] Elinson, 'Loss Written in Stone', p. 87.

the swaying and repetition of God's name in the context of a Sufi *dhikr*'.[52] To these, we may add the ritualized movements of professional mourners, typically women, at funerals. The formulaic repetition of *kam* to enumerate the glories of the fallen city occupies the second segment of Abū Isḥāq's elegy (lines 4–8):

٤. وكم مـن مُجيبٍ كانَ فيها لصارخٍ   تُجابُ إلى جدوى يديهِ السَّباسبُ
٥. وكمْ مِن نجيبٍ أنجَنَتْهُ وعالِمٍ   بأبوابِهمْ كانتْ تُناخُ الرَّكائبُ
٦. وكمْ بَلَغتْ فيها الأماني وقضِّيتْ   لِصَبٍّ لُباناتٌ بها ومآرِبُ
٧. وكمْ طلعتْ الشُّموسُ وكم مَشتْ   على الأرضِ أقمارٌ بْها وكواكِبُ
٨. وكمْ فرستْ فيها الظباءُ ضراغماً   وكم صرعتْ فيها الكُماةَ كواعِبُ

4. How many, there, answered to a cry for help! Deserts are traversed in search of the generosity of their hands.
5. And how many noblemen she engendered! And how many scholars stopped their camels at her doors,
6. How many realized their hopes there, satisfying their wishes and desires,
7. How many suns rose from her, and how many moons and stars walked on her soil
8. How many gazelles there hunted young lions, and how many buxom girls defeated great heroes!

The images evoked by the poet celebrate aim to celebrate a society, more than a place. No physical attribute of the city is recalled. No monuments or architectural features are evoked, as in Ibn Shuhayd's ode: we are left thirsting for a glimpse of local colour, of the physical remnants of the city. It is a different city, the one mourned by Abū Isḥāq, a city of ideas: a cathedral of learning, a stronghold of holy warriors, a locus of mutual help and solidarity, an alcove for romantic encounters. The poet immortalizes Elvira by evoking its inhabitants, the population displaced to Granada. Rather than the city itself, the Arabo-Andalusian citizens of Elvira are the real subject of Abū Isḥāq's elegy. The poet crafts their praise by counting their merits: their generosity (line 4), extolled with imagery borrowed from the pre-Islamic ode; their learning (line 5) and the liberality of Elvira's patrons (line 6), the beauty of its women and the prowess of its men (the suns, moons, and stars of line 7). Thus we discover that the

[52] Elinson, 'Loss Written in Stone', p. 85.

persona of Abū Isḥāq cannot be simply, and simplistically, read as the lone voice of a dissenter. As he mourns and praises Elvira, the poet is in fact eliciting an emotional response from his fellow citizens, who have been forced to abandon their hometown. Abū Isḥāq is here appealing and giving voice to the swathes of people who saw their position suddenly overturned as they were forcibly displaced from Elvira to Granada. Abū Isḥāq's fellow citizens, previously the members of an Arabo-Andalusian upper class, are now subjects of the once-despised Berbers. And probably Abū Isḥāq, who enjoyed the protection of influential religious figures such as Ibn Abī Zamanīn in Elvira and Ibn Tawba in Granada, was one of the few public voices who dared to express his discontent about the new rulers and their bold move to desert Elvira. His opening invective against the *ahl al-zamān* is, on the surface, a reproach to the Andalusians' complacency or cowardliness, while on a deeper level it subtly calls them to remember and re-live a shared past effaced by Zāwī b. Zīrī and his Sanhaja army. The poem is also a rumination on the dire fate of the Andalusian Muslims, now fettered and gagged by the new Berber lords of Granada.

Perhaps, therefore, the most compelling aspect of this poem is that, as he praises Elvira, Abū Isḥāq crafts an implicit praise for al-Andalus before the *fitna*. The ruins of Elvira that he evokes contain the memories of the refinement of the society effaced by civil war (and one may here draw a comparison with Ibn Ḥazm's own '*Ṭawq al-Ḥamāma*', a work that is ultimately one of nostalgia for the bygone era of Umayyad Cordoba). It is easy to gauge how, as he praises Elvira, Abū Isḥāq is also casting a disguised invective against the Sanhaja Berbers: the poet's accusations against the Berbers, who had ordered the dismantling of Elvira, would not be lost on his contemporaries. Implied in this praise of Elvira is the Arab-Andalusian contempt for the Berbers, and quite possibly also, the blame the poet suggests they must bear for the civil unrest that eventually brought down the Umayyad caliphate. We read in this poem the germ of the later, far-reaching critiques which Abū Isḥāq would level against his contemporaries and his own rulers, culminating in his invective against the Jews of Granada, which will be discussed further on in this chapter.

Abū Isḥāq was never timid in criticizing and rebuking even the powerful and influential. In another poem, he rebuked a vizier of Granada, Hāshim ibn Abi Rajā', for dressing too sumptuously during a public holiday.

Abū Isḥāq, no. 16[53]

١. ما عيدُكَ الفَخمُ إلا يَومَ يُغفرُ لك   لا أنْ تَجُرَّ به مُسْتكْبِراً حُلَلَك
٢. كمْ من جَديدِ ثِيابِ دِينُهُ خَلَقٌ   تَكادُ تَلعنُهُ الأقْطارُ حيثُ سَلَك
٣. وكمْ مُرَقَّعِ أطمارٍ جديد تُقًى   بَكَتْ عليهِ السَّماء والأرضُ حين هَلَك
٤. ما ضرَّ ذلك طمراهُ ولا نَفعَتْ   هذا حُلاهُ ولا أَنَّ الرِّقابَ مَلَك

1. Your sumptuous feast day will only occur the day you are forgiven — on that day, you will not prostrate yourself boasting your exquisite clothes
2. How many a man wears new garments, while his religion is discarded rag, the streets nearly curse him when he passes by.
3. And how many a man, who mends his old clothes, has a renewed fear of God! Heaven and earth cry upon his death!
4. Those old tattered clothes do not harm, nor does foppish attire do you any good.

These public chastisements, addressed even to influential personalities, must have made our poet particularly disliked by the ruling elites of Granada. Loyal to his persona of public censor, he seems entirely unafraid to attack those in power when he felt that they trespassed the boundaries of propriety or did not act in accordance with Islam. In Granada, a city governed by a drunk, illiterate Berber warlord and a Jewish minister, Abū Isḥāq's staunch criticism of any extravagance (*bidʿa* — innovation or a breach in custom) was to eventually meet with catastrophic results. When his patron Ibn Tawba passed away in 1058, the poet lost his protector and became vulnerable to the attacks of his professional and political rivals. What happened at this point in his life is unclear, but it appears that Abū Isḥāq fled, or was forced to leave, Granada. It is probably at this point that he withdrew to the hermitage of al-ʿUqāb, near the ruins of his beloved Elvira. Information about this occurrence may be garnered from a short poem in which he makes reference to al-ʿUqāb. In the poem Abū Isḥāq seems to complain of the attacks he suffered at the hands of his close friends: perhaps his colleagues in the profession of religious scholar?

[53] Abū Isḥāq, *Dīwān*, ed. by Muḥammad Riḍwān al-Dāya, p. 8.

Abū Isḥāq, no. 19[54]

١. ألا حـــي العُقــاب وقاطنيــه   وقــل اهــلاً بــه وبزائريــه
٢. حللــتُ بــه فنفّــسَ مــا بنفســي   وأنَّسَــني فمــا استوحشــتُ فيــه
٣. وكــم ذِيــبٍ يجــاوره ولكــن   رأيــت الذئــب أســلم مــن الفقيــه
٤. ولــم اجــزع لفقــد أخ لأنّــي   رأيــتُ المــراء يؤتــي مــن أخيــه

1. May God bless al-ʿUqāb and its inhabitants, welcome to its visitors!
2. I have been absolved in it, and alleviated of what was in my soul and tamed of my bestial inclinations.
3. How many a wolf wanders around it, but I have found that the wolf is more docile than the *faqīh*
4. I don't regret the absence of a brother: I found that a man is often ruined by his own brother!

It is difficult to gauge whether the lines above contain an actual accusation against those who forced Abū Isḥaq to repair to al-ʿUqāb: is the word '*faqīh*', in line three, to be interpreted as some actual rival of Abū Isḥāq, or perhaps as the poet himself? Is this Abū Isḥaq's own rumination on his shortcomings as a Muslim (the word '*aslam*' in fact has the double meaning of 'more docile' but also 'better Muslim'), a type of rumination which filled his many ascetic poems (*zuhdiyyāt*)? Is the word '*akh*' in line four a reference to someone close to the poet who backstabbed him after Abū Isḥāq lost his precious patron and protector Ibn Tawba? These questions remain unanswered, and yet the poem testifies to the growing resentment and misanthropy of Abū Isḥāq, characteristics that ageing will only accrue.

After his period of retreat at al-ʿUqāb, it seems that Abū Isḥāq managed to return to Granada, where he resumed his involvement in politics. As he ages, the poet appears more and more concerned with the local politics in Granada. In his late poems, Abū Isḥaq crafted for himself a stronger voice as censor of public morality, going as far as to reprimand the very king of Granada, Bādīs ibn Habbūs (r. 1038–1073) and to confront the political protagonists of the time.

[54] Abū Isḥāq, *Dīwān*, ed. by Muḥammad Riḍwān al-Dāya, pp. 83–84.

III. *Abū Isḥāq's Last Years: His Invective Against the Jews of Granada*

A brief historical 'detour' is necessary here to contextualize the last phase of Abū Isḥāq's political poetry, which is dominated by his infamous invective against the Jews of Granada.

Not long after having resettled in Granada, Zāwī b. Zīrī opted for leaving al-Andalus for North Africa; the old warlord had hopes to gain mastery over Ifrīqiya, hopes that never came to fruition.[55] Meanwhile in Granada, Zāwī's nephew Habbūs, with the support of our old acquaintance, the qāḍī of Elvira, Ibn Abī Zamānīn, staged a coup and deposed Zāwī's son Halāla, who eventually repaired to North Africa with his father. Now secured on the throne of Granada, Habbūs strove for a government of integration and thus maintained good relations with the descendants of Zāwī who chose to remain. The new king was also aware of the simmering resentments of the Andalusians against the Sanhaja: he had to choose his trustees very carefully in the treacherous rivalries of the post-*fitna* period. Habbūs turned to the neutral element of the Andalusian Jewish community, who had largely remained outside the ferocious power struggle that had been savaging al-Andalus for three decades.[56] Habbūs found a perfect candidate for his vizier in the Jewish Samuel (Arabic Ismāʿīl) ibn Naghrīla, also known as Ha-Nagid (993–1056). A secretary of Habbūs had discovered him accidentally in Malaga, where Samuel ran a spice shop. Recognizing him as a man of exceptional learning, literary taste, and linguistic proficiency, the secretary recommended him to the king, who was only too eager to introduce him to his entourage. In Granada, Ibn Naghrīla's prestige rose steadily both at court and among his coreligionists, due to his brilliant intellect and skill in public administration. In 1027 he was appointed *nagid*, the highest official in the Jewish community. Habbūs died in 1038 leaving a pacified, thriving capital.[57] His son Bādīs succeeded him to the throne of Granada, and confirmed Ibn Naghrīla as his personal advisor. The *nagid* was able to gain the complete confidence of, particularly after he helped the king to unveil the conspiracy of his cousin Yaddayr, who was plotting to assassinate him.[58] The *Nagid* died in 1056, hoping to have secured the post of vizier for his twenty-one-year-old son Yūsuf, whom he had carefully groomed for the post. However, king Bādīs was hesitant to appoint Yūsuf, whom he found inexperi-

[55] Ibn Bulukkīn, *Kitāb al-Tibyān*, pp. 38–40.

[56] Ibn Bulukkīn, *Kitāb al-Tibyān*, pp. 40–41.

[57] Ibn Bulukkīn, *Kitāb al-Tibyān*, pp. 41–44.

[58] Ibn Bulukkīn, *Kitāb al-Tibyān*, pp. 47–51.

enced as compared to his charismatic father. The king found an alternate solution by appointing his own advisor ʿAlī ibn al-Qarāwī as vizier, and the young Yūsuf as the latter's secretary. But the ambitious Yūsuf was determined to reach the vizierate, for which his father had carefully groomed him. He resorted to plotting against al-Qarāwī and his family. Using his influence on Bādīs, who had fallen into the habit of immoderate drinking and living in perpetual intoxication, Yūsuf succeeded in having al-Qarāwī removed and gaining the post of vizier for himself. He also obtained the position of *nagid* that had been his father's.[59] However, in his rise to power, Yūsuf was quick to make enemies in and out of court. Among them, was Bādīs' own son Bulukkīn. The latter was close to the Banū al-Qarāwī, and openly opposed Yūsuf. When Bulukkīn was assassinated in 1064, strong suspicions arose in Granada that the Jewish vizier was behind the murder.[60] Bādīs, perpetually drunk, was reduced to a puppet in the hands of his minister. Granada simmered in resentment against Yūsuf. He found no sympathy at court and even less among the population of Granada, whereupon he withdrew to a fortified palace on top of the Sābiqa hill (probably the site of the Nasrid Alhambra some two-hundred years later).[61]

Feeling that his power was vacillating, or maybe overconfident of his grip on Granada, Yūsuf opted for a bold attempt. Sometime around 1065, he plotted with Ibn Ṣumādiḥ (r. 1051–1091), king of Almería, to depose Bādīs. According to the *Tibyān*, he invited Ibn Ṣumādiḥ to attack Granada: he would facilitate his entrance to the city.[62] In 1066, the Almerian army encamped at the garrison of Cabrera, a stone's throw from Granada.[63] Also according to the account in the *Tibyān*, it was Yūsuf himself who, intoxicated, incautiously uncovered his plot at a drinking party held at his palace. The conspiracy was publicized. Rumours spread that Yūsuf had assassinated the king and was waiting for the Almerians to seize power for himself.[64] The Granadines, Arabs and Berbers alike, were outraged by the news. It was around this time that Abū Isḥāq once again stepped in with his vitriolic verse, circulating a poem in which he incited Bādīs and the Sanhaja to kill off the Jews and to rid themselves of Yūsuf. On 30 December 1066, the population of Granada fell upon the Jewish quarters and spread out

[59] Ibn Bulukkīn, *Kitāb al-Tibyān*, pp. 53–56.

[60] Ibn Bulukkīn, *Kitāb al-Tibyān*, pp. 56–59.

[61] Ibn Bulukkīn, *Kitāb al-Tibyān*, p. 59.

[62] Ibn Bulukkīn, *Kitāb al-Tibyān*, pp. 69–74.

[63] Ibn Bulukkīn, *Kitāb al-Tibyān*, pp. 72.

[64] Ibn Bulukkīn, *Kitāb al-Tibyān*, pp. 73.

all the way to Yūsuf's palace.[65] The vizier tried desperately to calm down the mobs by bringing out the drunk Bādīs, but the popular rage could not be dispelled. Yūsuf b. Naghrīla was captured and lynched, and as many as four thousand Jews, according to Arabic sources, were murdered.[66] After the commotion's end, Bādīs had to sober up, calm the frenzied mobs and set out to repel the Almerians, who were now entrenched at Guadix.[67] He sought the help of the ruling family of Toledo, the Dhū al-Nūn, who sent an army. Ibn Ṣumādiḥ, eager to abandon the risky enterprise, negotiated a peace treaty with Bādīs and retreated to Almería.[68] Bādīs died on 30 June 1073.

As is to be expected, Abū Isḥāq's invective against the Jews of Granada has often been read as the spark behind the 1066 riot against the Jews of Granada.[69] In his commentary on Abu Isḥāq's invective, James Monroe sketched a description of the poet as a member and defender of the Andalusian *Mālikī fuqahā'*. Monroe summarized the situation in Granada in Abū Isḥāq's time as follows:

> Abu Isḥāq had the misfortune, for an Arab, of living under the Zirid dynasty of Granada who were Berbers. The latter had found it impossible to rule the Arabs without the support of a neutral element of society, and so they had raised the Jewish Banū Naghrīla family to a position of power over the hostile Arab population. The king Badīs ibn Ḥābbūs was ignorant, old, and an alcoholic to boot. Insensitive to the feelings of his Muslim subjects he allowed matters to get out of control. The fuqahā' who were orthodox and narrow-minded were forced to lead a marginal life in a kingdom ruled by a religiously indifferent monarchy.[70]

Monroe explains how the *fuqahā'* had enjoyed influence and prestige under the Amirids, former rulers of al-Andalus; 'now relegated to obscurity, they expressed their dissatisfaction and discontent'.[71] While it is perhaps an exagger-

[65] See Monroe, *Hispano-Arabic Poetry*, p. 27; García Gómez, *Un alfaquí Español,* Abū Ishāq de Elvira, p. 38, García Sanjuán, *Violencia contra los Judíos: el pogromo de Granada*, pp. 167–205.

[66] García Sanjuán, 'Violencia contra los Judíos: el pogromo de Granada', pp. 181–85. The *Tibyān* states that after murdering Yūsuf 'the population (*al-'āmma*) killed by the sword every Jew in the city, and seized exorbitant riches from their possessions': see Ibn Bulukkīn, *Kitāb al-Tibyān*, p. 73.

[67] Ibn Bulukkīn, *Kitāb al-Tibyān*, pp. 73–74.

[68] Ibn Bulukkīn, *Kitāb al-Tibyān*, pp. 74–76.

[69] See Carpentieri, 'Abū Isḥāq al-Ilbīrī', pp. 68–69.

[70] Monroe, *Hispano-Arabic Poetry*, p. 27.

[71] Monroe, *Hispano-Arabic Poetry*, p. 27.

ation to state that the *fuqahāʾ* were 'relegated to obscurity' (they still enjoyed important administrative positions such as that of chief *qāḍī* in Granada), their tense relationship with both Zirid power and the Muslim citizenry is evident in some of Abū Isḥāq's poems. In modern scholarship, Abū Isḥāq has been repeatedly quoted for his invective, the vehemence of which has largely overshadowed the rest of his production. Teresa Garulo, in her wide-ranging study of Andalusian Arabic literature, only briefly addresses Abū Isḥāq's ascetic poems, without foregrounding his overall poetics.[72] Yet another study by Alejandro García Sanjuán inscribed the infamous invective within the political context of Zirid Granada, without addressing the rest of the poet's oeuvre.[73]

It is unclear why Abū Isḥāq wrote the poem at this time, and where precisely he was writing from: whether from al-ʿUqāb or Granada. It is, however, safe to assume that when Yūsuf ibn Naghrīla's prestige at court began to wain, Abū Isḥāq felt safe enough to return to the city and even to attack the minister directly. The poem is composed of three main sections: in the first section (lines 1–3), Abū Isḥāq invokes the Sanhaja, praising them while calling their attention to their prince Bādīs' mistake of appointing a Jew as his vizier.[74]

Abū Isḥāq, no. 25[75]

١. ألا قل لصنهاجة أجمعين بدور الزمان وأسد العرين
٢. لقد زلّ سيدكم زلة تقر بها أعين الشامتين
٣. تخير كاتبه كافرا ولو شاء كان من المؤمنين

1. O say to all of the Ṣanhāja, the full moons of the time, and the lions of the thicket
2. Your lord has made a [fatal] slip whereby the enemy derive joy.
3. He chose a nonbeliever to be his secretary, whereas had he so wished he could have chosen a Muslim.[76]

[72] Garulo, *La litêratura Árabe*, p. 214.

[73] García-Sanjuán, 'Violencia contra los Judíos', pp. 167–206.

[74] This poem has been previously translated and analysed by James Monroe, and it will be summarized briefly here, as its implications extend beyond the focus of the present book. For a full translation of the poem, the reader should refer to Monroe's excellent study. Monroe, *Hispano-Arabic Poetry*, pp. 206–13.

[75] Abū Isḥāq, *Dīwān*, ed. by Muḥammad Riḍwān al-Dāya, pp. 107–12.

[76] Monroe, *Hispano-Arabic Poetry*, pp. 206–13.

In the following section of the poem (lines four to thirteen) Abū Isḥāq directs an acrid invective towards the Jews of Granada. These have, according to the poet, gained privileges over the Muslims, privileges that, sanctioned by the king Bādīs, are nothing short of a breach in religion:

٤. فعزّ اليهود به انتخوا   وتاهوا وكانوا من الأرذلين
٥. ونالوا مناهم وجازوا المدى   فحان الحلاك وما يشعرون
٦. فكم مسلم فاضل قانت   لأرذل قرد من المشركين
٧. وما كان ذلك من سعيهم   ولكل منا يقوم المعين
٨. فهلا اقدى فيهم بالأولى   من القادة الخيرة المتقين
٩. وأنزلهم حيث يستأهلون   وردّهم أسفل السافلين
١٠. فطافوا لدينا بأخراجهم   عليهم صفار وذلّ وهون
١١. وقمّوا المزابل عن خرقة   ملونة لدثار الدفين
١٢. ولم يستخفوا بأعلامنا   ولم يستطيلوا على الصالحين
١٣. ولا جالسوهم وهم هجنة   ولا راكبوهم مع الأقربين

4. Thus the Jews have waxed arrogant because of [that secretary] and have behaved with insolence and pride, whereas before they were base.

5. They obtained their desires going beyond the utmost limit, yet those living in misery have perished while [the Jews] have not noticed it.

6. For how many a Muslim of noble origin has abased himself before a miserable monkey from among the nonbelievers!

7. Nor was all this the result of their own efforts, but rather, their helper comes from us!

8. Why did he not follow with regard to [the Jews] the example of those good and pious leaders of yore,

9. And throw them down to the place they deserve, pushing them back to the [company of] the lowest of the low?

10. Then would they go about among us with their poll taxes upon them; being demeaned, contemptible, and base,

11. And they would rummage in the dung heap for a coarse cloak variegated in colour with which to cover their dead,

12. Nor would they hold our noble ones in light esteem, nor would they scorn our pious men.
13. Nor would they sit with them, since they are baseborn; nor would they ride with those near [to the King]![77]

Finally, there follows a long section (lines fourteen to forty-seven) in which Abū Isḥāq addresses Bādīs directly. The poet asks the king to open his eyes to the abuses committed by his vizier Yūsuf ibn Naghrīla and by his Jewish clients. These, he says, have grown arrogant and spiteful towards the Muslims citizens and the rulers themselves. They have split up the *taifa* of Granada in personal fiefdoms among themselves; they abuse and revile the Muslims on a daily basis; they impoverish the population by collecting taxes that they illicitly keep for themselves. Abū Isḥāq also accuses Bādīs's vizier Yūsuf ibn Naghrīla of deceiving the prince, distracting him with drinking parties. He states that Yūsuf has grown as rich and powerful as the prince himself and that his wealth is an offence in the face of the Muslims living in poverty. Based on all these accusations, the poet incites Bādīs and his Sanhaja to confront the Jews. His language is unequivocal and stark: Bādīs should execute his minister and rid Granada of the Jews by slaying them all (lines thirty-nine to forty-one). In the poem's closing lines (forty-two to forty-seven), Abū Isḥāq argues that killing the Jews, normally protected by their status of *dhimmī*, would not be a breach in religion because of their crimes.

Apart from the stark picture we get of Abū Isḥāq, this poem hints to some important changes in Granada and in the life of Abū Isḥāq at this time. First, Yūsuf b. Naghrīla was named vizier in 1056. Abū Isḥāq wrote his piece sometime around 1066. Is there any precise political reason for this attack at this moment? Was it perhaps because Yūsuf's favour at court had begun to dwindle by then, and Abū Isḥāq now felt safe to openly confront the still-powerful minister? And did Abū Isḥāq's occupation of *faqīh* have anything to do with his appeal to the Sanhaja?

The performative power of Abū Isḥāq's invective is perhaps most evident in lines forty-one and forty-four, where Abū Isḥāq (and let us here recall his status of *faqīh* and of a man ostensibly respected for his piety and devotion among the Muslims) promulgates a sort of *fatwā* that delivers the Sanhaja from the obligations of the *dhimma* status for the Jews of Granada. He declares it lawful for Bādīs to kill them and confiscate their property. He also makes it

[77] Monroe, *Hispano-Arabic Poetry*, pp. 206–13.

clear that killing the Jews would not be a breach of Islamic law since the Jews of Granada are guilty of many wrongs in relation to the Muslims. The incitations here are not formulated only against Yūsuf b. Naghrīla for his arguable political manoeuvres: Abū Isḥāq attacks the whole Jewish community of Granada. He also aims to arouse the greed of the Sanhaja by encouraging them to confiscate the Jews's properties. From the poem's language, it is clear that Abū Isḥāq is capitalizing on his position as a religious scholar to reinforce his attack against Yūsuf and Granada's Jewish community at large, which he qualifies as unworthy of the *dhimma* protection. The poem's *fatwa*-like lines forty-one to forty-four are a testament to this:

٤١. وفرق عراهم وخذ مالهم   فأنت أحق بما يجمعون
٤٢. ولا تحسبن قتلهم غذرة   بل الغذر في تركهم يعبثون
٤٣. فقد نكثوا عهدنا عندهم   فكيف تلام على الناكثين
٤٤. وكيف تكون لهم ذمة   ونحن خمول وهم ظاهرون

41. Distribute their property and seize their wealth, for you have a greater right to what they have collected.
42. Do not consider the slaying of them to be a breach of faith; nay, the real breach of faith would consist in leaving them to cause harm,
43. For they have already broken the pact with us; so how could you be blamed among pact breakers?
44. How can they enjoy [the security of] the *dhimma* when we are abased and they are notorious?[78]

Reading these lines against the account of the *Tibyān*, one wonders if Abū Isḥāq, with his poem, was indeed stoking the flames of an already simmering resentment among the Sanhaja elite. The poem's language supports this idea: its message is explicit and straightforward. Abū Isḥāq made his message unequivocal for Bādīs and the Sanhaja, who could hardly appreciate the subtleties of the Arabic *qaṣīda*, by stating plainly that an attack against the Jewish population was permissible: their abuses against the Muslims nullified the *dhimma*. Such a statement by a *faqīh* who was also respected as a pious man among the population would have a powerful effect on both the Sanhaja Berber elite and the Andalusians of Granada.

[78] Monroe, *Hispano-Arabic Poetry*, pp. 206–13.

While scholarship has attempted to calculate the extent to which this poem may have unleashed the wave of violence against the Jews of Granada, the exact relationship between Abū Isḥāq's poem and the 1066 massacre remains unclear. The first to associate the poem with the massacre was Ibn al-Khaṭīb in his *Iḥāta*.[79] Yet Ibn al-Khaṭīb, a minister to the Nasrid emirs of Granada, was writing three centuries after the events; no previous historiographical source mentions Abū Isḥāq's poem in conjunction with the 1066 riot. This fact led Bernard Lewis and other contemporary scholars to put the repercussions of Abū Isḥāq's invective into perspective: according to Lewis, the poem may in fact have had very limited circulation in Granada, and therefore its role in the 1066 massacre would have been a minor one.[80] Obviously, Abū Isḥāq's poem cannot be read as the sole direct cause behind the Granada massacre. I find it is perhaps more fruitful to examine what insights this poem offers into the evolving relationship between the Sanhaja elite and the old guard of the Andalusian *fuqahā'* in Granada. This relationship had been a tense one, as we have seen in discussing Abū Isḥāq's elegy to Elvira. It is very likely that the citizens who were forcibly removed from Elvira harboured cold, if not outright hostile, feelings towards their new rulers. Abū Isḥāq, an uncompromising character to say the least, was one of the public voices of this resentment. For their part, the Sanhaja elite had found a neutral and politically capable element in the Jewish Andalusian community, but, as it transpires from the *Tibyān*, Yūsuf's schemes must have alienated many in Granada.[81] By 1066, Yūsuf had become an uncomfortable presence at court. Adding fuel to the fire, the population's resentment against Yūsuf and his co-religionists, eloquently channelled by Abū Isḥāq in his poem, were a potential threat to the Sanhaja's own rule. Led by an alcoholic ruler and at a low ebb in popularity, the Berbers could well do with a scapegoat. As they sought new support among the alienated Andalusians, an alliance with the old guard *Mālikī fuqahā'* would have proven a blessing. Did Bādīs and his court seek such an alliance? Was Abū Isḥāq's invective a spontaneous attack against a political rival or can it perhaps be read as a work of propaganda, if not commissioned or encouraged, at least welcomed? Is the deterioration of Yūsuf's favour at court a mere coincidence with Abū Isḥāq's attack at this point? While there can be no definitive answer to these questions based the evidence at hand, what is clear is that the poem is Abū Isḥāq's first and only praise (if backhanded) of Bādīs,

[79] Dozy, *Recherches*, pp. 71–72.

[80] Lewis, *Islam in History*, p. 172.

[81] Ibn Buluggin, *Kitāb al-Tibyān*, pp. 79–85.

and a poetic incitation (*taḥrīḍ*) that testifies to a dialogue, whether sought or actual, between the poet and the Berber court. If we combine this element with the historical background provided by such accounts as the *Tibyān*, we can see how the staggering rule of the Sanhaja could only benefit from such a dialogue: winning the approval of the *fuqahāʾ* and redirecting the popular resentment toward the Jews, the Sanhaja would be able to save their rule, and that was precisely the result of the bloodbath of December 1066.

A more nuanced and detailed picture of the *taifa* of Granada emerges from Abū Isḥāq's public poems. The *Mālikī fuqahāʾ*, who had been the political movers and shakers in Umayyad al-Andalus, had to re-assert or, at least re-negotiate, their power and influence once the Sanhaja Berbers established a new political order in Granada, a political order which included, for instance, a novel position of power for the city's Jewish elite. Abū Isḥāq's poems played a part in this process of re-negotiation of power and privilege. One example is found in the poet's praise of Ibn Tawba's display of authority in the 'Ibn al-Ḥājj's case'. The Sanhaja, on their parts, seem to have been wary of their competitors in power and authority: Abū Isḥāq's escape from Granada must be seen within the context of effort to 'purge' elements of social disturbance in a time of political adjustment. When he retired to the small monastery of al-ʿUqāb, Abū Isḥāq was leaving a position of power as the secretary of Ibn Tawba. From this post, he may have hoped to witness the re-emergence of the religious hierarchies as prominent political players in Granada, but his hopes must have been thwarted by the Sanhaja and their Jewish clients, who succeeded in securing the highest posts in the Berber administration. Yet, towards the end of the poet's life, a new collaboration between the Sanhaja and the Andalusian clergy was forged: the population's resentment towards the prospering Jewish community and Yūsuf's alleged plots and intrigues, the Sanhaja's precarious stance after 1050, the residual influence of the *fuqahāʾ*, and the performative power of the *qaṣīda* all played a part in the Granada massacre of 1066.

IV. Ibn Ḥamdīs: A Privileged Upbringing

In stark contrast with Abū Isḥāq's austere persona of an ascetic and a moral censor, Ibn Ḥamdīs's persona emerges from his *dīwān* as diametrically opposite: a true *bon-vivant*, a professional panegyrist who revelled in the pastimes of the medieval Muslim court: wine-drinking, song, dance, and amorous escapades. A sophisticated and highly appreciated poet, Ibn Ḥamdīs found work at various Muslim courts across the Mediterranean: Seville, Majorca,

Mahdiyya, and Bijāya.[82] With his poetry, Ibn Ḥamdīs celebrated the political and social life of the elite, praising the powerful figures of his times, congratulating them in their victories, and providing consolation in their defeats. The panegyric is, in fact, the most prominent poetic aim (*gharaḍ*) in the *dīwān* of the Sicilian poet, who earned his living and fame largely thanks to his poetic praises to various princes in al-Andalus and North Africa.[83] His *dīwān*, containing three-hundred and sixty poems, survives in two manuscripts: Rome, Biblioteca Vaticana, Vat. Ar. 447 and Saint Petersburg, Asiatic Museum, Ar. 294.[84]

The full name of our poet was ʿAbd al-Jabbār Abū Muḥammad ibn Abī Bakr ibn Ḥamdīs al-Azdī. He was born in Syracuse, about 1055–1056, in a family that traced its origins in the tribe of al-Azd. He took his *nasab* (patronymic) from a Ḥamdīs ibn ʿAbd al-Raḥmān, a Ḥimyarite chief who, in 802, had rebelled against the Aghlabid emir Ibrahīm ibn al-Aghlab.[85] Ibn Ḥamdīs's family would therefore hark back to the Arab aristocracy who initially settled in North Africa after the great wave of Islamic conquest. It is likely that the family resettled in Sicily after the failed rebellion, to escape Aghlabid retaliation. The choice of Syracuse over Palermo, the seat of Islamic power in Sicily, may be explained with the family's need to stay as much as possible out of the reach of the Aghlabids.

Ibn Ḥamdīs grew up during the Norman conquest of Sicily, and practically nothing is known of his youth. What evidence we have must be inferred from literal readings of his poems about Sicily. Michele Amari speculated, based on such readings, that the young poet-to-be spent his early years fighting the Normans, having love affairs, and carousing.[86] Around 1078, aged — probably — twenty-four, Ibn Ḥamdīs fled Sicily. It is again Amari who suggested, and again based on literal readings of the poet's early verse, that an unfortunate love affair may have hastened the young man's flight.[87] Romance aside, it is not unthinkable that the poet's family participated in battles or skirmishes against

[82] For an exhaustive biography of Ibn Ḥamdīs see the newly published Granara, *Ibn Ḥamdīs the Sicilian*, pp. 6–144.

[83] William Granara has, of late, focused his research on Ibn Ḥamdīs's panegyrics: see Granara, *Narrating Muslim Sicily*, pp. 99–141.

[84] For everything concerning these MSS see Ibn Ḥamdīs, *Dīwān*, ed. by Iḥsān ʿAbbās, pp. 22–26.

[85] Amari, *SMS*, vol. 2, p. 593.

[86] Amari, *SMS*, vol. 2, p. 593.

[87] Amari, *SMS*, vol. 2, pp. 593–94.

the Normans, as they advanced in Sicily.[88] They may have suffered retaliation in the aftermath of Norman conquest, and the ravages of war and conquest may also have played an important role in the poet's decision to abandon his native island. Be this as it may, if Ibn Ḥamdīs had it in mind to earn a living as a court poet, clearly he would have had to look elsewhere, as the prospects of patronage in Sicily at this point were dire. When the poet came of age, the courts of the Sicilian *taifas* had fallen one after the other before the Norman avalanche, and the Christian invaders were yet to demonstrate their eclectic taste and propensity to patronize scholars and poets regardless of their language and religion. Even then, it is unlikely that the uncompromising poet would have accepted an accommodation with the Norman rule: his *dīwān* contains multiple invectives against the 'barbarians' and 'dogs' who snatched his Sicily from *Dār al-Islām*.[89]

It is unclear as to how Ibn Ḥamdīs attained his poetic mastery: his verse is conversant both with the pre-Islamic *qaṣīda* as well as with *muḥdath* poetry, but with no concessions to strophic poems, which are absent from his *dīwān*. These details open compelling questions about Arabic poetics in Muslim Sicily.[90] What books were available and where? In Palermo, most probably, but what about Syracuse, Ibn Ḥamdīs's birthplace? Did poets frequent local *majālis*, perhaps at the *taifa* courts or in private gatherings? Did itinerant poets, akin to the figure of Ibn Quzmān in al-Andalus, contribute to the evolution of Sicilian Arabic poetics, as some of Ibn Ḥamdīs's poems seem to suggest? What kind of patronage was available in Eastern Sicily for court poets right before the Norman invasion (and after)? These questions remain unanswered to this day, and will need a dedicated study. Some of Ibn Ḥamdīs's poems, if read literally, attest, however, to the poet's privileged upbringing, a background that would have provided for him the keys to the elite education which backed his poetic mastery. One example of the aforementioned poems follows:

[88] In *Dīwān*, 49, Ibn Ḥamdīs describes, for instance, a raid into Christian territory. It is not specified if this was Norman-controlled territory, however. The numbering of Ibn Ḥamdīs's poems adopted in this book is based on ʿAbbās's edition. See Ibn Ḥamdīs, *Dīwān*, ed. by Iḥsān ʿAbbās, pp. 75–76.

[89] Ibn Ḥamdīs, *Dīwān*, 28, see Ibn Ḥamdīs, *Dīwān*, ed. by Iḥsān ʿAbbās, pp. 34–37.

[90] For preliminary study on the subject see Carpentieri, 'Adab as Social Currency'. See also Granara, *Narrating Muslim Sicily*, p. 99–125.

Ibn Ḥamdīs, no. 110[91]

١. قضتْ في الصّبا النفسُ أوطارَها   وأبلغها الشيبُ إنذارها
٢. نعمْ وأُجيلتْ قداحُ الهوى   عليها فقسّمْنَ أعشارها
...
١٢. وراهبةٍ أغلقتْ دَيرَها   فكنّا مع الليل زوّارها
١٣. هدانا إليها شذا قهوةٍ   تذيعُ لأنفك أسرارها
١٤. فما فاز بالمسك إلا فتىً   تيمّمَ دارينَ أو دارها
١٥. كأنّ نوافجَهُ عندها   دنانٌ مُضَمَّنَةٌ قارها
١٦. طرحتُ بميزانها درهمي   فأجرتْ من الدنّ دينارها
...
٢٤. يرى ملكُ اللهو فيها الهمومَ   تثورُ فيقتلُ ثوّارها
٢٥. وقد سكّنتْ حركات الأسى   قيانٌ تُحرّكُ أوتارها
٢٦. فهذي تعانقُ لي عودها   وتلك تقبلُ مزمارها
٢٧. وراقصةٍ لقطتْ رجلُها   حسابَ يدٍ نقرتْ طارَها
...
٣٢. ذكرتُ صقلّيّةً والأسى   يُهيّج للنّفس تذكارها
٣٣. ومنزلةً للتصابي خلت   وكان بنو الظرف عمّارها
٣٤. فإن كنت أُخرجت من جنةٍ   فإني أُحدث اخبارها
٣٥. ولولا ملوحة ماء البكاء   حَسِبتُ دموعيَ أنهارها
٣٦. ضحكتُ ابن عشرين من صبوة   بكيتُ ابن ستين أوزارها
٣٧. فلا تعظمنّ لديك الذنوب   فما زال ربّك غفّارها

1. My soul was reckless in youth; afterwards, white hair made me wiser
2. Yes! The arrows of love were cast for me, and and many a time I was awarded its prizes

   ...

12. I recall an abbess, once, who bolted up her convent for us, night-visitors.

[91] Ibn Ḥamdīs, *Dīwān*, ed. by Iḥsān ʿAbbās, pp. 180–83.

13. We had been guided her by the fragrance of wine, who told her secrets to our noses.
14. Only a youth who travelled to Darin, or to that monastery may find such a fragrance.
15. There, her fragrance casks are pitched wine jars.
16. I cast my golden coin on her scale, and she poured her silver from her jar.

…

24. The sovereign of passion kept watch over the worries that might surge among our companions, and killed off even the more recalcitrant.
25. And the singing girls dispelled all sadness plucking the strings of their instruments.
26. One, with her fingers, was stroking a lute, another, with her lips, was kissing a flute!
27. A dancing girl lifted her feet in time with her beating her hand drum

…

32. I remember Sicily, and its memory brings me sharp pain
33. A mansion in which we caroused freely, surrounded by noble people.
34. I have been banished from heaven, how can I tell about it?
35. Were the waters of crying not bitter, I would believe my tears to be its rivers
36. In my twenties I laughed over my youth; in my sixties I cry over my sins
37. Do not reprehend me for my sins, for your Lord is their great forgiver.

These lines reveal Ibn Ḥamdīs's ease with the *qaṣīda*'s various registers, which he deploys in close succession and tampers with, while maintaining the poem's conceptual unity. The thematic arrangement is at once contrasting and complementary: the bacchic motif (*khamriyya*) occupies a large section of the poem, but is framed within its antithetical themes of old age (*shayb*), the nostalgia for the homeland (*al-hanīn ilā al-waṭan*), and pious poetry (*zuhdiyya*). The poem opens with an antithesis: the contrast of youth vs. old age, and, following this, it digresses on sensual pleasure (*lahw*) in a long section from lines two to twenty-seven. This section is dominated by the bacchic motif (*khamriyya*): the description of wine, and the petit-récit of the escapade to a Christian monastery to purchase wine, much reminiscent of Abū Nūwās. Ibn Ḥamdīs inscribes his own poetic persona in the *khamriyya* by evoking Sicily in line thirty-two: it is in this final part that the poem reaches its climax, coming full circle with its opening line. In this section the poet revives the initial motif of youth and old age, and he finishes the poem with a supplication to God (*duʿāʾ*). In lines thirty-two to thirty-six, the poet binds the *khamriyya* to the memory of his homeland, contextualizing the bacchic scene in Sicily, the land of his youth, pleasure and hope, as opposed to his present of exile. The closing lines redeploy a set of contrasts centred on the motif of youth vs. old age, with which Ibn Ḥamdīs opened the poem. The poet's sombre reflections upon his own sins, unexpected after the festive mood of the *khamriyya*, are perhaps the most apparent of these contrasts. The contrast lies in the juxtaposition of two antithetic genres: the bacchic and the gnomic. We must read closely lines thirty-four to thirty-six, in order to appreciate the transition from the *khamriyya* to the final *duʿāʾ* of line thirty-seven: in this transition lies both a key aesthetic feature of the overall *qaṣīda* (its *ḥusn al-takhalluṣ*) and the key to the poem's meaning or aim, its *gharaḍ*. In line thirty-four, Ibn Ḥamdīs draws an analogy between the banishment from Eden and his own exile from Sicily. He does so by defining Sicily as 'heaven', a metonymy that often recurs in his verses of longing for his homeland. Line thirty-five reinforces the image of Sicily as a paradise lost, evoking at once its fresh-water rivers and the tears of the exile away from his homeland. Then in line thirty-six, the poet alludes to such an exile as being a divine punishment: as Adam was chased out of Eden for his disobedience, so the poet was banished from Sicily for his sins. The poem then concludes with the final supplication to God of line 37. These lines condense, in a way, the poet's own reading of his life and exile as an old man: Sicily was the realm of pleasure, but also of sin and of transience: was it perhaps on account of his sins that the poet was doomed to exile and to a roving life?

V. Leaving Sicily

Ibn Ḥamdīs was about five years old when the Norman armies, aided and abetted by the Sicilian warlord Ibn al-Thumna, disembarked at Messina and moved into Sicily. When Palermo fell in 1072, the hopes for a revival of Muslim sovereignty on the island began to wane. By the end of the 1070s the Normans were moving southward to complete their conquest of Sicily. Trapani fell in 1075 and Syracuse would fall in 1078. Ibn Ḥamdīs, like so many others, set sail to Ifrīqiya with his family, to reach some of his relatives in Sfax. He was about twenty-four. On this occasion, once again the poet employed one of the classic themes of the *qaṣīda*, the *raḥīl*, to recount the difficult separation from his homeland. An opening note to the poem in the *dīwān* indicates that Ibn Ḥamdīs composed it upon his departure from Sicily.

Ibn Ḥamdīs, no. 98[92]

[وتوجه] عبد الجبّار من صقلية إلى إفريقية سنة أحدى وسبعين وأربعمائة وهو في سن الحداثة وصحب العرب. وأشعارها تعرب نفسها إذا ثبتت مواضعها [كذا]، فقال

٥. ما لي أطيلُ من الديارِ تغرّبا أفبالتغرّب كان طالعُ مولدي
٦. أبداً أُبدّد بالنوى عزمي إلى أملٍ بأطراف البلاد المبدّد
٧. كم من فلاةٍ جُبتُها بنجيبَةٍ عن منسمٍ دامٍ وخطمٍ مزبد
٨. أبقى الجزيلُ لها جميلَ ثنائه في العيس موصولاً بقطع الفدفد
٩. ضربتْ مع الأعناق أعناق الفلا بجسامِ ماءٍ في حشاها مغمد

ʿAbd al-Jabbār moved from Sicily to North Africa in the year 471, being in the prime of youth, and he accompanied the Arabs. When they settled in those places, their poems became more attuned to the ways of the Arabic speech.

5. What is it with me, that I stretch my wandering away from my country, as if wandering was my fate from birth?
6. Will I dissipate my resolution forever, by chasing a hope in remote and distant lands?
7. How many a desert have I crossed on a noble she-camel, her hooves bleeding, her mouth foaming!
8. May eloquent verses reserve a beautiful praise for her, distinguished above camels, for her crossing a scorching desert
9. With her stride, she overcame the desert with a blade of water sheathed within her belly.

The poem's introduction is compelling: it sheds some light on the still obscure literary formation of Ibn Ḥamdīs. I will return on this passage later in this chapter. According to this introductory remark, the poet travelled to Africa in AD 1078, when he was still a young man. There is no clear evidence of a single reason behind Ibn Ḥamdīs's choice to leave. It is, however, logical to assume

[92] Ibn Ḥamdīs, *Dīwān*, ed. by Iḥsān ʿAbbās, pp. 167–68.

that the Norman invasion of Sicily played a major role in this choice: like so many other Muslims, Ibn Ḥamdīs chose exile over accepting being ruled by the invaders. It is unclear whether he intended to earn a living with his verses: was the young Ibn Ḥamdīs seeking a patron to pursue a career as court poet? If indeed he had this in mind, Sicily, torn by internecine struggle and ravaged by the restless advance of the Normans, was no longer a propitious place for the patronage of poets. The splendour of the Kalbid age was past, and even the modest courts of the Sicilian *taifas* were being swept away by the Norman avalanche: a wave of migration began for all those Sicilian Muslims who could afford a passage. Many of them had relatives in North Africa and so did Ibn Ḥamdīs, who could count on the help of a maternal aunt in Sfax, eulogized in one of his dirges.[93] After leaving his home in Syracuse, the poet thus headed for the most logical destination: the nearby North Africa, where he could find the support of his relatives in Sfax.[94] It was not long, though, before Ibn Ḥamdīs must have grown restless to improve his position and obtain a post as a court poet.

In the precarious scenario of western Islam of the eleventh century, court poets from Sicily turned to al-Andalus or North Africa for patronage. The Andalusian *taifa* kings, greedy for professional panegyrists to grace their courts and enhance their reputations, competed to sponsor poets. Among the *taifa* kings, one stood as the *arbiter elegantiae* in literary taste, a first-class poet himself, and a generous patron of the arts: al-Muʿtamid ibn ʿAbbād, king of Seville. Attracted by his reputation, Ibn Ḥamdīs left Ifrīqiya for Seville, hoping to earn his living and to make his name as a court poet in al-Andalus. Doing so, he followed the example of his fellow countryman and colleague in the poetic trade Abū al-ʿArab, who had travelled to Seville from Sicily some years before.

VI. Ibn Ḥamdīs's Life in al-Andalus: A 'Sicilian' Poet?

Departing from North Africa not long after his arrival, Ibn Ḥamdīs reached Seville in 1078 accompanied by his wife and children, hoping for the generous reception that al-Muʿtamid had lavished upon so many other poets who sought his protective wing. The beginnings were shaky: Ibn Ḥamdīs was initially not received by al-Muʿtamid and was instead made to wait until, disheartened, he set to leave. Only at the last moment did al-Muʿtamid make

93 Ibn Ḥamdīs, *Dīwān*, 27, see Ibn Ḥamdīs, *Dīwān*, ed. by Iḥsān ʿAbbās, pp. 28–33.

94 Ibn Ḥamdīs, *Dīwān*, 27, see Ibn Ḥamdīs, *Dīwān*, ed. by Iḥsān ʿAbbās, pp. 28–33.

a surprise appearance at the poet's lodgings and, after a poetic tournament, convinced himself of Ibn Ḥamdīs's talent and admitted him to his entourage.[95] With the doors of al-Muʿtamid's palace opened to him, Ibn Ḥamdīs could finally revel in *la dolce vita* of a professional poet working at a thriving Muslim court. In Seville, Ibn Ḥamdīs lived happy and productive years. The court was resplendent and the king a famously generous patron. Ibn Ḥamdīs voiced his gratitude to al-Muʿtamid in many panegyrics which provide us with useful biographical information. Formally, these public poems stay loyal to the archetypes of the professional courtly praise: they celebrate the patron's military prowess, his foresight and political acumen, his pedigree, his generosity and magnanimity. But, while adhering strictly to the codified aesthetic of the Islamic panegyric, they are not devoid of the poet's own voice. In a panegyric devoted to al-Muʿtamid, the poet crafts a final section, the most important in the business of professional praise since in it the poet asks for payment, with a singular praise. Extolling the patron's generosity (and thus nudging to compensation), Ibn Ḥamdīs deploys the news of the death of his father in Sicily. Al-Muʿtamid, the poet says, has bound him to Seville with his hospitality, and even the death of his own father will not make him abandon the king's court. In so doing, the poet suggests that al-Muʿtamid himself became a fatherly figure for the exiled poet.

Ibn Ḥamdīs, no. 101[96]

٢١. طارت إليكَ بنو الآمال وانتشقتْ   من ذكرك الندّ استشفين منك يدا
٢٢. فما انحرفتَ براجٍ عن بلوغ مُنىً   ولا تركتَ لصادٍ بالعطاء صدا
٢٣. لا نأيَ لي بتنائي السّيرِ عن بلدي   فقد رضيتُ بحمصٍ بعدَهُ بلدا
٢٤. بدّلتُ من معشري الأدنين معشرها   لا فرّقَ الله فيما بيننا أبدا
٢٥. وكم حوى التّربُ دوني من ذوي رحمي   وما مقلتُ لبُعدي منهمُ أحدا
٢٦. ولم يسرني من مثواكَ موتُ أبي   وقد يقلقلُ موتُ الوالد الولدا
٢٧. وما سددتَ سبيلي عن لقائهمُ   لكن جعلت صفادي عنهمُ الصفَدا
٢٨. وحسنَ برٍّ إذا فاضتْ حلاوتهُ   على فؤاديَ من حرّ الأسى بردا

[95] See Granara, *Sicilian Poets in Seville*, pp. 199–216.

[96] Ibn Ḥamdīs, *Dīwān*, ed. by Iḥsān ʿAbbās, pp. 170–71.

21. Those who hope fly to you, sensing the scent of your generosity, asking to be healed by your hand.
22. You have not turned your back on those who hoped to have their desires fulfilled, you did not cease to lavish favour on those who were thirsty for it.
23. There was no path opened for me after I abandoned my homeland, but I was satisfied when I took Seville for my home.
24. I have changed the company of my kin with its kin, may God never separate me from these bonds.
25. How many a relative my country keeps away from me, not a single one can I see, due to the distance between us
26. Not even the death of my own father made me leave your abode, though the death of a father is a great distress for the son!
27. You did not prohibit me from visiting them, but you chained me away from them with your bounty.
28. and with a sincere affection, whose sweetness, once poured into my heart, cooled its scorching heat.

In the lines above, and particularly from line twenty-three onwards, we see how Ibn Ḥamdīs redeployed the classical tropes of poetic praise to construct his own poetic persona in public occasions. The poet binds his personal experience of exile to the praise of al-Muʿtamid, who redeems the poet after the loss of his homeland and kin. By the time he wrote this poem, Ibn Ḥamdīs was well aware that a return home was improbable. In line twenty-five, in particular, the poet states that his own country is keeping him apart from his relatives, that is, the political collapse of Muslim Sicily prevented his return. These lines, notwithstanding the loss they express, are charged with a positive message: the loss of Sicily is compensated for by the patron's protection. Ibn Ḥamdīs, in the poem, replicates the customary token exchange between patron (*mamdūḥ*) and poet, masterfully explored by Gruendler:[97] the patron is the redeemer of the poet for his many losses, but he is also redeemed by the latter through his inscription in the sacred poetic lore of the *qaṣīda*.

The *madḥ* required a festive or at least celebratory mood, and Ibn Ḥamdīs would avoid lines of sorrow and regret within a poetic praise. Instead, he

[97] Gruendler, *Medieval Arabic Praise Poetry*, pp. 3–47.

played on intimacy: while he lost his relatives in Sicily, he acquired a new family in Seville. While mourning the death of his father, he blessed the protection of al-Muʿtamid. All in all, these lines indicate that Ibn Ḥamdīs was hopeful for a safe and secure life in Seville. His glory days in the Andalusian capital are immortalized in many a poem: wine-parties in luxuriant gardens, summer evenings on boats on the Guadalquivir, and all the sundry bonuses of a first-rate entertainer. These come through as the happiest times in the life of the Sicilian poet.

I should here open a parenthesis: I have used the adjective 'Sicilian' for Ibn Ḥamdīs, and I will do so throughout this book. Yet, at this point, one may question the extent to which we can classify Ibn Ḥamdīs's poetry as 'Sicilian'. After all, Ibn Ḥamdīs left Sicily when he was no older than twenty-five. His poetic formation may have taken place, in earnest, elsewhere. Would it not be more accurate, then, to think of Ibn Ḥamdīs's poetry as, for instance, Andalusian? This is a concept articulated by Granara in his *Narrating Muslim Sicily*, where he maintains that, in al-Andalus, Ibn Ḥamdīs would 'hone his poetic skills'.[98] This idea is recurrent in debates among critics of Ibn Ḥamdīs — that is, that we could think of Ibn Ḥamdīs as an Andalusian poet, but I beg to differ. Firstly, the poetry of Ibn Ḥamdīs, formally, is deliberately crafted to erase all trace of locality: that was its power and that was what it made a marketable good across *Dār al-Islam*. Formally, Ibn Ḥamdīs adhered strictly to the revered code of the *qaṣīda* as enshrined by poetic giants such as Al-Buḥturī, Abū Tammām, and al-Mutanabbī. He made no concessions to vernacularisms or to the strophic modes that arose, particularly in al-Andalus, during his lifetime. Moreover, it makes very little sense to talk about 'national' boundaries when thinking about classical Arabic poetry, an art honed on the example of a quasi-sacred canon whose essential quality was that of uniting, through language and through the mythopoiesis of a lost world,[99] a vast and culturally heterogeneous universe: the *Dār al-Islām*. It was in the content of Ibn Ḥamdīs's poems, and not in its formal aspects, that one finds the poet's deliberate choice of a literary identity: that is, to be associated with Sicily. The only true trace of localism in the *dīwān* of Ibn Ḥamdīs is found in *ṣiqilliyyāt*: his poems of nostalgia for his lost homeland. From these poems, it is clear that if ever there was an adjective that Ibn Ḥamdīs would have wanted associated with his name, that would have been, without a shade of doubt, 'Sicilian'. It was in his poems for Sicily that Ibn Ḥamdīs carved for a space for his autobio-

[98] Granara, *Narrating Muslim Sicily*, p. 101.

[99] On this, see Stetkevych, *The Mute Immortals Speak*.

graphical voice and for his poetic persona. Through these poems, Ibn Ḥamdīs chose to become the enduring poetic voice of Muslim Sicily.

Finally, a word on Ibn Ḥamdīs's poetic formation. It has been suggested (more recently by Granara, as stated above), that Ibn Ḥamdīs honed his poetic skills in al-Andalus. This may be true to a certain degree, but a number of factors tell us otherwise. I should here like to recall an excerpt from Ibn Ḥamdīs's poem ninety-eight quoted above, a *dāliyya* in *kāmil* metre, whose introduction reads as follows:

Ibn Ḥamdīs, no. 98[100]

وتوجه بد الجبّار من صقلية إلى إفريقية سنة أحدى وسبعين وأربعمائة وهو في سن الحداثة وصحب العرب. وأشعارها تعرب عن نفسها إذا أثبتت مواضعها [كذا]، فقال

ʿAbd al-Jabbār moved from Sicily to North Africa in the year 471, being in the prime of youth, and he accompanied the Arabs. When they settled in those places, their poems became more eloquent.

This is virtually the only piece of evidence in our hands about the poetic formation of Ibn Ḥamdīs. Yet, this snippet of information seems to raise more questions than it answers. We have evidence that the poet left Sicily in 471 *hijrī*, that is to say sometime in AD 1078/1079, when he was a young man (*fī sinn al-ḥadātha*), but who were the 'Arabs' he accompanied? Does this refer to Sicilian Arabs? Can we read this as opposed to the Sicilian Berbers — an opposition that indeed fares in historical accounts of civil strife in Muslim Sicily? These questions remain open, but this short paragraph does provide us with some precious information about Ibn Ḥamdīs's craft as a poet. According to the passage, Ibn Ḥamdīs (along with his 'Arab' companions) was already composing verse in his early youth in Sicily, and his poetic taste improved after settling in North Africa. In North Africa, a land germane to Muslim Sicily in so many ways (politically, culturally, ethnically) the poet would have made a name for himself. This thesis is reinforced by the fact that Ibn Ḥamdīs was well received at the court of al-Muʿtamid, obtaining a 'post' as a court poet. Ibn Ḥamdīs was granted access to the Seville after a long wait at the door of al-Muʿtamid and that the king himself examined his poetic skills, as it is described in Ibn Ḥamdīs's very *dīwān*.[101] It is safe to assume that only an already accomplished

[100] Ibn Ḥamdīs, *Dīwān*, ed. by Iḥsān ʿAbbās, pp. 167–68.

[101] Ibn Ḥamdīs, *Dīwān* 344: see Ibn Ḥamdīs, *Dīwān*, ed. by Iḥsān ʿAbbās, p. 543. On Ibn Ḥamdīs's arrival in Seville see Granara, 'Sicilian Poets in Seville'.

poet would have passed the test to enter al-Muʿtamid's entourage and to work at al-Andalus's most prominent and arguably most sophisticated court. It was therefore in North Africa, and not in al-Andalus (which he reached some years later) that Ibn Ḥamdīs's poetic skills ripened. In sum, three factors combined depose in favour of my labelling Ibn Ḥamdīs as a 'Sicilian' Muslim poet: firstly, it is Sicily, and not al-Andalus or North Africa that the poet chose to be associated with through his verse, secondly, his poetic formation took place mainly in Sicily, and ripened in North Africa, thirdly, Ibn Ḥamdīs avoided all vernacular contaminations in his poems, it is through the themes of his poetry, and not in its formal aspects, that we must look for traces of locality: in this sense, it is Sicily and not al-Andalus that dominates the poetics of Ibn Ḥamdīs.

During the thirteen years he spent in al-Andalus, Ibn Ḥamdīs participated in the political events that involved the *taifa* kingdoms; the Christian onslaught coming from the North, and the looming Almoravid conquest. While at the ʿAbbādid court, Ibn Ḥamdīs recorded many of the political and military events of his time in his poems. In 1086, for example, the Almoravid armies helped al-Muʿtamid in inflicting a sound defeat on Alfonso VI of Castile at Zallāqa in 1086.[102] On this occasion, Ibn Ḥamdīs wrote ceremonious praises of the Almoravid Yusuf b. Tāshūfin, who had come to the rescue of his patron al-Muʿtamid. But Ibn Ḥamdīs would live to regret his poetic praise of the Almoravids when, five years later, they returned to al-Andalus as enemies and conquerors, deposed al-Muʿtamid and went on to conquer each and every one of the Andalusian *taifas*: al-Andalus was now a province of the sprawling Almoravid empire. Ibn Ḥamdīs was left mourning the loss of al-Muʿtamid as a sovereign and benefactor and had to behold the killing of the king's male heirs, some of whom were personal friends of his. We imagine the poet standing at the docks on the Guadalquivir, a shocked witness to how al-Muʿtamid is dragged in chains and forced to watch, helpless, the execution of his children, to be eventually shipped towards his prison in North Africa.

VII. On the Road Again

1091 was an *annus horribilis* not only for the *taifas* of Spain, but also for Ibn Ḥamdīs personally. As the Andalusian *taifas* were falling one after the other to Yūsuf ibn Tāshūfin's armies, Muslim Sicily's last stronghold capitulated to

[102] Ibn Ḥamdīs, *Dīwān*, 277 and 283. See Ibn Ḥamdīs, *Dīwān*, ed. by Iḥsān ʿAbbās, pp. 424–28 and 435–38.

the Normans and the island was forever lost to the Christian invaders. After this new set of traumatic events, Ibn Ḥamdīs opted to leave al-Andalus. He first went to console his former patron, embarking on a perilous sea-journey to reach North Africa. It was during this sea-voyage that Ibn Ḥamdīs lost one of his dearest life companions: Jawhara, an enslaved girl whose death he lamented in three dirges, some of which will be analysed in the third chapter.[103]

Once in North Africa, reaffirming his sincere affection for al-Muʿtamid, Ibn Ḥamdīs went to visit his former benefactor at his prison in Aghmāt, nearby the Almoravid capital of Marrakesh. There, the two exchanged verses,[104] as they used to during the merry days of Seville. But on this occasion, those verses reflected the bitter twist of fate they both suffered. In one of these poems, an epistle dispatched by the king to his former court poet, al-Muʿtamid begs Ibn Ḥamdīs to forgive him for an incident that had occurred in Aghmāt.

Ibn Ḥamdīs, no. 153[105]

ومضى عبد الجبار لزيارة المعتمد في أغمات فصرفه بعض خدمه بأنّه لا يوجد في ذلك الوقت، فرجع عبد الجبار إلى منزله، فأخبر المعتمد بمجيئه ورجوعه، فعسر ذلك عليه، وعنف خدمه، وكتب إليه بالغداة الشعر يعتذر إليه، فقال:

١. حجبتَ فلا والله ما ذاك عن أمري   فأصغِ فدتك النفس سمعاً إلى عذري
٢. فما صار إخلال المكارم لي هوى   ولا دارَ إخجالٌ لمثلك في صدري
١٠. وأنت إبن حمديس الذي كنت مهديا   لنا السحر إذا لم يأت في زمن السحر

فجاوبه عبد الجبار يقول:

١. أمثلكَ مولىً يبسطُ العبدَ بالعذر   بغيرِ انقباض منك يَجري إلى ذكرِ
١٣. ليالي لا أشدوكَ إلّا مطوفاً   بنعماك في أفنانِ روضاتك الخضر
١٧. فخذها كما أدري وإن كلّ خاطري   وإن لم يكن منها البديعُ الذي تدري

ʿAbd al-Jabbār went to visit al-Muʿtamid in Aghmāt, and a servant of his turned him away, saying that in that moment he was not there. ʿAbd al-Jabbār returned home and wrote to al-Muʿtamid saying that he had gone to visit him, but he was sent back. This upset the prince, who

[103] Ibn Ḥamdīs, *Dīwān*, 131. See Ibn Ḥamdīs, *Dīwān*, ed. by Iḥsān ʿAbbās, pp. 212–13.

[104] Ibn Ḥamdīs, *Diwān*, 152, 153, and 335. See Ibn Ḥamdīs, *Dīwān*, ed. by Iḥsān ʿAbbās, pp. 262–72 and 530–33.

[105] Ibn Ḥamdīs, *Dīwān*, ed. by Iḥsān ʿAbbās, pp. 270–72.

scolded his servants and the next day wrote back to the poet, begging pardon.

1. You have been turned away:, by God, that was not my order. Lend your ear to my apology, may I be your ransom.
2. It was not my will to forsake the generous, nor in my heart I ever wanted to confuse someone like you!
10. You are Ibn Ḥamdīs, who brought us magic, when it eluded us in times of magic

ʿAbd al-Jabbār replied, saying:

1. How can it be, my Lord, that someone of Your stature begs pardon to his servant, who, not forgetting your gifts, still remembers you?
13. I remember the nights, when I wore your favour as a wreath, among your luxurious gardens.
17. Accept these verses, that I made as good as I could, although their magic is not the one you once knew.

Amari defined these lines as 'pious tears' and 'mediocre verses'.[106] I find, instead, that these snippets of poetry provide us with a fascinating document of the lives of these two men: the famed and unfortunate Muslim king of Seville and his loyal court poet and friend. The lines are charged with a unique pathos thanks to an unexpected inversion of roles: the former king dispatches a poetic apology (*iʿtidhār*) to his former protégée. To have a better grasp of this scene, one must return to the days of the two poets in Seville, when al-Muʿtamid and Ibn Ḥamdīs exchanged similar verses in much different circumstances. Then, the patron would ask his court-poet to best his own lines, matching them in metre and rhyme, and completing their meaning. Now, destitute and in exile, the same patron received his former protégée as a benefactor, begging his pardon for the bad manners of his Berber warden and seeking consolation in his downfall. These lines are far from being stale maxims of pious resignation: they encapsulate the two men's realization that, in Aghmāt, the final act al-Muʿtamid's tragedy would be consummated, and that with his demise, there would come the end of a great historical moment for western Islam. Even on this occasion, the two friends used the code of the *qaṣīda* to write this final act. Surrounded by Berber guards, despoiled of the refinement of his courtiers, a

[106] Amari, *SMS*, vol. 2, p. 595.

chain at his foot, the former king revived his heydays through the medium of the *qaṣīda* finding a ready audience and interlocutor in Ibn Ḥamdīs. Two exiles from different countries, the two men rekindled their past glories with a common language: poetry.

Having paid a visit to his former patron in prison, having accompanied him in his misfortune for some time, nothing was left to Ibn Ḥamdīs but the open road. He journeyed North to reach the Mediterranean ports (we do not know where he sailed from, but Tangiers seems a plausible candidate), and embarked on a ship that would take him to the island of Majorca, then the seat of a thriving emirate. While we have no exact date for the poet's arrival in Majorca, it is probable that Ibn Ḥamdīs landed there a few years after the deposition of al-Muʿtamid (1091), perhaps in the company of his friend and colleague Ibn al-Labbāna from the Seville brigade.[107] Ibn al-Labbāna himself landed in Majorca in 489/1096, a year after the death of al-Muʿtamid in Aghmāṭ. As both poets had followed their former patron in his exile at Aghmāṭ, it is likely that they embarked for Majorca together, after the death of their former Maecenas.

After a short stay in Majorca, attested by a couple of poems that he wrote for the island's ruler Nāṣir al-Dawla, Ibn Ḥamdīs left his friend Ibn al-Labbāna and headed for Ifrīqiya, drawing closer to his beloved Sicily. He obtained a position as a court poet in Mahdiyya, where he eulogized the Zirid princes. There he settled permanently, as attested by his panegyrics for the Zirids emirs Yahyā b. Tamīm, ʿAlī b. Yahyā and al-Ḥasan b. ʿAlī. This was a momentous period for both the poet and his homeland, as the Zirids became increasingly involved in sea warfare against the increasing naval power of Normans, now established rulers of Sicily.

VIII. Growing Old in North Africa: 'Fitna' and the End of Muslim Sicily

Throughout his many journeys, Ibn Ḥamdīs was a witness to the turbulent life of a Mediterranean where new rising powers clashed and met with increasing frequency: the Hauteville Normans, the Almoravids, the Zirids, the Fatimids, and the kings of Castile were among the new movers and shakers of this tumultuous age. Islam itself was divided: Muslim Sicily had drowned, both socially and politically, in a protracted *fitna* (civil war). The Sicilian Emirate of Palermo (approximately 948–1050) had been effaced by family squabbles for power and

[107] On Ibn al-Labbāna see Foulon and Tixier du Mesnil, *Famille princière et poésie*, pp. 310–25.

replaced by a fragmented political scenario with local warlords at the head of warring fiefdoms: the short-lived Sicilian *taifas*, soon to be swept away by the Norman avalanche. From his long exile in Iberia and North Africa, Ibn Ḥamdīs devoted many a poem to his beloved Sicily, remembering the heydays of his youth there and mourning its demise. The following excerpt is taken from one such poem:

Ibn Ḥamdīs, no. 28[108]

٣٦. ولو أنّ أرضي حُرّةٌ لأَتَيْتُها　　بِعَزْمٍ يَعُدُّ السَّيْرَ ضربةَ لازبِ
٣٧. ولكنّ أرضي كيف لي بفكاكها　　من الأسرِ في أيدي العلوج الغواصبِ
٣٨. لئن ظفرت تلك الكلاب بأكلها　　فبعد سكون للعروق الضواربِ
٣٩. أحينَ تفانى أهلها طوعَ فتنةٍ　　يضرّم فيها نارَه كلُّ حاطبِ
٤٠. وأضحت بها أهواؤهم وكأنما　　مذاهبهم فيها اختلاف المذاهبِ
٤١. ولم يرحم الأرحامَ منهم أقاربٌ　　تروّي سيوفاً من نجيع أقاربِ

36. If my land was free, I would go to her, with a resolve that deems travelling an absolute necessity
37. But my land, how can I liberate her from the chains held by infidel usurpers?
38. Indeed, if those dogs have seized their food, it was only after our arteries had stopped pulsing.
39. How? while her people annihilated each other at the beck and call of civil strife (fitna), every wood-gatherer kindled his fire there
40. In its light their heretic views were revealed and it was as if their beliefs were all different
41. No mercy was shown on blood-relations — relatives washed their swords in each other's blood

The excerpt above contains what amounts to a poetic narrative of the demise of Muslim Sicily. It is a narrative drawn by allusion and, yet, its reach is clear and would not be lost to the poet's audience. It contains also a 'hefty' word

[108] Ibn Ḥamdīs, *Dīwān*, ed. by Iḥsān ʿAbbās, pp. 28–37.

to deploy in a poem, the word *fitna,* which I have translated as civil strife, but whose semantic reach is far wider.

In order to fully appreciate Ibn Ḥamdīs's *récit* it is essential to address here, albeit summarily, the main historical narratives about the end of Sicilian Islam and to sketch the meaning of the semantically loaded term *fitna*. While medieval Arabic chronicles provide us with a reasonable amount of information about the beginnings and the apogee of the Sicilian Muslim venture, they are far more reticent about its demise. The master narrative, which later accounts are largely derivative of, is found in Ibn al-Athīr's *Al-Kāmil fi al-Tārikh*. A quick glance at Ibn al-Athīr's work is important to gauge the importance of Muslim infighting in the collective imaginary, when it came to the Norman conquest of Sicily. Thus, Ibn al-Athīr immortalized the conflict:

ذكر ملك الفرنج جزيرة صقلية:

في هذه السنة استولى الفرنج -لعنهم الله- على جميع جزيرة صقلية أعادها الله تعالى إلى الإسلام والمسلمين، وسبب ذلك أن صقلية كان الأمير عليها سنة ثمان وثمانين وثلاثمائة أبا الفتوح يوسف بن عبد الله بن محمد بن أبي الحسين ولاه عليها العزيز العلوي صاحب مصر وإفريقية فأصابه هذه السنة فالج فتعطل جانبه الأيسر وضعف الجانب الأيمن، فاستناب ابنه جعفراً فبقي كذلك ضابطاً للبلاد حسن السيرة في أهلها إلى سنة خمس وأربعمائة، فخالف عليه أخوه على أعانه جمع من البربر والعبيد فأخرج إليه أخوه جعفر جنداً من المدينة فاقتتلوا سابع شعبان وقتل من البربر والعبيد خلق كثير، وهرب من بقي منهم وأخذ علي أسيراً فقتله أخوه جعفر وعظم قتله على أبيه فكان بين خروجه وقتله ثمانية أيام. وأمر جعفر حينئذ أن ينفى كل بربري بالجزيرة فنفوا إلى إفريتية وأمر بقتل العبيد فقتلوا عم آخرهم وجعل جنده كلهم من أهل صقلية.[109]

(Year 484 (1091–1092) How the Franks took the Island of Sicily.

In this year the Franks, God curse them, occupied the whole island, may God return it to Islam and to the Muslims. The cause of this was that in the year 338 (AD 998) the Emir of Sicily was Abu al-Futūḥ Yūsuf... In this year he was struck by a hemiplegia that paralysed his left side and weakened his right. He thus appointed his son Jaʿfar to rule in his stead. The latter ruled wisely and behaved justly to the people up to the year 405 (AD 1014–1015). Then, his brother ʿAlī led a revolt against him, backed by Berber troops and black slaves. Jaʿfar mobilized the army against them. On 7 Saʿban (31 January 1015) the two factions faced each

[109] Ibn al-Athīr, *Al-Kāmil*, vol. 8, pp. 481–82.

> other in pitched battle. Many Berbers and black slaves died on the battlefield, while the others fled. ʿAlī was taken prisoner and executed by his brother Jaʿfar. Only 8 days had elapsed since the start of the rebellion to the execution of Ali, which caused great sorrow to his father. Jaʿfar immediately proscribed all the Berbers, who were forced to leave the island, and executed all black slaves. The first were all deported to Africa, while the latter were killed to the last man. Jaʿfar thus rebuilt his army completely out of Sicilians.

The first remarkable feature of Ibn al-Athīr's narrative is how the historian links the Norman conquest to the Kalbids' infighting and to the civil war which ensued: he describes the catastrophic plunge of Sicily into civil war in a graphic account that places the Kalbid princes under the spotlight and follows the unfolding of their family drama and political downfall. Ibn al-Athīr explains how Jaʿfar's mutilation of the army led to the Kalbids being unable to tame a series of uprisings that ensued in Palermo and all across Sicily. The uprisings exploded in response to Jaʿfar's harsh fiscal policies imposed by his minister Ḥasan b. Muḥammad al-Baghā'ī in 1019, when landowners and farmers were forced to pay exorbitant taxes in kind on their crops. This calamitous new taxation probably arose from the need to recruit new troops after the Berbers' expulsion from Sicily. The uprisings reached a climax in 1019: Jaʿfar was besieged in his palace in Palermo, 'by both the plebes and the elite', who set out to lynch the unpopular ruler, according to Ibn al-Athīr. But just when the mob was about to seize Jaʿfar, his father Yūsuf, once a popular ruler but now incapacitated by a stroke, was carried on a stretcher before the frenzied citizens. Yūsuf succeeded in appeasing the rebels, mainly by conceding to their demands of deposing Jaʿfar and appointing his other son al-Akḥal as emir.

But even this al-Akḥal proved a calamitous ruler. He had started out under the best of auspices, resuming *jihād* against the Val Demone region, still predominantly Christian, and replenishing the dwindling public treasury with booty. Throughout the 1020s he even led various expeditions into the Italian mainland. But even this did not suffice to heal the public treasury and al-Akḥal had to concoct a new plan to extort taxes from the Sicilians. He decided to play two factions against one another. As in al-Andalus, these factions represented the first generations of Muslims who settled on the island, on the one hand, and recently arrived Berbers on the other. The latter can most likely be identified with troops that entered the island during the insurrection of 947. Historians referred to the former as *ahl Ṣiqilliya*, 'the people of Sicily', and to the latter as *ahl Ifrīqiya*, 'the people of North Africa'. Al-Akḥal proposed to the

Sicilians that they be exempt from a new tax that he would impose only on the North Africans. To this proposal the Sicilians replied that making a distinction between them and the 'Africans' had become impossible since they had been intermarrying for so long. Unperturbed, al-Akḥal went on to proposed the very same offer to the North Africans. The North Africans, apparently less scrupulous than their Sicilian cousins, accepted. As a consequence, a land tax (*kharaj*) was imposed only on the 'Sicilians'. The Sicilians responded with open rebellion, sending envoys to the Zirids. Ibn al-Athīr summarizes this mission as follows. The Sicilians said to al-Muʿizz (the Zirid emir):

نحب أن نكون في طاعتك وإلا سلمنا البلاد إلى الروم.[110]

> We want to become your subjects. But if you do not accept, we'll give the island to the Byzantines.

We can pin down this incident as the definitive turning point of the Sicilian civil war: the moment that unleashed internal fighting of various factions within. The Zirids immediately dispatched an army to remove al-Akḥal. He was besieged in his palace by the joint Sicilian and Zirid forces and killed by the mob. But, at this point, the Sicilians had a sudden change of heart. In the words of Ibn al-Athīr:

ثم إنَّ الصقليين رجع بعضهم على بعض وقالوا: أدخلتم غيركم عليكم والله لا كانت عاقبة أمركم فيه إلى خير، فعزموا على حرب عسكر المعز وقتل منهم ثمانمائة رجل ورجعوا في المراكب إلى إفريقية. وولّى أهل الجزيرة عليهم حسناً الصمصام أخا الأكحل...[111]

> Then, the Sicilians turned against each other, saying: You have brought foreigners upon yourselves, and by God, the outcome of this will be no good! So they resolved to attack the encampment of al-Muʿizz: they rallied together and fell upon them, they fought them and they routed them; 800 of them were killed, the rest fled and returned to Africa. The Sicilians then elected to the rulership. the brother of the deceased al-Akḥal, Ḥasan al-Ṣimṣām.

From this point onwards, Ibn al-Athīr's detailed and coherent narrative evaporates. The historian liquidates the turbulent and disturbing events of the Sicilian civil war in only one paragraph:

[110] Ibn al-Athīr, *Al-Kāmil*, vol. 8, p. 482.

[111] Ibn al-Athīr, *Al-Kāmil*, vol. 8, p. 483.

فاضطربت أحوالهم واستولى الأرزال وانفرد كل إنسان ببلد وأخرجوا الصمصام[112]

Then everything went upside down — the basest of the base took power, each man proclaimed himself independent on his own land, and they even ousted al-Ṣimṣām.

If we search through other Arabic sources to try and add flesh to the bones of Ibn al-Athīr's tale we are bound to be disappointed: these narratives appear to derive their accounts from Ibn al-Athīr's, to which they add very little. Thus in al-Nuwayrī:

ثم اختلف أهل صقلية وأراد بعضهم نصرة الأكحل. فقتله الذين أحضروا عبد الله بن المعز غدراً وأتوا برأسه إلى عبد الله...ثم رجع بعض الصقليين عن بعض وندموا على إدخال عبد الله إلى الجزيرة واجتمعوا على حربه وقاتلوه فانهزم عسكر عبد الله وقتل منهم نحو ثلاثمائة رجل ورجعوا في المراكب إلى إفريقية.[113]

Then the Sicilians disagreed with one another and some wanted al-Akḥal to prevail. But the faction that had brought ʿAbd Allah b. al-Muʿizz in killed him [al-Akḥal] and brought his head to ʿAbd Allah...then the Sicilians repented having brought ʿAbd Allah to their island, they rallied together against him, fought him, defeated him killing over 300 people...everything went upside down then, each faction declaring itself independent in a portion of the island.[114]

And in Ibn Khaldūn:

ثم ندم أهل صقلّيّة على ما فعلوه وثاروا بأهل إفريقية، وقتلوا منهم نحوا من ثلاثمائة وأخرجوهم. وولوا الصمصام أخا الأكحل فاضطربت الأمور، وغلب السفلة على الأشراف. ثم ثار أهل بليرم على الصمصام وأخرجوه، وقدموا عليهم ابن الثمنة من رءوس الأجناد، وتلقب القادر بالله[115]

The Sicilians regretted what they had done [i.e. putting al-Akḥal to death], they took arms against the Africans, killed over 300, chased out the rest and elected al-Simsām instead of the defunct al-Akḥal. Then everything went upside down — the basest prevailed against the noblest,

[112] Ibn al-Athīr, *Al-Kāmil*, vol. 8, p. 484.

[113] Al-Nuwayrī, *Nihāyat*, vol. 6, p. 207.

[114] Amari, *Biblioteca Arabo Sicula*, pp. 141–42.

[115] Ibn Khaldūn, *Kitāb al-ʿIbar*, vol. 4, p. 269.

> the people of Palermo rose against al-Simsām and ousted him, electing a chief from the army officer, Ibn al-Thimnah, who took the title al-Qādir bi-llah as their emir.

Finally, in Abū al-Fidāʾ:

> ...وقتل الأكحل في الحصار. ثم إنّ أهل صقلية كرهوا عسكر المعز، فقاتلوهم فانهزم عسكر المعز وابنه عبد الله وقتل منهم ثمانمائة رجل، ورجعوا في المراكب إلى إفريقية وولّى أهل صقلية عليهم أخا الأكحل واسمه الصمصام بن يوسف، واضطربت أحوال أهل صقلية عند ذلك واستولى الأرذال...[116]

> Al-Akḥal was killed in the siege. But then the Sicilians grew tired of al-Muʿizz's army, they fought it, routed it with their general Abd Allah, son of al-Muʿizz and they killed 800, then they proclaimed as their ruler the brother of al-Akḥal whose name was al-Ṣamṣām b. Yūsuf, there was great turmoil in the island, and the basest men rose to power.

As the Muslims' ranks broke, Byzantium took advantage of their disarray to launch an offensive in 1038. It was headed by George Maniakes, who counted among his mercenary troops a group of Normans. Maniakes was able to take most of the Val Demone with great ease. Although he was suddenly recalled to Constantinople, and the Muslims were eventually able to regain most cities except for Messina, Maniakes's campaign accelerated the destabilization of Muslim Sicily. By 1040, the Kalbid kingdom had disintegrated. In place of centralized rule, local warlords had seized the main urban centres across the island and proclaimed themselves independent. Soon a power struggle would ensue, drawing the island into civil war. Once again, the Muslims turned against one another. From the chaos of the Sicilian civil war there emerged a strongman: Ibn al-Thumna, lord of Syracuse and Catania.

Despite incongruences in the accounts of Arabic historians, it is clear that Ibn al-Thumna possessed a powerful army, with which he swallowed up smaller principalities such as that of Ibn al-Maklatī in Catania. It was during his struggle against his main rival, Ibn al-Ḥawwās, that Ibn al-Thumna forged a perilous alliance with the Normans. Aided and abetted by Ibn al-Thumna, the Normans crossed the Strait of Messina over to Sicily. They found no resistance all the way to Castrogiovanni and took possession of one town after the next. When Ibn al-Thumna was ambushed and killed by fellow

[116] Abū al-Fidāʾ, *Al-Mukhtaṣar*, vol. 2, p. 15.

Muslims in 1062 the Normans continued in their enterprise, possibly still aided by Ibn al-Thumna's Muslim army.

As the Normans advanced in their conquest of Sicily, large numbers of Muslim refugees fled to North Africa, reporting the news of the dire situation on the island, and possibly exhorting the emir al-Muʿizz him to stem the Norman tide. Al-Muʿizz responded to the Norman attacks dispatching a fleet in aid of the Sicilians. But the Zirid enterprise was a disaster: the fleet was sunk by a sea storm, and no Zirid troops actually made it to Sicily. A-Muʿizz's successor, Tamīm, refused to abandon the hope of recovering Sicily. In 1063 he dispatched a larger army commanded by his son Ayyūb. These reinforcements were received by Ibn al-Ḥawwās, who was holding out in his impregnable citadel of Castrogiovanni. Ayyūb and his army were encamped at Agrigento, some fifty miles from Castrogiovanni, devising a strategy to strike the Normans. Once again, however, the Muslims started bickering. Ibn al-Athīr described the events as follows:

فلما أقام أيوب فيها أحبه أهلها فحسده ابن الحواس[117]

while Ayyūb tarried there [at Agrigento], the people there grew fond of him and Ibn al-Ḥawwās grew jealous of him.

Then Ibn al-Ḥawwās dispatched letters to Agrigento, intimating to the Muslims that they should oust the North African contingent, which they did not do. So he marched against Ayyūb with his own army, and fought him in pitched battle. But the people of Agrigento stood by the North Africans, and fought with them against Ibn al-Ḥawwās. In the fray, the latter was struck and killed by an arrow. The army hailed Ayyūb as king of the Sicilians.

Ibn al-Athīr's narrative thus tells us of the birth of a new polity: a new Sicilian *umma* ruled by a North African, Zirid king. This is a crucial detail, for Ibn al-Athīr's use of *fitna* in the very next paragraph is meant to underscore the sudden fracture in this new polity. The historian is suggesting that the 'last chance' for Muslim Sicily was lost in this final episode of infighting, aptly labelled with the semantically loaded term *fitna*:

ثم وقع بعد ذلك بين أهل المدينة وبين عبيد تميم فتنة أدّب إلى القتال، ثم زاد الشر بينهم فاجتمع أيوب وعلي أخوه ورجعا في الأسطول إلى إفريقية سنة إحدى وستين وصحبهم جماعة من أعيان صقلية الأسطولية، ولم يبق للفرنج ممانع فاستولوا على الجزيرة[118]

[117] Ibn al-Athīr, *Al-Kāmil*, vol. 8, p. 484.

[118] Ibn al-Athīr, *Al-Kāmil*, vol. 8, p. 484.

> Then, *fitna* broke out between the people of the city and the slaves of Tamīm, which degenerated into open war. The slaughter reached such a point that Ayyūb and his brother gathered their forces and returned to North Africa with their fleet. Most of the Sicilian notables and warriors went with them, so that no one remained to face the Franks, and the latter took over the island.

Such was the end of Muslim Sicily in Ibn al-Athīr's account. A survey of the historical narratives also stops at this point, where we finally encounter the contentious term: *fitna*. Annliese Nef has maintained that the civil war that ushered the Normans into Sicily, i.e. the quintessential 'Sicilian *fitna*', was not addressed as *fitna* at all in the Arabic sources.[119] But her survey of the Sicilian civil wars did not include this rather late episode of hostility among the Muslims, as she focused only on the turmoil that preceded the Norman invasion. My study therefore complements her findings, since Ibn al-Athīr's narrative raises our interest exactly here, with this one instance of the semantically loaded term of *fitna*. In order to illustrate its importance, it will be appropriate to explore the significance of this term.

In Islamic historiography, the term *fitna* is generally applied to disturbances or outright civil war. It suggests the idea of dissension within the *Umma*, that borders on apostasy and the loss of divine guidance. The word also evokes with immediacy the *Fitna* par excellence: that which opposed the followers of ʿAlī ibn ʾAbī Ṭālib to those of Muʿāwiya ibn Sufyān between 656 and 661, and which would eventually determine the first and most important rift within the *Umma*, between *Sunnī* and *Shīʿa*.

The semantic reach of the term is wide-ranging and rather surprising. The Encyclopaedia of Islam has the primary meaning of *fitna* as 'putting to the proof, a discriminatory test';[120] and this meaning is also the first one to appear in the *Lisān al-ʿArab* (*al-ibtilāʾ*, *al-imtiḥān*). The verb *fatana*, from which the noun derives, refers to the process of purifying gold and silver from the dross by burning these metals in fire, hence the idea of separating what is bad from what is good. By extension, *fitna* is for the Muslim a test of faith ('tentation d'abjurer', according to R. Blachère) whereby the believer is examined and purified.[121] This meaning of *fitna* extends, however, to the general idea of seduction (particularly by evil) and temptation, and specifically the temptation to stray

[119] Nef, 'La Fitna Sicilienne', p. 104.

[120] *Encyclopaedia of Islam*, 2nd edition: Fitna.

[121] *Encyclopaedia of Islam*, 2nd edition: Fitna.

from the 'straight and narrow', giving adjectives such as *fattān*: 'charming' but also 'seductive'. And *fitna*, particularly in the Qur'ān, is itself the punishment (a 'burning in fire') for succumbing to seduction: the term appears in conjunction with the torment of sinners in hell. It is by means of such trials and punishments that the heart of the believer is purified: *fitna*, in its many semantic shades, emerges as a sieve that sets hypocrites apart from true believers. Thus, in 51 *al-Dhāriyāt* (The Winnowing Winds) we read:

٨. إِنَّكُمْ لَفِي قَوْلٍ مُّخْتَلِفٍ ٩. يُؤْفَكُ عَنْهُ مَنْ أُفِكَ ١٠. قُتِلَ الْخَرَّاصُونَ
١١. الَّذِينَ هُمْ فِي غَمْرَةٍ سَاهُونَ ١٢. يَسْأَلُونَ أَيَّانَ يَوْمُ الدِّينِ.
١٣. يَوْمَ هُمْ عَلَى النَّارِ يُفْتَنُونَ ١٤. ذُوقُوا فِتْنَتَكُمْ هَـٰذَا الَّذِي كُنتُم بِهِ تَسْتَعْجِلُونَ

> (8. Truly ye are in a doctrine discordant, 9. Through which are deluded [away from the Truth) such as would be deluded. 10. Woe to the falsehood-mongers, 11. Those who [flounder] heedless in a flood of confusion: 12. They ask, When will be the Day of Judgment and Justice? 13. [It will be] a Day when they will be tried [and tested] over the Fire! 14. Taste ye your trial! This is what ye used to ask to be hastened!)[122]

This cluster of *āyāt* (Qur'ānic verses) reveals the quality of *fitna* as a religious breach, manifest in the accusations against the 'falsehood mongers', those following 'discordant doctrines' and 'floundering...in a flood of confusion'. The word *fitna* appears in *āya* 14 ('trial' in Yusuf Ali's translation): it condenses the wide semantic range of disturbance, heterodoxy, unbelief, trial, and burning in hellfire. As a state of rebellion against the divine law, it is at once crime and punishment. In the light of these semantic nuances, it is clear that when Islamic writers define a revolt or a civil war as *fitna*, they imply that these episodes arise from or are accompanied by divisions of a schismatic sort. In other words, such writers are in fact pointing an accusatory finger at those Muslims who, espousing 'discordant doctrines', fracture the cohesion of the community, plunging it into strife. It is important at this stage to underscore how the Qur'ānic excerpt above establishes a relationship between dissension, infighting, and *fitna*. 'Dissension' appears in *āya* 8 as *qawl mukhtalif* ('doctrines discordant' in Yusufali's translation): The adjective *mukhtalif* points to the root *khalafa* and the verbal form *khālafa*: to contradict, diverge, clash, be at variance, but also to contradict an order and to breach. The derivative verbal noun *khulf* conveys the meanings of 'difference', 'contrast', 'variance', while *khulfa* 'sin', 'corruptness' and

[122] *The Holy Qur'an* , trans. by Abdullah Yusuf Ali.

'want of wit'. The Qur'ānic excerpt is unequivocal in drawing a parallel between *khulf* and *fitna*: contrast and disagreement lead to *fitna* understood as infighting, trial, and punishment. In the previous section, we have seen how Muslim historians referred to the disorders in Sicily with *khulf, ikhtilāf* and, eventually, *fitna*.

In light of the above, the usage of such terms reveal a scenario of 'internal otherness', a term adopted by Akasoy in her study of al-Andalus.[123] These powerful terms subvert, to different degrees, narratives of confessional confrontations of Islam vs. Christianity that characterize this period of Maghribī Islam and even intrude, regrettably, on contemporary political and academic discourse. By conjuring the great schisms that plagued the *Umma* since its very early days, the terms *khulf* and *fitna* disturb such narratives in their acknowledgment of the rifts that, particularly from the tenth century onwards, with the rise of the Fatimids, undermined the cohesion of western Islam and made it vulnerable to the rising inference of Christian powers. The moral taint of *fitna* aggravates these accusations, by shaping what Denaro has recently defined as 'narratives of defeat', as opposed to the triumphalist tales of the *futūḥāt*, i.e. the accounts of the period of the great Islamic conquest.[124] As Nef and Denaro have pointed out, such moral taint, in the teleological narratives of Islamic historians, equates religious breaches to political decadence and military downfall.

Arabic poets, traditional voices of their communities, would themselves tap into such teleological narratives, amplifying them in their own tales of mourning over the losses of Maghribī Islam in the eleventh century. Thus, having clarified the main implications of the word *fitna*, we can fully appreciate the gravity of Ibn Ḥamdīs's accusations in his poem quoted above. His verses insist on how turmoil and infighting breach religious and social codes, conjuring the spectre of sectarian antagonism as the great puppeteer behind the scenes of the *fitna*. In lines thirty-seven and thirty-eight, in particular, the poet casts an invective against the Normans, belittled as 'barbarians' and 'dogs' throwing themselves upon a dead body. But at the same time he constructs an invective against the very Muslims of Sicily: it is the Muslims, 'our people', not the Normans, who have murdered Sicily, causing her arteries to stop. The insistence on religious trespassing and the loss of divine guidance, that is, the quintessential meaning of *fitna*, features prominently in lines thirty-nine and forty, where Ibn Ḥamdīs denounces the fragmentation of the Sicilian polity's social cohesion through the

[123] Akasoy, 'Al-Andalus in Exile'.

[124] Denaro, 'And God Dispersed Their Unity', pp. 105–08.

terms *fitna*, 'heretic views' and 'differing beliefs'. The message is reinforced with the deployment of the familiar word *ikhtilāf*, seen above, whose root *khalafa* conveys at once the meaning of difference but also of contrast and sin. In these two lines we may read an allusion to a *sunnī/shīʿa* divide that, for over a century, had lain dormant in Muslim Sicily. Sicily, in fact, thrived as a predominantly Mālikī Sunnī ecumene even after the Fatimid takeover in 909. The *Cambridge Chronicle* tells us that the Fatimid Caliph al-Mahdī (reigned 909–934) had 'introduced' Sicilian notables to Ismāʿilī doctrines, but the extent of the conversions to the *shīʿa* in Sicily remains unclear.[125] It seems in fact that the island remained predominantly Sunnī until the Norman conquest. Ibn Ḥamdīs's use of the word, in particular, *madhāhib* points to a possible breaking out of hostilities along confessional lines, pitching *Sunnī* against *Shīʿa*.

In the key terms there deployed, Ibn Ḥamdīs's poetic excerpt is highly reminiscent of *Sūra al-Dhariyāt*. Ibn Ḥamdīs taps into the religious lexicon of *fitna* to decry the fratricidal war that consigned Sicily to the Normans: the Muslims of Sicily, split by 'heretic views' have literally murdered their own country, whose carcass has fallen in the clasp of the rapacious Normans.

IX. The Last Days of Ibn Ḥamdīs: Fleeting Revenge and Hopes for Revival

But the poet would have, in his old age, a final, if ephemeral, moment of revenge against the usurpers of his homeland. It happened in July 1123, when Roger II of Sicily mounted a failed expedition against al-Mahdiyya, which the poet describes in a congratulatory ode to his Zirid patron. Then, Ibn Ḥamdīs had his revenge on the Normans: the expedition resulted in a sound defeat for them. Now seventy, the old poet rejoiced in their defeat, and sung the exploits of the Muslims who had crushed the invading Christian fleet.[126] Towards the end of his life, an old man of eighty, Ibn Ḥamdīs journeyed to the Hammadid court of Bijāya (modern-day Algeria) where he wrote laudatory poems for al-Manṣūr ibn al-Nāṣir ibn ʿAlā' al-Nās.[127] Ibn Ḥamdīs died in July 1133: an elegy dedicated to the *qā'id* Abū al-Ḥasan ʿAlī ibn Ḥamdūn al-Ṣanhājī in the *dīwān* records the year. We have scant information about this *qā'id*: according

[125] See Metcalfe, *The Muslims of Medieval Italy*, pp. 44–46.

[126] Ibn Ḥamdīs, *Diwān*, 143.

[127] Ibn Ḥamīs, *Diwān*, 347, on the Zirids in North Africa in this period see Idris, *La Berbérie orientale*, pp. 314–41.

to ʿAbbās, the Banū Ḥamdūn were viziers to the Banū ʿAlannās of Bijāya. A second elegy (*dīwān,* 103) is dedicated to Ibn Ḥamdūn. We learn from these two elegies that the poet was present at Ibn Ḥamdūn's burial in 527/1133; the year of his own death. In light of this evidence, the idea that the poet may have died in Majorca, proffered until recently, must be abandoned.[128] Only one poem (no. 213) attests the presence of Ibn Ḥamdīs in Majorca: a congratulatory ode which he composed for the ruler of the island, Nāṣir al-Dawla Mubāshir. But the latter died in 1115 during the Genoese attack on the island — and in no other instance does the *dīwān* mention Majorca.[129] Ibn Ḥamdīs was therefore in Majorca before 1115, and in Bijāya, to attend the funeral of Ibn Ḥamdūn in 1133, the year in which he himself died. It is thus safe to assume that the poet did in fact die in North Africa and that his last residence was Bijāya.[130]

Growing old in North Africa, Ibn Ḥamdīs witnessed, through the accounts of the Sicilian refugees to North Africa, and through the incessant military confrontations between Zirids and Normans, the final stages of the Christian conquest that put an end to the Muslim rule of Sicily and threatened the Zirid supremacy in North Africa. These traumatic events appear clearly in his poems, just as the demise of caliphal al-Andalus and the sectarian strife in Granada appeared in those of Abū Isḥāq. Ibn Ḥamdīs was able to adopt the poetic thoughts of the classical Arabic *qaṣīda* to give voice to such events. As a court poet, Ibn Ḥamdīs would perform his poetry in public, on formal occasions or in the context of the *majlis al-uns*, informal court gatherings for the entertainment of the Islamic princes and their court. Ibn Ḥamdīs's profession of court poet required that he adhere to an established literary tradition, redeploying familiar imagery, tropes and structures, but this is not to say that Ibn Ḥamdīs wrote simply to appease the taste of his patrons. Using the mould of the *qaṣīda*, he reflected upon his life-experience and, by using a codified language as a *koiné*, he involved his different audiences — Iberian, North African, Sicilian — in his own mythopoiesis of Muslim Sicily. As Granara has pointed out, Ibn Ḥamdīs adopted a 'literary conservatism' by means of which he built a literary memorial to his lost homeland. He avoided emerging 'hybrid' modes such as the *zajal* and the *muwwashshaha*, to stick to the classicist aesthetics of the *muḥdath*, without disdaining occasional forays into the archaizing motifs

128 See Granara, *Remaking Muslim Sicily*, pp. 189–93, and Carpentieri, 'Towards a Poetics of Ageing', p. 128.

129 Amari, *SMS*, vol. 2, pp. 253.

130 Abbās already favoured this hypothesis: see Ibn Ḥamdīs, *Dīwān*, 139. Ibn Ḥamdīs, *Dīwān*, ed. by Iḥsān ʿAbbās, pp. 240–43.

of the pre-Islamic *nasīb*. As Granara has it, his conservative aesthetic choices allowed him to carve a place for Sicily in the literary canon of Arabic poetry.[131] He re-imagined his homeland through the shapes and functions of the classical Arabic ode: the elusive phantom of the beloved (*ṭayf*), the abandoned encampment (*aṭlāl*) from which the poet rides away (*raḥīl*), the locus of pleasure and merriment for a drinking session (*khamriyya*).

As for the final stage of Ibn Ḥamdīs' *oeuvre*, that of maturity and old age, it assumes very defined thematic contours. Its first distinctive trait is the predominance of the war motif (*ḥarbiyya*) on the one hand, and of ascetic poems (*zuhdiyyāt*) on the other. In his *ḥarbiyyāt*, Ibn Ḥamdīs eulogized the Zirids, portraying them as defenders of Islam against the Normans in Sicily and leaders of various naval incursions against North Africa. It is natural to assume that proximity to his homeland brought the poet to a more active involvement with Sicilian politics: it is likely in this period that he dedicated a poem to the Muslims of Syracuse, advising them against leaving Sicily and inciting them to active resistance against the Normans. The military confrontations between the Zirids and the Normans occupied much of Ibn Ḥamdīs's public poems of this period. On various occasions, the poet rejoiced in the Zirids's victories against the 'usurpers' of his beloved island. One of these occasions was aforementioned the 'Battle of Cape Dīmās', where a Zirid flotilla inflicted a crushing defeat on the Normans in 1123. In another poem, addressed to the Zirid al-Ḥasan ibn ʿAlī ibn Yaḥyā the poet used the war motif to actively spur the young prince to wage war to the Normans. Although the poem uses a highly stylized language, its message would not be lost on its audience:

Ibn Ḥamdīs, no. 142[132]

٨. فإن نصرتَ على طاغٍ ظفرت به   فما حليفاك إلا النصر والظفر
٩. وإن خفضتَ عُداةَ الله أو خذلوا   فأنتَ بالله تستعلي وتنتصر
١٠. أصبحتَ أكبر تعطي كلّ مرتبة   حقاً وسنّك مقرونٌ بها الصغر
١١. يُخشى حسامُك مغموداً فكيف إذا   ما سلّ للضرب وانهدّتْ به القصر

8. If the rebel [against God] is always vanquished, then you will triumph, your sole allies are victory and triumph!

[131] Granara, 'Remaking Muslim Sicily', p. 168.

[132] Ibn Ḥamdīs, *Dīwān*, ed. by Iḥsān ʿAbbās, pp. 249–52.

9. When you debase the enemies of God, or they are vanquished, by God you are exalted and made victorious.
10. You have become the greatest and every honour is given to you by right, though you are still in young age.
11. Your sheathed sword is fearful; how will it be when it is unsheathed and aimed at hitting, smashing the collar bones?

The lines above create a singular praise for the young prince. In a customary, almost formulaic fashion (particularly in these North African poems), Ibn Ḥamdīs portrays his patron as a defender of Islam against its many enemies. In this poem specifically, his reference to the Normans of Sicily would be easily recognized by the audience. However, lines eight and nine articulate a subtler message: certainly, the prince has been installed for his dynastic right, but will his deeds match his inherited rank? One has to recall that at the time of this praise, the Normans of Sicily were actively engaged in naval warfare against the Zirids, as they attempted to extend their influence in the Mediterranean. Based on the climate of protracted aggressions, back and forth of inconclusive victories and defeats on both sides, one could argue that by means of such rhetoric, the old poet was in fact spurring the young prince to a more aggressive form of *jihād* against the Normans. After all, they had snatched Sicily from the Muslims thanks only to a fortunate series of conjunctions in a very swift campaign: could the Zirids not do the same in their turn? Ibn Ḥamdīs's poems of old age points to the fact that the poet never ceased to harbour hopes for a return to a Sicily restored to Islam. In the last part of his life, he occasionally rose his voice to support the Muslim resistance against the Christian onslaught in the Mediterranean, an onslaught that was ever more apparent in the territories where Ibn Ḥamdīs spent his life: Sicily, Iberia, and North Africa. A further document of the poet's appeals for Muslims to restore Sicilian Islam is found, for example, in the following exhortation directed to the Muslims who remained in Sicily. Ibn Ḥamdīs incites them to hold their ground against the Normans:

Ibn Ḥamdīs, no. 270[133]

١. بني الثغرِ لستم في الوغى من بني أمي　　إذا لم أصل بالعرب منكم على العجم
٢. دعوا النوم إني خائفٌ أن تدوسكم　　دواهٍ وأنتم في الأماني مع الحلم

[133] Ibn Ḥamdīs, *Dīwān*, ed. by Iḥsān ʿAbbās, pp. 416–17.

1. Sons of the frontier! You are not of my kin on the battlefield, was I not to face the barbarians with the Arabs among you!
2. Wake up! I fear calamity will hit you, while you chase false hopes!

The 'sons of the frontier' whom the poet addresses in the first line are the Sicilian Muslims, and the poet's appeal becomes ever clearer in the next line: the 'false hopes' may be read as a reference to the dangerous alliance that some Muslims have struck with the Normans. From this snippet of poetry, it is clear how Ibn Ḥamdīs never ceased to participate in the political life of his homeland, taking upon himself the role of Poet of Muslim Sicily. Could his North African patrons wrest Sicily back from the Normans? Could Sicily be restored to Islam? This (vain) hope, let us say in passing, would be reiterated a century later by Muslim travellers to Sicily such as Ibn Jubayr.

Until the end of his life, Ibn Ḥamdīs did not cease to include in his panegyrics to the Zirids long sections of war-poetry, portraying his patrons as defenders of Islam and inciting them to prosecute their *jihād* against the Normans. But while these poems reveal the poet's active engagement in the public life of the Zirid kingdom during his twilight years, another facet of his late verses stands in sharp contrast with such an engagement. In his final days, afflicted by multiple losses, consumed by his desire to return to his homeland, and tormented by an ophthalmia that almost took his sight, Ibn Ḥamdīs also wrote more and more frequently about growing old and his desire to abandon his false hopes and withdraw into a sort of existential retreat. He lamented the fatigue of old age, his many disappointments, the loss of family members and friends, and his apprehension for the afterlife. These themes found increasing voice in his panegyrics, in gnomic pieces on the vicissitudes of time and the caprices of fate, and in religious and ascetic poems. And if at the beginning of his long exile Ibn Ḥamdīs evoked Sicily mainly with nostalgia, as he grew old he reflected with bitterness and angst on the dissolution of Islamic political supremacy there. Ibn Ḥamdīs dialogued with such losses using the many modes and moods of the *qaṣīda*, including old age poetry (*al-shayb*), the vicissitudes of time (*al-dahr*), and ascetic poetry (*zuhd*). In so doing, the old poet immortalized at once the demise of his world and his own decline: to his physical demise, the poet coupled the dissolution of the 'old' Maghrib, best symbolized by the loss of Muslim Sicily.

Chapter Two

THE POETICS OF AGEING: *AL-SHAYB WA-L-SHABĀB* AS A POETIC MOTIF

Following fleeting appearances in the pre-Islamic ode, the motif of old age gained favour among *badīʿ* poets and, particularly with Abū Tammām and al-Buhturī in the ninth century AD, it became one of the canonical poetic genres of the *qaṣīda*.[1] Verse on old age is largely referred to, in Arabic poetics, with the label *al-shayb wa-l-shabāb* (literally: white hair and youth, perhaps more idiomatically translatable as 'youth and old age').

After the era of *muḥdath* poets, *al-shayb wa-l-shabāb* became almost a *passage obligé* in the thematic arrangement of an ode, taking its place alongside more traditional poetic thoughts such as *nasīb, raḥīl*, and *madḥ*. Yet, the Arabic poetics of ageing have received limited attention in contemporary scholarship. A survey of literature on Arabic verse on old age has been provided in this book's introduction. In the introduction, I have also brought attention to the lack of a systematic study of the Arabic poetics of ageing, particularly concerning Maghribī poets. In particular, I have underscored how little attention has been paid to how Arabic critics classified verse on old age, and to the interactions between verses on old age and other themes of the *qaṣīda* such as the love-poem, the wine-song, and the ascetic poem.[2] This chapter surveys selected Arabic critical works, in order to offer a clearer picture of what we may define as an 'Arabic poetics of ageing': its formal aspects and its appeal to medieval audiences. After such a survey, the attention will shift to our two poets, Abū Isḥāq and Ibn Ḥamdīs, investigating how they reworked the motif of ageing into their own oeuvre, and for which purposes.

[1] Thus, Arazi asserts: 'This poetic theme of the Arabs has known a long and prolific history and has played, in urban post-Djahilī poetry, a role analogous to that of the nasīb in the moulding of the kasida', Encyclopaedia of Islam, 2nd edition: *al-Shayb wa-l-shabāb*.

[2] See Carpentieri, *Towards a Poetics of Ageing*, pp. 119–43.

I. Critical Sources: Medieval Arabic Critics on al-shayb wa-l-shabāb

The first set of questions that I would like to address concerns the classification of *al-shayb wa-l-shabāb* in some of the most important medieval works of poetic criticism in Arabic. Did Arabic critics count *al-shayb wa-l-shabāb* among the *aghrāḍ al-shiʿr*? What aesthetic appraisals of this poetic motif can we garner from classical works of Arabic criticism? And what exactly made old age so popular among Arabic poets and with their audiences, according to these critics?

Hardly any Arabic critical work includes *al-shayb wa-l-shabāb* in its classifications of poetic genres/motifs.[3] Thaʿlab, in *Qawāʿid al-Shiʿr*, makes no mention of the theme in the categories derived from the basic elements (*uṣūl*) of a poem (command, prohibition, predication, and question)[4] which, let us recall, are: praise (*al-madḥ*), invective (*al-hijāʾ*), dirges (*al-marāthī*), verse for asking forgiveness (*al-iʿtidhār*), love poetry (*al-tashbīb*), simile (*al-tashbīh*), and report (*iqtiṣāṣ al-akhbār*). *Al-Shayb wa-l-shabāb* is also absent from Qudāma b. Jaʿfar's famous division of *aghrāḍ al-shiʿr* into praise (*al-madīḥ*), invective (*al-hijāʾ*), dirges (*al-marāthī*), simile (*al-tashbīḥ*), description (*al-waṣf*), and love poetry (*al-nasīb*). The absence of *al-shayb wa-l-shabāb* from among the main *aghrāḍ al-shʿir* may reflect Qudāma's focus on pre-Islamic poetry on the one hand, and, on the other, the fact that *al-shayb wa-l-shabāb* can be legitimately included within one of the above wider categories. But which one? The first plausible candidate from among Qudāma's rubrics is *waṣf*: the description of white hair customarily has the lion's share in the overall development of the theme. But one may also think of *tashbīḥ,* and even again *hijā* (poets elaborated a whole panoply of vituperative assaults on the loathed whiteness) and *madīḥ* (indeed, some poets even praised decrepitude as a bringer of *waqār* — dignity — and forbearance — *ḥilm*).

The fact is, we must revert to Qudāma's famous idea of 'poetic aims' — *aghrāḍ* — a definition which will find much favour among later critics. Qudāma uses the word '*gharaḍ*' literally: the aim of the poet in crafting a given *qaṣīda*. If we follow this logic, a poet could do a number of things with old age: praise it, blame it, describe it, allude to it, and so on (hardly mourn it, I'm afraid).

[3] The concept of 'poetic genre' is in itself only partially adequate to reflect Arabic criticism on the issues of *maʿāni al-shiʿr* , and *aghrāḍ al-shiʿr*. (cf. Schoeler, *The Genres of Classical Arabic Poetry*). I will be using this term to translate the Arabic *funūn/ḍurūb*, or will specify case by case when it refers to a different Arabic term.

[4] Shoeler, *The Genres of Classical Arabic Poetry*, p. 10.

The next question to be addressed here is the relationship, according to Qudāma, between the *maʿnā* and *gharaḍ*. In this respect, Schoeler's interpretation is convincing: Qudāma was specific in his usage of the term *gharaḍ* as 'poetic aim', and of *maʿnā* (pl. *maʿānī*) as 'poetic thought', the latter being included in the former. In Schoeler's words:

> the 'aims' are 'poetic thoughts' (maʿānī) — in a wider sense; the latter term, however, is used by Qudāma also more specifically, something like in the sense of 'motifs' which constitute the 'aims'.[5]

According to the above, we can read *al-shayb wa-l-shabāb* as a '*maʿnā*'[6] in the sense of a motif capable of informing a wider poetic aim (*gharaḍ*). The ubiquitousness of this motif in poems spanning the most disparate aims (dirges, love poems, bacchic poems, and so on) reinforces this idea. Considering *al-shayb wa-l-shabāb* as a *maʿnā* in conformity with Shoeler's reading of Qudāma also suggests an interdependence between the theme of old age and the whole array of poetic aims of the *qaṣīda*: segments on old age are deployed as subservient to the poem's overall aim. They also bend, influence, and modify the main aim of a given poem of poetic segment. The efficacy in reaching a given aim thus relies partially on the proper deployment of the ageing segment(s). This interdependence may be found both on the level of meaning, as described above, and structure. A survey of poems containing segments on ageing reveals that *al-shayb wa-l-shabāb* recurrently serves for *ḥusn al-takhalluṣ*: proper transitions between thematic segments, and, specifically, from the *nasīb* towards the *madḥ*.[7]

The idea of the interdependence between *maʿnā* and the overall economy of a given poem must, however, be put in perspective. Like Thaʿlab before him, Qudāma did not contemplate whole poems in his classification: his *shawāhid* comprise verse groups extrapolated from larger poems. This of course does not hamper the validity of hypothesis formulated above (particularly if we consider the function of *maʿnā* within a given poetic segment as opposed to whole poems) but only limits the efficacy of Qudāma to back it up.

Classifications in the follow-up to Qudāma are no more specific than the latter's for what concerns *al-shayb wa-l-shabāb*. ʿAlī b. ʿIsā al-Rummānī's and

[5] Schoeler, *The Genres of Classical Arabic Poetry*, p. 11.

[6] I must here underscore that I found no reference, in the *dīwān* of Ibn Ḥamdīs, to *al-shayb* as a 'maʿnā', as, for instance, happens with *zuhd* (as in '*wa qāla fī maʿnā al-zuhd*' *vs.* '*wa qāla fi-l-shayb*'). My choice to define *al-shayb wa-shabāb* as '*maʿnā*' is subservient to my reading, informed by al-Murtaḍā's classification of this motif as one capable of informing, and transforming, 'larger' poetic aims (*aghrāḍ*).

[7] See Carpentieri, *At War with the Age*, pp. 39–50.

Abū Hilāl al-ʿAskarī's lists are mainly derivative of Qudāma's and make no mention of the theme at all. A paradigm shift in the classification of poetic motifs appears with Qudāma's contemporary Ibn Wahb, who produced a much more meticulous subdivision of poetic themes in his *Kitāb al-burhān fī wujūh al-bayān*. Of particular interest is Ibn Wahb's mention of gnomic poetry (*ḥikma*) with its three subcategories: adages (*al-amthāl*), summons to renunciation (*al-tazhīd*), admonitions (*al-mawāʿiz*). The absence of *al-shayb wa-l-shabāb* is remarkable here, as the theme often informs the three subcategories mentioned above. In particular, *zuhd* (or *tazhīd*, as Ibn Wahb has it) poems often open with the motif of old age, to the point that this motif can be considered an integral part of the overall aim. In *zuhd* poems, adages may take the form of musings upon the fragility of life and admonitions may be proffered by ageing poetic personae to themselves or their audience. Ibn Wahb's list of poetic genres (*funūn al-shiʿr*) reflects the author's attention to themes made popular by *muḥdath* poets: why then does he not contemplate *al-shayb wa-l-shabāb*? A possible answer lies in the fact that Ibn Wahb only mentions themes that can appear as independent poems:[8] the theme of old age, as we will see later on, is largely used within multi-partite odes. This all goes to reinforce what said above for Qudāma. Rather than a poetic aim *per se*, *al-shayb wa-l-shabāb* can be best read as a motif (*maʿnā* according to Schoeler's reading), capable of informing the main themes, or poetic aims, of the *qaṣīda*.

In a study devoted to Maghribī poets, a couple of critics deserve a separate and more detailed discussion. First is Ibn Rashīq, one of the most illustrious men of letters of Ifrīqiya, who spent the last part of his life in Sicily. Ibn Rashīq died at the time (1071) when Ibn Ḥamdīs must have been an adolescent beginning to compose verses and perfect his poetic formation. It is therefore very likely that Ibn Ḥamdīs, whose verse displays a keen awareness of the poetic debates of his time, may have had access to Ibn Rashīq's work.

In *al-ʿUmda fī sināʿat al-shiʿr wa naqdi-hi*, Ibn Rashīq classifies poetry according to a strict understanding of *gharaḍ* as aim, in a way analogous to Qudāma's. Ibn Rashīq divides poetry into person-directed and private. Consequently, he proffers the following division of *aghrāḍ al-shiʿr wa ṣunūfu-hu* (aims and categories of poetry): love poetry (*al-nasīb*), praise (*al-madīḥ*), self-praise (*al-fakhr*), dirge (*al-rithāʾ*), demand and plea to fulfil a promise (*al-iqtiḍāʾ wa al-istinjāz*), reproach (*al-ʿitāb*), threat and warning (*al-waʿīd wa al-indhār*), invective (*al-hijāʾ*), and apology (*al-iʿtidhār*).

[8] Shoeler, *The Genres of Classical Arabic Poetry*, p. 16.

Each of these categories is person-directed, and as is to be expected, *al-shayb wa-l-shabāb* does not figure among them. Yet, *al-shayb wa-l-shabāb* appears in the *ʿUmda* under the following headings:

1. Poetry of Caliphs, *Qāḍīs* and *Fuqahāʾ* [ʿUmar ibn ʿAbd al-ʿAzīz][9]
2. Pleas and instigations of poets: [opening of a *qaṣīda* by ʿAlqama al-Faḥl][10]
3. Rhymes: [ʿAlqama al-Faḥl, on *murdaf rhyme* — the *rawī* is preceded *ālif, wāw* or *yāʾ* — called *ridf*-][11]
4. Beginning, transitioning and ending: [al-Nābigha al-Dhubyānī — *ḥusn al-takhalluṣ*][12]
5. *Majāz* [al-Farazdaq][13]
6. Proverbs [al-Mutanabbī][14]
7. *Tajnīs* (paronomasia) [Ibn al-Rumī][15]
8. *Tardīd* (repetition of the same word with different meanings) [anonymous][16]
9. *Taṣdīr* (repetition of a word without a change in meaning in the first and second hemistich) [Manṣūr ibn al-Faraj][17]
10. *Tikrār* (repetition) [Abū Kabīr al-Hudhalī, Ibn al-Zayyāt][18]
11. *Taḍmīn* and *Ijāza* (alluding to a line and continuing a line of poetry with the same rhyme and metre) [Kushājim][19]
12. Censoring: [al-Mutanabbī][20]

[9] Ibn Rashīq, *al-ʿUmda*, pp. 31–43.
[10] Ibn Rashīq, *al-ʿUmda*, pp. 73–88.
[11] Ibn Rashīq, *al-ʿUmda*, pp. 243–76.
[12] Ibn Rashīq, *al-ʿUmda*, pp. 350–71.
[13] Ibn Rashīq, *al-ʿUmda*, pp. 429–34.
[14] Ibn Rashīq, *al-ʿUmda*, pp. 457–67.
[15] Ibn Rashīq, *al-ʿUmda*, pp. 530–52.
[16] Ibn Rashīq, *al-ʿUmda*, pp. 553–59.
[17] Ibn Rashīq, *al-ʿUmda*, pp. 560–64.
[18] Ibn Rashīq, *al-ʿUmda*, pp. 698–711.
[19] Ibn Rashīq, *al-ʿUmda*, pp. 819–33.
[20] Ibn Rashīq, *al-ʿUmda*, pp. 852–62.

Like other critics before him, Ibn Rashīq' does not single out *al-shayb wa-l-shabāb* in his classification of poetic genres and it does not figure as a discrete aim within private verse either. As seen above, verses on old age appear scattered in the *ʿUmda*, mainly as examples of certain rhetorical figures and *aghrāḍ*. It is all the more disappointing that Ibn Rashīq, a Maghribī author, quotes exclusively from Eastern poets, contributing next to nothing to the subject of a Magribī poetics of ageing. Yet, the list above does provide interesting information about the usage of *al-shayb wa-l-shabāb* in Arabic poetry, and particularly concerning the history of the motif of ageing in Arabic poetics. Ibn Rashīq uses old age verses to illustrate the figures of speech most appreciated by *badīʿ* poets. Of his twelve quotations on *al-shayb wa-l-shabāb*, at least five illustrate examples of the figures of speech that *badīʿ* poets employed more frequently (*tajnīs*, *tardīd*, *taṣdīr*, *tikrār*, and *taḍmīn*). To these figures of speech, one must add the theme's key role in the *takhalluṣ* or *khurūj*, a feature that will be discussed further on in this book. A common example of *ḥusn al-takhalluṣ* obtained through the deployment of *al-shayb wa-l-shabāb* is the poet voicing nostalgia for his youth after the *nasīb* in order to disengage from the mood of the amatory preface and move on to the next section of the ode. *Al-shayb wa-l-shabāb* replaces, in such an instance, the quaint images of the *raḥīl*: the hardships of travelling are replaced by those of ageing. This feature, and the many examples proffered by Ibn Rashīq point to the malleability of *al-shayb wa-l-shabāb*, such that it can be turned towards the crafting of a type of urban poetry more in tune with *muḥdath* poetics.

The tight bond between *al-shayb wa-l-shabāb* and *badīʿ* poetic that can be inferred from Ibn Rashīq's usage of the motif in his critical work, is reinforced by yet another, albeit later, Maghribī work of poetic criticism: Ḥāzim al-Qartājannī's *Minhāj*. A survey of the work reveals a rather meagre total of four quotations on *al-shayb wa-l-shabāb*. The first of these occurs in a heading on *muṭābaqa*, mostly translated as 'antithesis'.[21] The quote, from Diʿbil al-Khuzāʿī, is presented as an example of *muṭābaqa maḥḍa* or 'pure antithesis': that is to say, an antithesis construed by means of two words of directly opposite meaning (as in to weep and to laugh) as opposed to *ghayr maḥḍa* which contrasts words whose meaning is close to opposite yet not directly opposite as in 'to smile' and 'to weep' and words with different yet not opposite meaning, such as white as opposed to red:

[21] Encyclopaedia of Islam, 2nd edition: *Tibāḳ*.

لا تعجبني يا سلم من رجل ... ضحك المشيب برأسه فبكى[22]

Do not marvel, O Salma, at a crying man whose white hair laughs on his head

Ḥāzim's example reveals a quintessential feature of the motif of old age: it lends itself extremely well to deploy contrasts and antitheses which are the bread and butter of *badīʿ*'s poetics. The two examples from Ibn Rashīq and al-Qarṭājannī are most telling in this sense. Opposition, as in white and black hair, for example, is charged with a host of ancillary meanings, mostly with reference to the moral sphere. It is not by accident that the second appearance of *al-shayb wa-l-shabāb* in Ḥāzim's work happens to be under the heading '*taḥsīn wa taqbīḥ*', 'to make something good or repellent'.[23] The heading describes how verse can be meant to convey the propriety, or lack thereof, of a certain act, and thus serve as an admonishment to the poet's audience. The goodness or badness of an act can be inherent or not inherent: i.e., related to accidents such as time, place, the reason and outcome of the act. As a fitting example, Ḥāzim presents the case of an old man infatuated with a young girl and says that, should we wish to dissuade the hoary Romeo from pursuing such a love affair, we could rely (*iʿtimadnā*) on poetic sayings (*aqāwīl shiʿriyya*) that shame old men who run after young girls.[24]

Ḥāzim's work contains two more references to *al-shayb wa-l-shabāb*. The first is an excerpt from Qudāma: two lines by Abū Nūwās on the description of wine. The quotation illustrates simile (*tashbīh*), with wine bubbles as white hair, and the wine underneath these as black hair. Ḥāzim engages with both Qudāma and Abū Faraj (al-Isfahānī) on the criticism of Abū Nūwās's simile, but this debate remains on the periphery of our topic. While we find no discussion, on the part of Ḥāzim, of the motif of *al-shayb wa-l-shabāb*, as such, his quotation substantiates the pervasiveness of *al-shayb wa-l-shabāb* in *badīʿ* poetry: from the *nasīb* to the *khamriyya* to the *zuhdiyya*, virtually no *gharaḍ* among the *aghrāḍ* of the *qaṣīda* is left unscathed (we will see how the theme found its way even into encomiastic verse) by the theme of old age.

The *Minhāj*'s final example of *al-shayb wa-l-shabāb* occurs under the heading '*tahsīn al-qubḥ wa taqbīḥ al-husn*': i.e. making what is ugly look beautiful, and what is beautiful look ugly. Ḥāzim classifies this among the *aghrāḍ al-shiʿr*.

22 Al-Qarṭājannī, *Minḥāj*, p. 63.

23 Encyclopaedia of Islam. 2nd edition: *taḥsīn wa taqbīḥ*.

24 Al-Qarṭājannī, *Minhāj*, p. 157.

According to Ḥāzim, some poets really excel in this, some are rather weak at it, and a third category stands in between the two. As one among the finest examples of the above, Ḥāzim quotes Ibn al-Rūmī, who described the narcissus using *tahsīn al-qubḥ wa taqbīḥ al-husn*, 'beautifying' love in old age:

لاح شيبي فظلت أمرح فيه ... مرح الطرف في اللجام المحلى[25]

When my white hair appeared, she rejoiced in it, with the joy of one who gazes upon an embroidered garment.

In this line, white hair replaces the blossoming white petals of the narcissus, and Ibn al-Rūmī obtains semantic layering with the description of the flower opening up to the psychological dimension of a lover's acceptance or rejection in old age. At this point, we may take stock of the development of *al-shayb wa-l-shabāb* in classical Arabic poetics. We have seen how Arabic critics appear concerned with more prominent poetic genres: *al-shayb wa-l-shabāb* does not figure among their classifications *aghrāḍ*, *ṣunūf*, and *ḍurūb*. We have also seen how Maghribī critics such as Ḥāzim al-Qarṭājannī and Ibn Rāshīq do not include *al-shayb wa-l-shabāb* in their classifications of poetic themes. They both consistently use passages on old age poetry, however, in order to illustrate certain *aghrāḍ* (as in the quotation above from Ḥāzim al-Qarṭājannī) or figures of speech (as in Ibn Rashīq). Based on such evidence, and on a partial survey of eastern authors, we cannot speak of a poetic aim or 'type' for *al-shayb wa-l-shabāb*. I suggest the English 'motif', a term which conveys the idea of a malleable trope that could be deployed within a variety of aims (*aghrāḍ*) and poetic genres, as was the case particularly after the *muḥdath*. But even though a lesser element within the overall economy of a poem, *al-shayb wa-l-shabāb* became so prominent a motif as to compete with its more illustrious cousins such as the *nasīb* and the *raḥīl*, which it sometimes replaced. When we analyse the poetry of Abū Isḥāq and Ibn Ḥamdīs we find some notable examples of the prominence of this motif, as we will see shortly.

[25] Al-Qarṭājannī, *Minhāj*, p. 317.

II. Al-Sharīf al-Murtaḍā: The Allure of Old Age and the Idea of 'Thematic Displacement'

As the critical works surveyed do not provide us with any critical appraisal of the motif of ageing from the viewpoint of rhetoric and aesthetics, we must resort to an altogether different type of work, namely, an anthology. Al-Sharīf al-Murtaḍā's *al-shihāb fī al-shayb wa-l-shabāb*, a thematic anthology devoted exclusively to the motif of ageing, provides us with the first, albeit succinct, aesthetic appraisal of Arabic old age poetry. After listing the salient features of *al-shayb wa-l-shabāb* and engaging in the debate over the merits of 'new' vs. 'ancient' poetics and of the merits of a *maṭbūʿ* over a *maṣnūʿ* poet, al-Murtaḍā formulates his own critical judgement on the overall motif of old age poetry. The judgement is worth quoting as it seems to address one of my central concerns in this book: what made the poetics of ageing so popular among Arabic writers and their audience?

> فأما بلاغة العبارة عنها وجلاؤها في معاريض الواصلة إلى القلوب بلا حجاب والانتقال في المعنى الواحد من عبارة إلى غيرها مما يزيد عليها براعة وبلاغة او يساويها او يقاربها حتى يصير المعنى باختلاف العبارة عنه وتغير الهيئات عليه وإن كان واحدا كأنه مختلف في نفسه.[26]

> That which makes it [i.e. the motif of youth and old age] superior, or equal, or close [to other *maʿanī*] is eloquence and clarity of expression about it (ʿibāra) in propositions that reach the heart without a veil, and the shifting, within a single meaning (maʿnā), from one expression to another, so that the meaning itself becomes the opposite of the expression, changing its exterior appearance and, while remaining one, it is as if was, in itself, different.

Al-Murtaḍā not only refers in his work to *al-shayb wa-l-shabāb* as a *maʿnā* — I have opted to render the word, with Shoeler, as 'poetic thought', but he also makes reference to *maʿānī al-shayb wa-l-shabāb*. 'Meanings' of old age poetry can be thus rendered as 'poetic thoughts': something larger than and inclusive of the individual image (*ʿibāra*), but narrower and included in the 'poetic aim'. According to al-Murtaḍā, the progressive layering of poetic images allows for a bending of the original poetic theme: in the case proffered by al-Murtaḍā, the genre boundaries of *al-shayb wa-l-shabāb* are pushed by such a layering until the

[26] Al-Sharīf al-Murtaḍā, *Al-Shihāb*, p. 2.

original image is altered. The beauty of old age poetry resides, in al-Murtaḍā's words, in its immediacy and its power to alter the original aims and themes of the *qaṣīda*. In his words: its capacity to 'reach the heart without a veil' — with images that change constantly so as to surprise the audience, altering each poetic thought indefinitely.[27] This reiterated shifting in images opens up a variety of meanings, and the original description of old age acquires semantic depth drawn from the many poetic genres of the *qaṣīda*. In turn, these poetic genres acquire new meanings through the juxtaposition of old age imagery. We may call this process 'thematic displacement': the shifting of images within a discrete thematic unit confers to the poem a polysemy which enriches its meta-textual dimension.

Al-Sharīf al-Murtaḍā's introduction underscores such rich semantic layering as the marker of an accomplished poem. We may also read more into his phrase '*al-maʿāriḍ al-wāṣila ilā al-qulūb bi-lā ḥijāb*' (propositions that reach the hearts without a veil): al-Murtaḍā engages with critics of *al-muḥtadhūn* by defending their decision to favour new poetic genres, such as *al-shayb wa-l-shabāb*, as opposed to the quaint traditional themes of the *qaṣīda*. The poetics of ageing speaks directly to the hearts of those whose youth has passed, it allows for unmediated communion between a poet and their audience: a poetics that strives for universality, familiar to audiences from Córdoba to Samarkand and beyond.

The main 'themes' summarized by al-Sharīf al-Murtaḍā in his introduction recur in Arabic poetry from Abū Tammām and al-Buḥturī up to Ibn Ḥamdīs and Abū Isḥāq three centuries later. Poets redeployed tropes of old age in compliance with poetic trends, once the motif had become canonical. Often, but not necessarily, these 'images' or 'themes' appeared in succession one after the other within discrete sections on old age in the *qaṣīda*. They can be summarized as follows:

Appearance of White Hair

Descriptions of the first white hair, often with elaborate metaphors and other figures of speech such as puns, used to describe the contrast of black and white hair. Abū Tammām and al-Buḥturī were the first to develop a wide repertoire of stock-phrases and similes on white hair, which were adopted and reworked

[27] One may argue that this is not at all a feature unique to *al-shayb wa-l-shabāb*, and one may refer, for instance, to Sells's work on the *nasīb* (see Sells, 'Guises of the *Ghūl*', pp. 130–64).

by later poets. Some examples include the representation of white hair on the head as stars appearing in the night sky; a lamp that is lighted on top of one's head, or the appearance of the dawn. These metaphors are often expanded and elaborated in multiple lines. This imagery fits within the aesthetics of descriptive poetry (*waṣf*), in which the poet exhibits his poetic bravado deploying lexical oddities and daring analogies.

The Departure of Youth

Youth has passed, and the poet reflect on his old age (I use the masculine pronoun, as *al-shayb wa-l-shabāb* remained a heavily gendered motif adopted, to my knowledge, solely by male poets), and contemplates his physical decay. This theme includes the description of the loss of agency on behalf of the poet due to the weakness of old age, the lack of self-reliance, and inability to face life's trials as one used to when young. This section on the departure of youth is often filled by a longing for the heydays of youth and maturity in which the poet was, or portrays himself as he was, a fearless warrior and a conqueror of women's hearts.

Unrequited Love

When youth passes and hair turns grey, young women shun men and sensual desire is bound to remain unrequited. This motif often occupies multiple lines of the sections on old age. The poet remembers his exploits as a Casanova and compares them with his present inability to capture the attention of young girls. This is an important motif, for it is in open antithesis with the *nasīb*, or amatory preface, customary in the *qaṣīda*; however, it is not rare to find the *nasīb* followed by a reflection on old age and unrequited love, as will be seen later on particularly in the poetry of Ibn Ḥamdīs. The contrast allows for a creative re-elaboration of one the *qaṣīda*'s most traditional openings.

Dye

The poet mentions the use of dye to cover white hair. The practice is described and either criticized or praised. Dye becomes a metaphor for disguise and deception, opening the realm of the physical to the moral and psychological: the deception of Time, men's deception, the boundaries of truth and lies.

Appeals to Abandon Sensual Pursuits

When we grow old, we should abandon sensual pleasures (sex, in particular) as these become both unattainable and ludicrous. The poet reflects that, since old age forbids him sexual gratification, he would be better off looking for spiritual pursuits. This last theme brings the motif of *al-shayb wa-l-shabāb* within that of *zuhd*, or ascetic poetry, which will be the subject of this book's final chapter.

These themes were commonly developed in the context of longer poems that may have included other sub-genres of the classical ode: the amatory preface, the night journey, the praise, the satire or the boast, as well as bacchic, hunting, naturalistic, and gnomic themes. Both Ibn Ḥamdīs' and Abū Isḥāq adopted most of the themes summarized above in their own poems, and the theme of old age poetry is pervasive in their overall production. In what follows, I explore each of these two poets' own appropriation of these themes and their personal reworking of *al-shayb wa-l-shabāb*.

III. Abū Isḥāq: Old Age as Asceticism

In what follows, I will discuss how Abū Isḥāq's own poems on old age fit within the canonical imagery of *al-shayb wa-l-shabāb*, and how they stand out as original. A total of thirteen poems out of the thirty-three contained in Abū Isḥāq's short *dīwān* make explicit reference to his growing old, to the whitening of his hair, and to his bodily decay. However, hardly any poem by Abū Isḥāq is devoid of some reference to the twilight of man's life. As the principal Andalusian poet of *zuhdiyyāt*, ascetic poems in which he exhorted his audience to reflect upon the caducity of life, the poetics of ageing represent the pillar of Abū Isḥāq's overall poetic production. The theme of ageing is deeply entwined, for Abū Isḥāq, with his ascetic poems: it informs his overall poetic persona to such an extent that it is impossible to detach Abū Isḥāq's usage of *al-shayb wa-l-shabāb* from his ascetic verse, which will be dealt in detail in the fourth chapter. It is both natural and correct to assume that the description of white hair would take up long portions of Abū Isḥāq's ascetic poems, and that he would participate in the poetic discourse on the advantages and disadvantages of growing old. At first reading, however, Abū Isḥāq's stance on the theme of old age seems ambiguous: we see the poet regretting and crying over the loss of his youth and, at the same time, seeking repentance and forgiveness over the sins he committed while young. He claims to accept white hair as a warning to reconsider his sins and to strive for a saintly life, but at the same time, he bitterly mourns the vigour of youth and the end of pleasures reserved to the young: first and foremost, sex. He insists on the transience of all that is physical, as for instance on the decay of his own body, but at the same time he contemplates with dismay the loss of physical strength and sexual power. Such ambiguity remains unsolved, making it problematic to define Abū Isḥāq's poetic persona as a pious and ascetic individual who renounced the world to seek a spiritual dimension to his twilight years, that is to say, a *zāhid*. The poet, on the contrary, longs for youth and appears to complain about the fact in particular that young women shun his attentions. White hair is consistently portrayed as a precious warning of mortality. As such, it is a counsellor who diverts old men from earthly to spiritual concerns. White hair is also a censor: it shames those who, in their old age, still strive in pursuit of pleasure. Abū Isḥāq's poems often exhort men to abide by the warnings of white hair, to their great advantage, while vituperating the old men who, dismissing such a warning, still pursue amorous escapades and pleasures in their old age. But, surprisingly, the old poet appears to count himself first among of these 'dirty old men'! This fact has been underscored by Scheindlin, in his commentary to *Dīwān,* 1.[28] In this poem, Abū Isḥāq, an old man of sixty, preaches to a young man called Abū Bakr about the advantages of abstinence. The old poet rebukes the youth for pursuing adventures with young girls rather than focusing on pious deeds. However, Abū Isḥāq inverts the roles, spurring Abū Bakr to scold him instead, for he himself, an old man, is still pursuing such adventures! The originality of this poem has been underscored by Scheindlin in his article: Abū Isḥāq's poetry often takes the shape of a pious advice or rebuke, based on the recognition of man's ageing and mortality. This is one pertinent example:

Abū Isḥāq, no. 1[29]

١. تفــتُّ فــؤادك الأيــامِ فــتّ   وتنحــتُ جســمك السّــاعاتُ نَحتــاً
٢. وتدعـوكَ المَنـونُ دُعـاءَ صِـدقٍ   ألا ياصــاحِ أنــتَ أُريــدُ أنتــا
٦. أبــا بكــرٍ دَعَوتُــكَ لــو أجَبتــا   إلــى مــا فيــه حظُّــكَ إن عقلتــا

1. Days crumble your heart into bits and hours reduce your body to emaciation
2. And doom calls out your name with a call that cannot be denied: O friend — it is you I want, yes, you!

[28] See Scheindlin, 'Old Age in Hebrew and Arabic "Zuhd" Poetry', pp. 89–90.

[29] Abū Isḥāq, *Dīwān*, ed. by Muḥammad Riḍwān al-Dāya, pp. 23–35.

6. Abū Bakr, I am calling you — if only you will respond — to something that will be good for you, if you are to be sensible

Lines one and two are *muqaddima ḥikamīya* or gnomic introduction, in which the poet reflects on mortality and physical deterioration. This introduction continues up to line six, in which the poet addresses Abū Bakr inviting him to abandon the pursuit of pleasure. After a long digression on the theme of sin and repentance, in line sixty-two the poet suddenly invites Abū Bakr to counterattack his rebuke. It is the poet who needs advice, we read, for he is still pursuing pleasures as an old man:

٦٢. و قل لي نصيحُ لأنتَ أولى بِنُصحِكَ لو بعقلكَ قد نظرتا
٧٢. لَيقبُحُ با لفتى فعلُ التّصابي وأقبَحُ منهُ شيخٌ قد تفتَّى

62. Why don't you say to me: 'O counsellor, if you look at the situation rightly, you are more in need of your counsel than I!'

72. True, it is ugly when a young man pursues illicit liaisons, but uglier by far is an old man playing the youth!

These two lines, which begin and end Abū Isḥāq's self-directed apostrophe, reverse the roles of advisor and advised: the old poet, and not the young Abū Bakr, is the one who needs advice the most regarding shameful amorous pursuits. This 'poetic dialogue' confers on the poem a unique character when compared to other, more standardized ascetic poems by Abū Isḥāq: with its unexpected reversal of roles, and through characterization of a poetic persona who rebukes others while being an impenitent sinner himself, Abū Isḥāq amplifies on the *zuhdiyya*'s fundamental aims: an exercise in self-deprecation, we could say. From this poem, there also emerges one of the more paradoxical aspects of Abū Isḥāq's poetics of ageing, namely, its focus on carnality. As he describes his own ageing, the poet denounces almost obsessively his many failed attempts to charm young women. A graphic example of this trend is found in *Dīwān,* 9, where Abū Isḥāq crafts this discourse on a strident dialectic between the linguistic lore and imagery of the *nasīb* and the motif of old age:

Abū Isḥāq, no. 9[30]

١.	قد بلغتَ السّتّينَ ويحكَ فاعلمْ	أنَّ ما بعدها عليكَ تلوّم
٢.	فإذا ما انقضَتْ سِنوكَ وولّت	فَصَلَ الحاكِمُ القَضاءَ فأبرمْ
٣.	أنت مِثلَ السّجِلّ يُنشَرُ حيناً	ثمَّ يُطوى من بعدِ ذاكَ ويُختمْ
٤.	كيفَ يلتَذُّ بالحَياةِ لَبِيبٌ	فوَّقتْ نَحوهُ المْمَنيّةُ أسهمْ
٥.	ليسَ يَدْري متى يُفاجيهِ منها	صائبٌ يقصِفُ الظهورَ ويقصِمْ
٦.	ما لِغُصني ذوى وكانَ نَضيراً	ولِظهري انحنى وكانَ مُقَوّمْ
٧.	ولِحَدّي نبا وكانَ مُبيراً	ولِجيشي انثنى وكان عرمرمْ
٨.	ولِدهري أدالَ شرخَ شبابي	بمَشيبٍ عندَ الحسانِ مُذَمَّم
٩.	فأنا اليومَ عن هواهُنَّ سالٍ	وقديماً بِهنَّ كُنتُ مُتيَّم
١٠.	لو بِرَوقِ الزمانِ يُنطَحُ يوماً	ركنُ ثهلانَ هدَّهُ فَتهدَّم
١١.	نحنُ في منزلِ الفناءِ ولكِن	هوَ بابٌ إلى البقاءِ وسلَّمْ
٢١.	ورَحى الْمَوتِ تستديرُ علينا	أبداً تطحَنُ الْجميعَ تهشِمْ
١٣.	وأنا مُوقنٌ بذاكَ عليم	وفعالي فِعالُ مَنْ ليسَ يعلمْ
١٤.	وكذا أمتطِي الهُوَينا إلى أن	أُتوفّى فَعندَ ذالكَ أندمْ
١٥.	فعسى مَن لَهُ أُعفّرُ وجهي	سَيَرَى فاقتي إليه فيرحمْ
١٦.	فشفيعي إليه حُسنُ ظنوني	ورجائي لهُ وأنّي مسلم
١٧.	ولهُ الحمدُ أنْ هذاني لهذا	عددَ القطرِ ما الحمامُ ترنَّم
١٨.	وإليه ضراعتي وابتهالي	في مُعافاةِ شيبتي من جهنَّمْ

1. You have reached your sixties, beware! Know that what is to come is but borrowed time
2. and if your life is not over yet, the judge has proclaimed a final verdict
3. You are like the scroll, which is briefly unfurled and then rolled back and sealed
4. How can a wise man enjoy life, while Death points arrows at him?

[30] Abū Isḥāq, *Dīwān*, ed. by Muḥammad Riḍwān al-Dāya, pp. 56–58.

5. He does not know when its infallible archer will suddenly hit him with a fatal shot
6. What of my branch, now withered, when once it was in full bloom, and what of my back, now curved, when once it was straight?
7. What of my knife, now dull, when once it was sharp and what of my army, retreating, and once almighty?
8. Time has exchanged the prime of youth for grey hair, despised by young girls
9. So now I am neglected by them, when once I was yearned for
10. If the side of Mount Thahlān was hit by the horn of Time, it would be cracked and demolished
11. We reside in the abode of annihilation; it is also a door and a staircase to eternal life
12. The mill of Death constantly revolving over us, forever grinding and crushing all,
13. And though I am aware of this, I act as if I did not know!
14. And so I travel calmly towards death, and on its verge, I repent!
15. But to whom will I now turn my face, that he may see my misery and be merciful?
16. My intercessors to Him: my good thoughts, my trust in Him, and my being a Muslim.
17. May he be praised as much as the constant thin rain falls, and as long as the doves coo
18. To him I submit in supplication: may He spare my grey hair from Hellfire!

We can say that these lines display the whole array of Abū Isḥāq's favourite poetic themes: old age, sin and damnation, wisdom (*ḥikma*), and the closing supplication to God (*duʿāʾ*). The poem's thematic arrangement is as follows: an introductory segment on old age [1–9], a second section on *ḥikma* [10–13], fear of damnation [14–16] and the final supplication to God [17–18]. The poem's central section, where Abū Isḥāq looks down on his ageing body [ll. 6–9] is particularly effective in depicting the poet's sexual impotence and physical decrepitude, through the images of a limp branch and a dull sword. Strength has vanished: the poet's army surrenders before the fight. The anti-climax in this description reaches its lowest point in line nine, where the poet concludes that young girls, who once favoured him, now shun him on account of his decrepitude. The whole section tampers with the archetype of the poet-hero: it parodies both the *nasīb* (amatory preface) and the *fakhr* (boast) sections of the *qaṣīda*, enhancing the metatextual density of the poem. Such allusion, as clarified by Gruendler, is meant to enhance the overall quality of the ode, by creating multiple semantic layers.[31] The allusion to *fakhr*, through the use of martial lexicon, is instrumental in increasing the satirical effect of the poet's portrait of himself as an old man. A similar usage is found in yet another *zuhdiyya* by Abū Isḥāq, which opens with an unlikely contextualization of the *nasīb*.

Abū Isḥāq, no. 2[32]

١. تُغازِلُنــي المَنِيّــةُ مــن قَريــبِ وتَلحَظُنــي مُلاحظَــةَ الرقيــبِ

1. Death is courting me closely, she looks at me with the look of a censor.

In this opening line, we find three staples of Arabic love poetry: first, the verb *ghāzala*, to court or flirt; second, the *laḥẓ* or glance which betrays love or causes one to fall in love; third, the *raqīb*, or censor, who scolds the enamoured poet over his childish infatuation. But embedding these tropes in a wider narrative on ageing creates a dramatic contrast: the *nasīb* is reproduced, as the customary opening of a tripartite ode, within an unexpected setting. This opening is thus a sort of anti-*nasīb* with a singular reversal of roles. The poet is the object, not the subject of the amatory preface, and his suitor is none other than his own death. The anti-*nasīb* leads to an anti-*fakhr* (boast), in which the poet describes himself as follows:

٥. أدال الشــيبُ يــا صــاحِ شــبابي فعُيِّضْــتُ البغيــضَ مــن الحبيــبِ
٦. وبُدّلــتُ التّثاقُــلَ مــن نَشــاطي ومــن حُســنِ النضــارَةِ بالشُّــحوبِ
٧. كــذاكَ الشــمسُ يعلوهــا اصفــرار إذا جنحــتْ ومالــت للغــروبِ

31 See Gruendler, *Medieval Arabic Praise Poetry*, pp. 3–48.

32 Abū Isḥāq, *Dīwān*, ed. by Muḥammad Riḍwān al-Dāya, pp. 36–37.

5. White hair, my friend, has vanquished my youth; once I was loved, now I am loathed
6. I was nimble, now I am slow, I was healthy, now I am withered and pale
7. like the sun going yellow, when it declines and sets

Abū Isḥāq laments his physical decay: beauty has vanished, vigour declines, he has become an unwelcome lover. The paleness of his countenance resembles the weak light of a fading sunset, harbinger of the night. Subsequently, the poet redeploys martial analogies in a succession of maxims:

٨. تحارِبُنا جنودٌ لا تجارى   ولا تُلقب آسادِ الحروبِ
٩. هي الأقدارُ والآجالُ تأتي   فتنزِلُ بالمِطبّبِ والطبيب
١٠. تفوّقُ أسهُماً عن قَوسِ غيبٍ   وما أغراضُها غيرُ القلوبِ
١١. فأنى باحتراسٍ من جنودٍ   مؤيّدَةٍ تُمَدُّ منَ الغيوبِ

8. Troops with no equal wage war on us; not even the champions of war can overpower them
9. They are Fate and Death approaching, who fall upon both patient and doctor
10. Arrows are aimed from an invisible bow, their target is but the heart
11. How to be on guard from such a mighty army, reinforced by divine powers?

The poet then apostrophizes himself over his heedlessness of the warning of old age:

٢١. وما آسى على الدنيا ولكن   على ما ركبتُ من الذنوبِ
١٣. فيا لهفي على طول اغتراري   ويا ويحي من اليوم العصيب
١٤. إذ أنا لم أنُحْ نفسي وأبكي   على حوبي بتَهتانِ سكوب
١٥. فمن هذا الذي بعدي سيبكي   عليها من بعيد أو قريب؟

12. I grieve not the world, but the sins I rode on
13. Woe unto me! How long my delusion! Woe unto me on reckoning day!

14. If I will not lament myself and my sins, as copious as raindrops in the storm
15. Who will, after me, cry over them, whether near or far?

The thematic arrangement of this excerpt is similar to that of the poem previously analysed: old age, *ḥikma*, sin, and fear of damnation. The poem's imagery closely adheres to the conventions of *zuhd* poetry, but Abū Isḥāq does not fail to endow these lines with personality. The meter, *wāfir*, is a fast paced one, which enhances immediacy; the initial reversed *nasīb* in which the poet is both courted and scolded by death itself opens the poem to an intertextual layering which enriches its meaning. Then the martial lexicon of lines eight to eleven resuscitates the glories of the Arabic war poem (*ḥarbiyya*) in another unusual inversion of roles: old age wages war on the poet, with its invisible weapons constantly waiting to deal their fatal blow; no respite is granted to the sinner. The poem's closing line, perhaps the nearest to modern audiences' sensibilities, openly voices our apprehension over oblivion after death. Thus, the two poems analysed above display a similar thematic structure, but the *dīwān* reveals how the majority of Abū Isḥāq's poems on old age display a common thematic structure. Once again, it can be summarized as follows: in the opening lines the poet contemplates his white hair and ponders his advanced age and his bodily decay. He scolds himself for his untimely insistence on pursuing pleasure, his continuous straying from the straight path in religion, and his incurable love for the world. Finally, he contemplates his imminent death, often pondering the long time he will spend in the grave before divine judgment. He then closes the poem with an appeal to God for salvation. We see these concepts strung together in three lines belonging to a thirty-three line *zuhdiyya*.

Abū Isḥāq, no. 5[33]

٧. شـاب القَذال فـآن لـي إن أرعـوي   لــو متعظــا بشــيب قَــذالِ
٨. ولـو اننــي مســتبصِر إذ حـلّ بـي   لعلمــت أنّ حلولَــهُ ترحالــي
٩. فنظــرت فــي زادٍ لــدار إقامتــي   وســألت ربـي أن يحـلّ عقالــي

7. Most of my hair has gone white. The time has come for me to repent, if I am to understand the warning of white hair!

[33] Abū Isḥāq, *Dīwān*, ed. by Muḥammad Riḍwān al-Dāya, pp. 44–47.

8. If I were a sensible man I would know that I shall be released, and my release is my departure! [from the world]
9. I have pondered long upon the abode of my residence, and I asked my lord to release me

A further example is found in the poem below, where Abū Isḥāq compares the first white hair to the first drops of rain announcing a storm:

Abū Isḥāq, no. 24[34]

١. بصرت بشيبة وخطت نَصيلي   فقلت له تأهّبْ للرحيل
٢. ولا يهن القليل عليك منها   ما في الشيب ويحك من قليل
٣. فكم قد أبصرت عيناك مزنا   صابك طلّها قبل الهمول
٤. وكم عاينت خيط الصبح يجلو   سواد الليل كالسيف الصقيل
٥. ولا تحرق بنذر الشيب واعلم   بأنّ القطر يبعث بالسيول

1. I noticed a white hair that was lining my beard and I said to it, you are calling me to death.
2. A white hair should never be dismissed as being too little for there is no 'too little' when it comes to white hair.
3. How many rain clouds have your eyes seen, whose drops have touched you before the pouring rain?
4. Have you seen the feeble first ray of sunrise cutting up the black night like a polished sword?
5. Do not dismiss the warning of white hair, and know that tiny raindrops can fill up a river!

These two poems evoke the transition from youth to old age with a powerful set of images that emphasize the all-too-quick withering of man. In line one of the second excerpt we see the poet contemplating a first white hair in his own beard, which he addresses as a messenger of his imminent departure from the world. The first white hairs are depicted as the initial drops of a rainstorm, slow at the beginning and then more and more abundant. Death impinges on men, who should be constantly mindful of its approach, and repent in a timely man-

[34] Abū Isḥāq, *Dīwān*, ed. by Muḥammad Riḍwān al-Dāya, pp. 105–06.

ner taking the afterlife into account. In this context grey hair is a God-given sign given to men as an opportunity to reconsider the mistakes of their youth.

In yet another poem Abū Isḥāq emphasizes his own heedlessness to the warning of white hair. The poet often questions his own purpose of abstaining from sin and ponders the little time that is left to him to change his conduct. He also considers that his age is too advanced for repentance, and that even knowing that time is short, he himself is not yet firmly determined to repent:

Abū Isḥāq, no. 6[35]

٧. أفي الستين أهجع في مقيلي   وحادي الموتِ يوقِظُ للرواح
٨. وقد نشر الزمان لواء شيبي   ليطويني ويسلبني وشاحى
٩. وقد سلّ الحمام عليّ نصلا   سيقتلني وإن شاكت سلاحى
١٠. ويحملني إلى الأجداث صحبي   إلى ضيق هناك أو انفساح
١١. فأُجزى الخير إن قدمت خيرا   وشراً إن خزيت على اجتراحي
٢١. وه أنا ذا على علمي بهذا   بطئ الشأو في سنن الصلاح

7. In my sixties, will I keep on slumbering in my resting place, while death is calling me to wake up and prepare for my journey?
8. Time has stretched the banner of white hair, making me wither and depriving me of my sword
9. Death has its arrow already drawn for me. It will kill me no matter my armour
10. My master, it will take me to my tomb and there [I will lie] wither in tightness or space
11. So I will be repaid with good if I have done any good, and with punishment if I have perpetrate a crime
12. And here I am, knowing this, slow in purpose at the age of piety.

In line seven, the poet ponders his impending death after crossing the threshold of sixty years. Line eight re-evokes the familiar images of white hair and the sword, while lines nine to eleven dwell on the theme of mortality and the afterlife, the reward for one's pious deeds, and the punishment for one's sin.

[35] Abū Isḥāq, *Dīwān*, ed. by Muḥammad Riḍwān al-Dāya, pp. 48–50.

These lines re-propose themes already analysed and outline once again the common aim of Abū Isḥāq's usage of the tropes poems of old age, which are consistently deployed in the context of his *zuhdiyyāt*. From the above overview of Abū Isḥāq's lines on old age, we can appreciate how the poetic thought of *al-shayb wa-l-shabāb* is, for this poet, entirely subservient to the ascetic poems which constitute the cornerstone of his overall poetics. Old age is, for Abū Isḥāq, a privileged locus for slowing down, pondering one's life and, ostensibly, finally ridding oneself of one's cravings and desires, in pursue of virtue. The poet adopts the persona of an old man as, in itself, it reinforces the self-directed appeals to abandon the pursuit of pleasure, and to make preparations for the long journey awaiting him after his impending death. Old age is the ultimate warner of man, and, loathed as it may be, it comes across as a precious ally in the Muslim poet's quest for redemption. In this sense Scheindlin's evaluation of Abū Isḥāq usage of old age poetry, namely that the focus of these poems is really that even in old age the poet is still incapable of fully abandoning the pursuit of pleasure, should be reassessed. It is clear that Abū Isḥāq's construction of an ageing poetic persona is subservient to the rhetoric enhancement of his ascetic message: the sharper the contrast between decrepitude and desire, and between a self-declared incapacity to forsake *al-dunyā* for *al-akhīra*, the more effective the poetic sermon and the exercise in self mortification that lies at the heart of the *zuhdiyya*. As I will dwell upon this *maʿnā*, in detail, in the fourth chapter of this book, there is no need for further discussion at this point. In what follows I will, instead, focus on Ibn Ḥamdīs's own usage of *al-shayb wa-l-shabāb*, that will prove much more diversified when compared to Abū Isḥāq's.

IV. Ibn Ḥamdīs: A Strategic Use of Old Age Verse

Abū Isḥāq's consistent usage of old age tropes within the *zuhdiyya* is entirely reversed when we look at Ibn Ḥamdīs's *dīwān*. There, we find lines on old age appearing in the most disparate contexts: from the love poem to the wine song. This is due to the radically different character of Ibn Ḥamdīs's poetic persona when compared to Abū Isḥāq's. The former was a professional poet, a court panegyrist, and an entertainer, while the latter was a *faqīh* who resorted to the poetic channel as a complement to his profession of jurist. Ibn Ḥamdīs's *dīwān* is many times the size of Abū Isḥāq's, hence, my study of Ibn Ḥamdīs's *shayb* lines occupies a much larger portion of this chapter. Ibn Ḥamdīs flourished as a professional panegyrist two hundred years after Arabic court-poetry had reached its creative zenith. The inventive era of the Arabic *qaṣīda* had stalled, particularly in the realm of praise poetry, as patrons across *dār al-Islām* sought and expected to have the forms of famous Eastern panegyrics replicated in their own praises. The twelfth century court poet had to display a thorough mastery of the classical poetic canon, both in form and in content and Ibn Ḥamdīs, who wrote at a time of political and professional uncertainty, adhered tenaciously to the literary conventions that his profession demanded. Formally, his poetry remained very much mainstream and as such it was a highly marketable good that could be adapted to the taste of different patrons. His verses covered the many poetic thoughts of the classical Arabic *qaṣīda*, with the notable exception of the invective (*al-hijāʾ*), a genre which, by his own admission, he rejected.[36] Ibn Ḥamdīs was capable of borrowing the magniloquence of the Eastern panegyrists to the great Abbasid caliphs for his eulogies to the Maghrib's precarious kings and dynasties. He appeased his audiences by tapping into contemporary taste for describing gardens and drinking parties, he also reproduced the more intimate registers of the *qaṣīda*: lines on old age, dirges, and ascetic poems, particularly as he grew old and faced his own mortality, the loss of patrons, family members, and of his own physical health. It is perhaps tempting, for the modern reader, to look for the Ibn Ḥamdīs' own voice in these more personal lines. However, the reader must be aware that Ibn Ḥamdīs, in writing on growing old and facing mortality, was tapping into a long-established tradition made up of distinct poetic thoughts, each possessing its own repertoire of images and tropes, some of which I have summarized above. Heinrichs and Gruendler have clarified how medieval Arabic poetry can be fully understood only by having a clear perception of the concepts of poetic 'quotation' (*taḍmīn*), 'allusion' (*talmīḥ*), 'taking over' (*akhdh*) and 'theft' (*sariqa*).[37] In the words of Beatrice Gruendler:

> A poet anticipated close scrutiny of his work and took care to ensure its linguistic soundness and ethical property. But he also relied on his audience to gauge his technical bravado. In particular he assumed their knowledge of themes and motifs, enabling them to identify how much of a line or hemistich came from an existing verse and how he enhanced it by giving it new form and meaning.[38]

There is no question that Ibn Ḥamdīs' versification is best appreciated in the context of the mannerist trends of his times. His adoption of the motifs of ageing, the subject of this study, abides by specific rules and conventions, similarly

[36] Ibn Ḥamdīs, *Dīwān*, 328, Ibn Ḥamdīs, *Dīwān*, ed. by Iḥsān ʿAbbās, pp. 520–21.

[37] Heinrichs, *The Hand of the Northwind*, p. 127; Gruender, *Medieval Arabic Praise Poetry*, pp. 3–48.

[38] Gruendler, *Medieval Arabic Praise Poetry*, p. 6.

to what we have seen discussing Abū Isḥāq. However, when we approach his late poems as a corpus, their intertextuality gives rise to new meanings, revealing a personal reworking of the classical forms and a high degree of individuality. These verses inform a personal poetics through which the poet chose to express both personal and collective concerns: mortality and the loss of youth on the one hand, and the political decline of Islam in the West and the fall of Muslim Sicily on the other hand. This reading reinforces the point made by Granara[39] in a previous study, that Ibn Ḥamdīs was at once a highly conservative as well as a progressive poet. The formal conservatism of Ibn Ḥamdīs' style was in fact a 'koine' which allowed the poet to share these private and collective issues with his varied audiences.

It is striking that critics of Ibn Ḥamdīs have barely focused on his verses of old age, for these pervade the larger part of his 'North African' poems, more than half his overall production, which are largely dedicated to his Zirid patrons. Ibn Ḥamdīs reached the Zirid court of Mahdiyya in his late thirties, and it was there that he reached the grand age of eighty. These poems thus constitute the production of his mature years and old age. From them, it appears that the poet embraced the persona of an ageing man wholeheartedly: hardly do we find a panegyric among those he dedicated to the Zirid emirs that is not peppered with lines on *al-shayb wa-l-shabāb*. This was an unlikely choice for panegyrics: typically, a festive mood was required to sing the praises of a patron. Yet, the ubiquitousness of segments on old age within the Zirid praises brings us to a set of questions that I will examine in what follows: how did Ibn Ḥamdīs deploy *al-shayb wa-l-shabāb* within these poems and for which purposes, and how did these segments on ageing enhance his praises to the Zirids? A response to these questions can be found in a panegyric dedicated to Abū al-Ḥasan al-Ḥasan b.ʿAlī b. Yaḥyā,[40] written when Ibn Ḥamdīs must have been somewhere between sixty-five and seventy-five years of age. The rule of al-Ḥasan in fact covers the last portion of Ibn Ḥamdīs's life: it began in 1121,

[39] Granara, *Remaking Muslim Sicily*, p. 171.

[40] The *qaṣīda* appears in the *dīwān* (ed. ʿAbbās) as the fourth within a succession of four poems all apparently dedicated to ʿAlī b. Yaḥyā. The series begins with 92, that the compiler of the *dīwān* introduces as: وقال يمدح الأمير أبو الحسن علي بن يحيى. The next three poems in the *dīwān* are simply introduced with وقال أيضاً يمدحه (93) and وقال يمدحه (94 or 95). It thus would appear that all poems would were written for ʿAli, but, instead, in 93 we read a dedication to Ibn ʿAlī, and in 94 and 95 to al-Ḥasan (Ibn ʿAlī). All three poems — 93, 94, 95 — were therefore written for al-Ḥasan ibn ʿAlī. We can attribute the confusion to an omission between poem 92 and 93 (a missing panegyric for al-Ḥasan), or, more likely, to a copyist error.

when Ibn Ḥamdīs was about sixty-five, and stretched beyond the time of the poet's death which probably happened in 1133.

The poem is a composite ode in which *al-shayb wa-l-shabāb* facilitates the transition from one thematic section to the next. It opens with an amatory preface (lines 1–7), followed by a section on old age (ll. 8–20), then a bacchic piece (ll. 21–29), and then yet another section on old age (ll. 30–33) that leads into a short description of a night-journey (ll. 34 and 35). It concludes with the praise of al-Ḥasan and a final boast. There follows, below, an abridged version of this 68-line ode:

Ibn Ḥamdīs, no. 95[41]

١. صادتك مهاة لم تصد فلواحظها شرك الأسد
٢. من تُوحي السحرَ بناظرةٍ لا تُنْفَثُ منه في العُقدِ
٣. لمياء تَضاحَكُ عن دررٍ بروقِ حياً وحصى برد
٤. يندى بالمسك لراشفه وسلافِ القهوة والشهد
٥. وَذَماءُ الليلِ على طرفٍ كترحّلِ روح عن جسد
٦. ورضابُ الماءِ بفيكِ جرى في جوهره عرضُ الصَّرَد
٧. كأنّ كليمَ الله بدا منه في الأفقِ بياضُ يد
٨. أسفي لفراق زمان صبا وركوبي قيد مها الخرد

...

١٣. نقضتْ وصلي بتتيّعها بالهجر ونومي بالسهد
١٤. وأصاب السود سهام البيض ببين البيض وبالنكد
١٥. عجبي لإصابة مرسلها من جوف ضلوعي في الخلد
١٦. يا نار نشاطي أين سنا ك وأين لظاك بمفأدي
١٧. زندي ولدتك وقد عقمت عن حمل السقط فلم تلد
١٨. أحييت بذكري ميت صباً أبكيه مسايرة الأبد
١٩. وطلبت الضد لأوجده وجموحي في الصد فلم أجد
٢٠. ولو أنّ كريماً تفقده يفدى بالنفس إذن لفدي
٢١. أذهبت الحزن بمذهبة وبها ذهبت لجين بدي

[41] Ibn Ḥamdīs, *Dīwān*, ed. by Iḥsān ʿAbbās, pp. 158–61.

٢٢. ولقد نادمت ندامى الراح بمطرفي وبمتلدي

...

٣٠. فالآن صددت كذي حذر عن ورد اللهو فلم أرد

٣١. وطردتُ منامَ الغي عن ال أجفان بإيقاظ الرشد

٣٢. ونقضت عهود الشرب فلا ودّ أصفيه لأهل دَدِ

٣٣. لا أشرب ما أنا واصفه فكأني بينهم قعدي

٣٤. ونقلت بعزمي من بلد قدم الإسراء إلى بلد

٣٥. في بطن الفلك مصارعة زمني وعلى ظهر الأُجد

٣٦. ووجدت الدين له حسنا سندا فلجأت إلى السند

1. You have been trapped by a wild ox that cannot be trapped, her glances are nets for the lion,
2. conjuring magic with a look, she needs not blowing on knots[42]
3. Dark-lipped, she laughs to uncover her pearls, flashing rain, hail, pebbles
4. sucking her lips you will taste redolent musk, old wine and honey
5. The last breath of the dying night is like that of the soul leaving the body
6. Her spittle running in your mouth has, in its essence, the accident of cold
7. and it is as if the white hand of an angel had appeared on the horizon.
8. My sadness comes from the departure of youth, and being a slave of gazelles and oxen

...

13. Leaving, she cut her bonds with me, and cut my sleep with insomnia
14. The arrows of the whites ones struck the black ones; she denied her favours and became stingy
15. I marvel at how their archers, from within my own ribcage, can strike into my mind

[42] A reference to Qur'ān 113:4.

16. Oh, flame of my vigour, where is your light? Where your heat in my fireplace?
17. The flint by which I lit you has turned barren from continually engendering sparks; no more will it procreate
18. I revived with my memories the dead youth. I am crying forever its departure
19. Recalcitrant to accept its abandonment, I sought its opposite to revive it, but I could not find it
20. If the departed could be brought back, even at the price of my own soul, I would ransom them!
21. I chased away sadness with a golden wine, that chased away the silver from my hand
22. I drank with my boon companions, squandering my wealth, both the acquired and the inherited!
30. Now I refuse the flower of pleasure; like one who stays on guard, I do not respond [to pleasure's allures]
31. I opened my lashes from the dream of error, I woke up to the straight path
32. I broke my deals with wine imbibers, and had no affection for drinking parties
33. I do not drink what I describe. Among my companions I look like a Qaʿadī[43]
34. With determination, I travelled at night from one country to the other
35. In the belly of a boat or on the back of a she-camel. I fought against the ravages of my time
36. And I found that al-Ḥasan is the upholder of religion, so I fled to him.

[43] *Qaʿadī*: a member of a sect of the Kharijites. In this line, the word conveys the meaning of a 'fundamentalist': someone who would be utterly out of place at a drinking party.

The poem opens with an amatory preface, where the poet declares his devotion to a young lover whose charms have bewitched him (ll. 1–2). Their love union is consummated at the end of a night meeting, and the description of the beloved and the rising dawn alternate in lines three to seven. The customary amatory preface is followed by a long section on *al-shayb wa-l-shabāb* introduced by line eight, in which the poet laments the all-too-quick passing of youth and this whole section is interspersed with further descriptive lines on the beloved. Line eight reverses the mood of the opening segment: the sensual *nasīb* turns into a memory of the love dalliances in the poet's youth, now departed, and the young lover rejects him on account of his old age (ll. 13–14). The motif of greying hair is introduced with the image of warring factions in white and black uniforms, with those in black quickly losing ground to those in white. The image extends into the next line, where Ibn Ḥamdīs alludes to his disappointment with his altered appearance, and the enfeeblement of his mental faculties. Line sixteen reinforces this idea, as the poet laments the loss of his strength, and his 'spark': youth is an extinguished fire that, no matter how hard one tries, cannot be revived. This *bukāʾ ʿalā faqd al-shabāb* (crying over the loss of youth) continues until line twenty-one, where, as is customary for him,[44] Ibn Ḥamdīs shifts to the *khamriyya* by using wine as a remedy for the sorrowful longing for his youth. The short bacchic section, a mere two lines, is largely occupied by the poet's boasting about his liberality in acquiring wine: he spends and always spent lavishly, both from his own wealth and from his inherited wealth, on wine. In line twenty-one, however, the mood is reversed again as Ibn Ḥamdīs returns to ponder his old age, which has undermined even his will and capacity to carouse with his boon-companions. This section (ll. 30–33) is perhaps the poem's most original. It has the poet standing at a party, sober, and abstaining from wine. He is like a Qaʿadī, a 'fundamentalist' *kharijite*: a sort of wet blanket, the spoilsport of the medieval Islamicate merry-making. But, we discover, it is old age that forces the recalcitrant poet to piety: making virtue out of a necessity, the ageing poet declares he will, from now on, take a virtuous path and abstain from sinful intoxication. And yet as a professional poet he will have to show up at work, crafting his wine songs for patrons and boon-companions while he himself will not touch a drop. This pearl of a line encapsulates the estrangement of the ageing persona from habitual social contexts, and we can, with Said, underscore the untimeliness of old age:[45] the old poet, out of place

[44] The use of wine to cure the nostalgia of lost youth is a recurrent motif in Ibn Ḥamdīs's poems. See Carpentieri, 'Towards a Poetics of Ageing', pp. 122–26.

[45] Said, *On Late Style*, p. 74.

and out of time, is left to perpetuate a message that rings hollow first and foremost to himself.

Ibn Ḥamdīs also tampers subtly with the pre-Islamic image of the *ṣuʿlūk* severing his bonds with his tribe, epitomized in the *lāmiyyāt al-ʿarab*. The poet's estrangement from the society of wine imbibers makes him an outcast in the familiar setting of the wine-party. As he 'breaks his deals with the winebibbers', nothing is left for him but to withdraw from their society. Obviously, the image makes for a perfect *takhalluṣ*, or disengagement from the *khamriyya*. Having achieved its *husn al-takhalluṣ* the poem moves on to the *raḥīl* in lines thirty-four and thirty-five. Here we find the familiar images of the warrior poet defying the hardships of journeying to travel towards his patron. The very short *raḥīl* is only two lines long, and the customary descriptions of the many hardships endured by the poet are here conflated in expression 'ravages of my time' (*maṣāriʿ zamanī*). The image encapsulates the very mood of this poem that now is reveals itself to be truly about the poet's ageing in a time of immense turmoil for Maghribī Islam; its meaning is completed only in the next line. There, the poem reaches its climax in the praise of al-Ḥasan, Ibn Ḥamdīs's patron, whom the poet addresses as the 'defender of religion'. Far from being empty praise, one must read it in the context of the circumstances of Ibn Ḥamdīs's arrival at the Zirid court. As he lands at the Zirid court at Mahdiyya, Ibn Ḥamdīs is a refugee, having fled from 'the ravages of his time' twice already. In *Ifrīqiya*, the poet would grow old, often looking longingly north towards the beloved island he would never again set foot on. It is in this context that we must read the praise to al-Ḥasan, the fact that the poet addresses him as a 'defender of religion', and, in particular, the verb *lajaʾtu*. Today we are sadly familiar with the word in its participle form *lājiʾ* (refugee) in relation to the catastrophe in Syria and to the tragedy of small boats crossing the Mediterranean and turning all too often into death traps for thousands of women, men, and children escaping war and famine. Ibn Ḥamdīs was himself a shipwrecked fugitive buffeted from shore to shore by the catastrophic political events of his time.

Against this historical backdrop, this panegyric dominated by the theme of ageing acquires a new and richer meaning: the ravages of time that have aged the poet, the military and political defeats of Islam in Sicily and across the Maghrib, and his final redemption at the hands of al-Ḥasan, portrayed as Islam's last bulwark against the Norman avalanche in the Mediterranean, all resound within this poem and shape Ibn Ḥamdīs's manipulation of *al-shayb wa-l-shabāb*. While in keeping with the traditional thematic arrangement of the *qaṣīda*, the interposition of *al-shayb wa-l-shabāb* between its main segments constructs a praise in which Ibn Ḥamdīs presents himself before al-Ḥasan as a refugee aged by misfortune: an old man redeemed only by his patron's protection. The age gap between the two was very great: over sixty years. Al-Ḥasan, who succeeded his father ʿAlī aged thirteen, was but an adolescent and, at the time of his writing, Ibn Ḥamdīs was probably on the verge of his eighties. We can picture the old poet addressing the boy king: his self-portrayal as an old man full of experience is most fitting. Ibn Ḥamdīs, the perpetual exile, the refugee escaped from the ruination of both his actual and adoptive homelands, the witness to the infighting of Maghribī Islam, places himself before al-Ḥasan as, at once, a seeker of protection and a counsellor and advisor. As he praises al-Ḥasan, bestowing upon him the title of upholder of religion (*sanad al-dīn*) Ibn Ḥamdīs is in fact making at once a statement and an injunction. After his father, grandfather, and great-grandfather before him al-Ḥasan is, in the poet's eyes, the defender of Maghribī Islam against Norman interference in the Mediterranean, and so Islam's hope to recover Sicily. Al-Ḥasan's rule had begun under the best of auspices in this sense, when his armies repelled a Norman incursion aimed at Mahdiyya. The Norman army, after raiding Pantelleria, landed north of Mahdiyya by Cape Dimas. Incapable of launching an attack against the fortified Zirid capital, the Normans fortified their troops at Dimas castle, but the Zirid army was not long in counterattacking. At the cry of '*Allahu Akbar*', the Muslim army besieged the castle: while part of the Norman army was able to take to the sea and escape, the remaining garrison was annihilated in the ensuing battle outside the city walls.[46] Ibn Ḥamdīs would describe the event in a celebratory ode in praise of al-Ḥasan.[47] While congratulating al-Ḥasan on his victories, the old poet also places upon the young ruler the responsibility to defend the Maghribī Muslim community against its enemies, and perhaps even to regain Sicily for the Muslim Maghrib. The poem's closing lines are telling in this sense:

٥٢. يـا غيـث المحـل بـلا كـذب وشـجاع الحـرب بـلا فنـد
٥٣. لحظـاتُ أناتـكَ جانِبُهـا أرسـى فـي غيظـك مـن أُحُـد

...

٦٧. وبذلّـة أهـلَ السـبت قضـى ويـذلّ لـه أهـل الأحـددف
٦٨. فانصـر وافخـر وأدر وأشـر وأبـر وأجـر وأغـر وَسُـدِ

[46] Amari, *SMS*, vol. 3, 2, pp. 256–61.

[47] Granara, 'Ibn Ḥamdīs's al-Dīmās Qaṣida'.

52. Oh rain of bounty in times of draught, without a lie, hero in war without deceit

53. A side-glance from your equanimous gaze is, in its anger, firmer than mount Uḥud

...

67. You humbled the people of Saturday, and now the people of Sunday are humbled too

68. So conquer proudly, reign and command, destroy and protect, attack and be Lord!

Line fifty-two exalts the two foremost virtues of the Islamic ruler: liberality towards his subjects, and courage in war. The ruler is the '*ḥalīm' par excellence*: equanimous and forbearing, yet firm and uncompromising. Line fifty-three extols such traits in al-Ḥasan using a compelling simile: he is firmer, in his anger, than mount Uḥud. To Muslims and those acquainted with early Islamic history, the very name of Uḥud conjures a host of images: the struggle between Islam and *kufr* — idolatry —, the first serious military setback for Islam, insubordination to the Prophet Muḥammad, and an instance of bickering among the Muslims who, driven by lust for the spoils of war, caused a major defeat for Islam. At Uḥud, Muslim archers deployed in the rearguard and instructed by the Prophet to hold their position broke loose when the battle seemed to be turning in their favour in order to secure booty for themselves.[48] This reckless manoeuvre hampered the overall strategy of the Muslims and soon the Meccans were able to overcome them, causing major losses among their ranks. The Prophet himself was badly injured and believed to be dead, which caused a general rout of Muslim forces. Uḥud epitomizes, in a nutshell, the strife and infighting that would recur within the Muslim Umma throughout the centuries. It contains the premises of all *fitna* to come. In a poem written in the Maghrib of the early twelfth century, the metaphorical Uḥud echoes with the strife and turmoil that are plaguing the region: both in the confrontations between Muslims and non-Muslims and in the infighting that Ibn Ḥamdīs was a witness to in both Sicily and al-Andalus. The history would replicate itself in al-Andalus some decades later, when al-Muʿtamid's perilous alliance with the Berbers of Ibn Tashufin soon backfired as the allies turned into foes. As for North Africa, the long-simmering conflict between the Zirids and the

[48] Robinson, 'Uḥud', *Encyclopaedia of Islam*, 2nd edition.

Fatimids, the ravages of the Banū Hilāl, the confrontations with the Ḥammādis of Bijāya,[49] and the precarious alliances with the Normans of Roger all spoke loudly of the internal fractures of Islam in that area. Ibn Ḥamdīs's choice to deploy Uḥud here — besides the convenient rhyming *dāl* — is instrumental to the aim of the whole *qaṣīda*: al-Ḥasan is 'firmer than Uḥud' and a 'defender and upholder of Religion'. The young al-Haṣān, scion of a long line of North African rulers who actively confronted the Normans of Sicily, is portrayed by Ibn Ḥamdīs as the hope of Islam against external aggressions and internal fractures. The penultimate line stalks the flame of a *jihād* rhetoric that imbues the final praise of al-Ḥasan: he humbled the Jews (the people of Saturday, a possible allusion to the Zirids' restrictive policies on the *dhimmī* in Ifrīqiya and the Jewish diaspora following the invasions of the Banū Hilāl) and now he has defeated the Christians.

The string of imperatives in the poem's closing line: 'conquer and be proud, reign and command, destroy and protect, attack and be Lord!', reinforces the message that Ibn Ḥamdīs chose to deliver to his patron: it is al-Haṣan's duty to defend Islam from inner and outer threats, to grant unity in North Africa, and to attack the Normans at sea (in Sicily?), for only by actively pursuing war against Islam's enemies will he prove himself to be a true ruler. In delivering this message, the persona of the ageing poet is a key element. As the voice of experience, Ibn Ḥamdīs can advise the young king. And advise him he does, warning al-Ḥasan of the dangers of complacency towards the enemy. Such complacency caused the downfall of both the Sicilian and the Iberian Taifa rulers, and one may read into this advice a veiled warning against the Zirids's ambiguous politics towards the Normans.[50] Ibn Ḥamdīs wishes for the young al-Ḥasan to prove himself worthy of his position as emir: he will make Islam triumphant provided that he avoids the compromises and dithering that have undermined other Muslim communities.

From the above, we see how *al-shay wa-al-shabāb* in Ibn Ḥamdīs's poem to al-Ḥasan is instrumental in crafting this praise and delivering its message. Throughout the ode, Ibn Ḥamdīs has construed the persona of an old man who, escaping the many upheavals that plagued the Maghribī Muslim community throughout his lifetime, finally found respite at the Zirid court of Mahdiyya. Addressing an adolescent king, the old poet presents himself as his advisor and counsellor; evoking both recent events and symbolic, historical events, he casts

[49] Amari, *SMS*, vol. 3, 2, p. 271.

[50] Amari, *SMS*, vol. 3 2, pp. 271–72.

his ruler as the guarantor of unity within the Maghribī Muslim ranks and the potential liberator of the Maghrib from the Christian threat. Ibn Ḥamdīs's deployment of *al-shayb wa-l-shabāb* performs at both the structural and semantic level. Structurally, and in keeping with Ibn Rashīq's examples drawn from the ʿUmda, it allows for *ḥusn al-takhalluṣ*, bringing the *nasīb* seamlessly into a *khamriyya* and then into a *raḥīl* that in turn ushers in the praise of al-Ḥasan, as summarized below:

I. al-*Nasīb*. Lines 1–7

II. *al-shayb wa-l-shabāb*. Lines 8–20

III. *Khamriyya*. Lines 21–29

IV. *al-shayb wa-l-shabāb*. Lines 30–33

V. *Raḥīl*. Lines 34–35

VI. *Madḥ/Fakhr*. Lines 36–68

The recurrence of *al-shayb wa-l-shabāb*, as shown above, draws attention to the persona of the ageing poet, allowing Ibn Ḥamdīs to negotiate a dialogic power relationship with the ruler: as a man of experience, he is in a position to advise, warn, and even rebuke. He is also in a position to remind the young king about the recent upheavals that so deeply affected his own life. Much of the turbulent history of medieval Maghribī Islam echoes through allusions in the poem: the external threats posed by the Norman expeditions against Zirid North Africa and other, internal threats — i.e. infighting and divisions — evoked through the image of Mount Uḥud.

In sum, the poem draws its meaning largely from the poet's persona of an old man, crafted by Ibn Ḥamdīs through a repeated deployment of *al-shayb wa-l-shabāb*. The overall poem is held together by this persona. There is a fundamental interdependence between the *nasīb*, the *raḥīl* and the *madḥ*: the lost beloved is replaced by the found patron; the perils of desert journeys are compensated for by the arrival at the patron's abode. Little has been said so far, however, about the interdependence between *madḥ* and *al-shayb wa-l-shabāb*: a tired old man would be poor company at a drinking party, and may be of scarce interest to an adolescent king; the beloved's rejection of the poet in the opening lines encapsulates these feelings. But it is precisely the poet's old age, and the very misfortunes that befell him, that make of him the most precious advisor to the enlightened ruler portrayed in the *madḥ*. This persona, an aged refugee who, pushed away by war and political upheaval, finally landed in Ifrīqiya is, at Zirid Mahdiyya, a living reminder of the calamitous consequences of Islam's internal rifts and its dangerous dalliances with Christian rivals. Positioning himself as the voice of experience, Ibn Ḥamdīs can warn al-Ḥasan against the challenges to his rule: the fragmentation of the Maghribī Umma and the increasing power of the Normans in the Mediterranean. Neglecting these threats would signify the end of the Zirids, as was the case for Muslim Sicily and for the Iberian *taifas*. The poet would not live to see his prophecy fulfilled: eroded by the Normans and reduced to a coastal strip in today's Algeria, the Zirid emirate would end with al-Ḥasan, swallowed by the Almohad empire.

Like Abū Isḥāq, Ibn Ḥamdīs reflected on the passing of time remembering youth with longing and nostalgia, and adopted the traditional imagery of old age poetry to describe his ageing body and mind. However, in contrast with Abū Isḥāq, who was a man of religion and a *faqīh*, Ibn Ḥamdīs, as a professional court poet, chose different contexts to write about old age. While Abū Isḥāq described old age mainly in ascetic poems, Ibn Ḥamdīs adopted the motif much in the trend set by his illustrious predecessors Abū Tammām and al-Buḥturī: in his *dīwān*, verses on old age are scattered in a variety of different types of poems, such as laudatory poems, love poems, wine poems, ascetic poems, and gnomic poems. One striking feature of Ibn Ḥamdīs' use of his lines of old age is their being deployed in close contact with different and at times antithetical sub-genres such as the *ghazal* or the *khamriyya*. In these instances, the intermingling of lines on old age with lines on love and revelry create a sharp contrast in theme, mood, imagery, and style: the poet plays between these through a liberal use of figures of speech such as puns (*muṭābaqa*) and paronomasia (*tajnīs*). Also, the antithesis between the festive mood of the *khamriyya*, the lyric mode of the *nasīb*, and the bitter and austere tone of old age poetry creates a polychromy of moods that resolve towards the end of the poem with the *duʿāʾ* (invocation to God), the *istisqāʾ* (the invocation for rain), or the *fakhr* (boast).

One further example of Ibn Ḥamdīs's deployment of *al-shayb wa-l-shabāb* is a tripartite *qasīda* on the themes of love, wine, and nature: a *ḥāʾiyya* in *ramal* metre of 34 lines, built upon three poetic thoughts among the dearest to classical Arabic poetry. The poem's opening lines nod to the *nasīb* with the apparition of the *ṭayf al-khayāl* (ll. 1–10), its central section is a *khamriyya* (11–20), or wine-song, and the conclusion is a *rawḍiyya:* the description of a garden (21–32). These three main themes appear to constitute separate sections of the poem: the poet shifts from one theme to the other, developing each one independently. Looking more closely, however, one notices a strategic deployment of transitional segments between each section. These transitional segments all pivot around the motif of *al-shayb wa-l-shabāb*: youth and old age. A structural analysis reveals that the theme of ageing is deployed to give the poem its overall thematic cohesion and enhance its metatextual dimension by embedding each of the poem's main sections within the larger subtext of *al-shayb wa-l-shabāb* — ageing.

In this poem, the motif of old age remains in the background, and is used to build a parallel narrative, largely through a process which I refer to as 'thematic displacement', with respect to three themes of the *nasīb*, the *khamriyya* and the *rawḍiyya*. It is this parallel narrative that gives cohesion to the *qaṣīda*, while enhancing its three main sections with a metatextual dimension. In what follows we will see how the poet, having appeased his audience's expectations with familiar imagery from the *nasīb* repertoire, will suddenly reverse the mood of this first section by superimposing the theme of ageing. From there, he meanders through the *khamriyya* to reach his forte: a descriptive section on a garden. The closing two lines return once more to the theme of old age and thus bring the poem full circle. The repeated insertion of lines on old age between the poem's three main segments is the crucial feature of this *qaṣīda*. These 'intermezzi' on old age shape a poetic persona acting as a narrating voice. They also create a subtle unsettling effect whereby the meaning (*maʿnā*) of each section is reversed or altered at its ending. The effect is built gradually, with strokes that progressively alter the habitual palette of each thematic section and eventually form a backdrop that redefines the entire picture. Let us have a closer look:[51]

Ibn Ḥamdīs, no. 56[52]

١. طَرَقتْ وٱللَّيْلُ مَمْدودُ الجَناحْ   مَرّحَبًا بِٱشَّمْسِ في غَيْرِ صَباح
٢. سَلَّمَ ٱلإيماءُ عَنْها خَجَلًا   أوما كَانَ لَهَا ٱلنَّطْقُ مُباح
٣. غَادَةٌ تَحْمِلُ في أَجْفانِها   سَقَمًا فِيهِ مَنيّاتُ ٱلصِّحاح
٤. بِتُّ مِنْها مُسْتَعِيدًا قُبَلًا   كانَ لي مِنْها على ٱلدَّهْرِ ٱقْتِراح
٥. أَلْثَمُ ٱلدُّرَّ حَصًى يَنْبَعُ لي   بِزُلالٍ ناقِعًا فيه ٱلْتِياح
٦. وأُرَوّيُ غَلَلَ ٱلشَّوْقِ بما   لَمْ يَكُنْ في قُدرَةِ ٱلماءِ ٱلقَراح
٧. بٱعْتِناقٍ ما ٱعْتَنَقْناهُ خَنًى   وٱلْتِزامٍ ما ٱلْتِزَمْناهُ سِفاح
٨. ما عَلَى مَنْ صادَ في ٱلنَّومِ لَهُ   شَرَكُ ٱلحُلْمِ مَهاةً مِنْ جُناح

[51] My translation is based on an original one prepared by James Monroe, during a 2003 graduate seminar at UC Berkeley, which I had the privilege of attending as an undergraduate.

[52] Ibn Ḥamdīs, *Dīwān*, ed. by Iḥsān ʿAbbās, pp. 82–85.

1. She came while the wing of the night was outstretched. Welcome to a sunshine without the dawn!
2. She greeted me waving her hand — out of shyness — and was speech not forbidden to her?
3. A young girl she is, whose eyelids carry a disease, that smites both the sound and the strong
4. I begged her for kisses, harassing her shamelessly, as the night passed along
5. And kissed her pearls, pebbles that poured me pure water to drink, quenching my thirst
6. And quenching the pangs of my passion, which no pure water could possibly quench
7. But there was no sin in our union, nor shame in our love
8. Is it shameful to stalk a gazelle in one's slumber? to seize her in the snare of one's dreams?

The poem opens with the visit of the phantom of the beloved (ll. 1–6), evoked by means of the verb *ṭaraqat*.[53] She is described as a sun coming before the dawn, eyelids imbued with the contagion of passionate love. A victim of this power, the poet importunes the young lady for a kiss, which she finally grants him. The love union is conjured through imagery of gushing water (ll. 5–6) but the sensuality of these lines is immediately broken in line seven. Here we have the denouement of this amatory preface: the love union is revealed to be a dream. The poet declares the virtuous nature of an unconsummated embrace: he 'hunted' his beloved 'with the snare of dreams' (l. 8). The transformation of the very tangible ghost of the beloved into an oneiric vision is in keeping with ʿAbbasid trends, as explained by Jacobi,[54] while the personal touch of the poet is found in the transitional section which follows. Lines nine and ten are the key transitional lines which project the *nasīb* into the bacchic song that follows. Both lines revolve around the theme of youth and old age (*al-shayb wa-l-shabāb*). The poet ponders the passing of time: in old age, love is destined to remain unrequited.

[53] See Stetkevych, 'Towards an Arabic Elegiac Lexicon'.

[54] Jacobi, 'The Khayāl Motif in Early Arabic Poetry'.

٩. همتُ بِٱلغيدِ فَلَوْ كُنْتُ ٱلصِّبا   لَمْ يَكُنْ مِنّي عَنْهُنَّ بَراح
١٠. ورَدَدتُّ ٱلشَّيْبَ عَنْها مُعرِضًا   بِكَلامِ السِّلمِ أَوْ كَلْمِ ٱلكِفاح

9. I have been madly in love with young girls: if I were youth itself I would never cease to chase them

10. I now avert my white hair from them, leaving with words of peace, or scars of war

These two transitional lines link the *nasīb* to the *khamriyya*; they also give the audience a glimpse of the persona of an ageing poet, dreaming of the woman he loved in his youth. It is this persona that surfaces again at the onset of the *khamriyya,* commending wine as the best remedy against the calamity of ageing (line eleven):

١١. عَلِّلِ ٱلنَّفْسِ بِرَيحانٍ وَراحْ   وأَطِعْ ساقِيَها وٱعْصِ ٱللُّواح
٢١. وأَدِرْ حَمْراءَ يَسْري لَطَفًا   سُكْرُها مِنْ شَمِّها في كُلِّ صاح
١٣. لا يَغُرَّنَّكَ مِنْها خَجَلٌ   إنَّها*1* تُبْديهِ في خدِّ وَقاح
١٤. وَٱعْلُها بِٱلماءِ تَعْلَمْ مِنْهُما   أَنَّ بَيْنَ ٱلماءِ وٱلنّارِ ٱصْطِلاح
١٥. وإِذا ٱلخَمْرُ حَماها صِرْفُها   تَرَكَ ٱلمَزْجُ حَماها مُسْتَباح
١٦. خَلِّني أَفْنِ شَبابي مَرَحًا   لا يُرَدُّ ٱلمُهرُ عَنْ طَبْعِ ٱلمِراح
١٧. إنّما يَنْعَمُ في ٱلدُّنيا فَتًى   يَدْفَعُ ٱلجِدَّ إِليها في ٱلمُزاح
١٨. فٱسْقِني عَنْ إِذْنِ سُلْطانِ ٱلهَوى   لَيْسَ يَشْفي ٱلرُّوحَ إِلَّا كَأْسُ راح
١٩. وٱنْتَظِرْ للحِلْمِ بَعْدي كَرَّةً   كَمْ فَسادٍ كانَ عُقباهُ صَلاحْ

11. Distract thy soul with basil and wine, obey the cupbearer and rebel against thirst!

12. Pass around the red that gushes forth generous, its smell is enough to get every sober man drunk

13. And don't let its blushing deceive you, for it blooms on the cheeks of the brazen and shameless

14. Mix water with wine, and witness the agreement of water and fire

15. Wine, when pure, is forbidden; mix it, and you will access its sanctuary

16. Let me squander my youth in debauchery, you cannot force the foal to forbearance

17. A young man will thrive in this world only by banning all seriousness and embracing amusement

18. So pour me a drink, as the Sultan of Passion commands! For only a cup of good wine can heal my soul

19. And wait for restraint to return when I'm gone; how often debauchery is followed by restraint

Let us here underscore how, within this bacchic section, lines sixteen to nineteen reintroduce the motif of youth and old age, creating, by associations of contiguity, a parallel with prominent images from the *al-shayb wa-l-shabāb* repertoire in the previous section. Thus we have white hair in the previous section (*shayb* l. 10) and youth in the latter (*shabāb* l. 16), wine as as the cure for a weary soul in both sections (*'allil al-nafs bi-rayḥānin wa-rāḥ* l. 12); *laysa yashfī al-ruḥ illā ka'si rāḥ* (l. 18), and the transience of time again in both sections (*law kuntu aṣ-ṣibā* l. 9); *intaẓir li–l-ḥilmi ba'di* (l. 19). Line nineteen seals the wine-song and gives way to the final descriptive section of the poem. The transition proper into the description of the garden (*rawḍiyya*) is achieved through the deployment anthropomorphic natural elements that draw a stylized image of a dancer:

٢٠. فَٱلْقَضِيـبُ ٱهْتَـزَّ وَٱلْبَـدْرُ بَـدا   وَٱلْكَثِيـبُ ٱرْتَـجَّ وَٱلْعَنْبَـرُ فـاح

20. Now the reed quivers, the full moon appears, the sand dune starts shaking, and ambergris wafts all around

Her (or his) lean torso, shaking to the rhythm of music, is a reed wavering in the wind; the undulating hips, a quivering sand dune and the dancer's wafting scent, ambergris. The description breaks the upbeat rhythm of the *khamriyya* and confers to the poem a quieter pace that permeates subsequent lines where the shape-shifting continues: thus, the setting Pleiades become a white heron folding its wings to sleep and the Western horizon is personified as a figure inhaling the scent of a bouquet of chamomile flowers; the first rays of dawn break on the scene horrified by the remnants of last night's debauchery:

٢١. وَٱلثُّرَيّـا رَجَـحَ ٱلجـوُّ بِهـا   كَٱبْنِ مـاءٍ ضَـمَّ لِلوَكْرِ جَنـاح
٢٢. وكَأَنَّ ٱلغَـربَ مِنهـا نـاشِـقٌ   بـاقَـةً مِـنْ يـاسِـمِينٍ أَوْ أَقـاح
٢٣. وكَأَنَّ ٱلصُّبْحَ ذا ٱلأَنْـوارِ مِـنْ   ظُلَمِ ٱللَّيْلِ عَلَى ٱلظَّلْمـاءِ صـاح

21. The Pleiades rise in the sky, like a heron folding its wings in its nest
22. And the West sniffs a bouquet of jasmine and camomile
23. And day breaks like a scream against the crimes of the night

The description reincorporates the bacchic element in the following lines (24 and 25), and overflows into the setting for a carousel: a garden at sunrise where the imbibers, intoxicated by drinking night and morning, are restored by the sight and scents of wildflowers and supple young branches (ll. 26–32):

٢٤. فٱشْرَبِ ٱلراحَ ولا تُخْلِ يدًا مِنْ يَدِ ٱللَّهْوِ غُدُوًّا ورَواح
٢٥. ثَقِّلِ ٱلراحَةَ مِنْ كَأْساتِها بِرَداحٍ مِنْ يَدِ ٱلخَوْدِ ٱلرَّداح
٢٦. في حَديقٍ غَرَسَ ٱلغَيثُ بِهِ عَبِقَ ٱلأَرْواحِ مَوْشيَّ ٱلبِطاح
٢٧. تَعْقِلُ ٱلطَّرْفَ أَزاهِيرُ بِهِ ثُمَّ تُعْطيه أزاهِيرَ صُراح
٢٨. فَتَرَبَّتْ فيهِ قاماتُ ٱلمِلاح أَرْضَعَ ٱلغَيمُ لِبانًا بانَهُ
٢٩. كُلُّ غُصْنٍ تَعْتَري أَعْتافَهُ رِعْدَةُ ٱلنَّشْوانِ مِنْ كَأْسِ ٱصْطِباح
٣٠. يَكْتَسي صِبْغَةَ وَرْسٍ كُلَّما وَدَّعَتْ في طَرْفِ ٱليَوْمِ بِراح
٣١. فَكَأَنَّ ٱلتُّرابَ مِسكٌ أَذْفَرٌ وَكَأَنَّ ٱلطَّلَّ كافورُ رَباج
٣٢. وَكَأَنَّ ٱلرَّوْضَ رَشَّتْ زَهْرَهُ بِمياهِ ٱلوَرْدِ أَفْواهُ ٱلرِّياح
٣٣. أفَلا تَغْنَمُ عَيْشًا يَقْتَضي سَيْرُهُ عَنْكَ غدُوًّا ورَواح
٣٤. وإِذا فارَقْتَ رَيْعانَ ٱلصِبّا فٱللَّيالي بِأَمانيكَ شِحاح

24. So drink wine, and don't let go of the hand of pleasure, morning or evening
25. Weigh down your palm with wine cups, offered by the hand of a buxom young girl
26. In a garden where bountiful rains have nurtured wafting aromas and embroidered pools
27. Where flowers capture your eye, and wine offers you its own flowers
28. There, the clouds' milk has nurtured each plant, rising in stately figures
29. Branches trembling like a drunk who stumbles after his morning draught
30. At the break of dawn, they don a robe yellow, waving their hands as if to greet us

31. And it is as if the soil was pungent musk, and the dew camphor from Rabāḥ
32. As if these gardens has sprinkled their flowers with drops of rose-water from the lips of the breeze
33. Oh, will you not take advantage of a pleasant life, whose days and its nights have been numbered
34. considering that when you leave the flower of youth behind, nights will be stingy in granting your desires?

Let us underscore once again how the two final lines, that close at once this last section and the whole poem reintroduce *al-shayb wa-l-shabāb*, bringing the poem full circle. We thus see how the ode is partitioned in three main sections, each sealed by a transitional segment featuring the motif of *al-shayb wa-l-shabāb*.These segments are devised to alter the mood of each section and to introduce a new section. Thus, the opposition of youth vs. old age concludes the *nasīb* and gives way to the *khamriyya*, which itself is sealed by a transitional line on ageing. The latter introduces the *rawḍiyya* which once again concludes on the theme of *al-shayb wa-l-shabāb*. At a glance, the poem is divided into the following main sections (alphabetical order) and transitional segments (T and cardinal numbers):

A. 1–10: *nasīb*

T1. 11–12: *al-shayb wa-l-shabāb*

B. 13–18: *khamriyya*

T2. 19: *al-shayb wa-l-shabāb*

C. 20–32: *rawḍiyya*

T3. 33–34: *al-shayb wa-l-shabāb*

The scheme above displays how *al-shayb wa-l-shabāb* functions as a unifying element in the poem. By introducing it repeatedly at the end of each section, Ibn Ḥamdīs composes a thematic framework whereby the three sections of the *nasīb*, *khamriyya* and *rawḍiyya* acquire new meanings. It should now be recalled that it was precisely this capacity to enhance the semantic layering of a *maʿnā* which was among the most prized features of *al-shayb wa-l-shabāb* as a poetic thought. Let us here quote one more al-Sharīf al-Murtaḍā, who in his introduction to his anthology '*al-Shihāb* fī *al-shayb wa-l-shabāb*' wrote:

فأما بلاغة العبارة عنها وجلاؤها في معاريض الواصلة إلى القلوب بلا حجاب والانتقال في المعنى الواحد من عبارة إلى غيرها مما يزيد عليها براعة وبلاغة او يساويها او يقاربها حتى يصير المعنى باختلاف العبارة عنه وتغير الهيئات عليه وإن كان واحدا كأنه مختلف في نفسه.[55]

That which makes it [i.e. the motif of youth and old age] superior, or equal, or close [to other *maʿanī*] is eloquence and clarity of expression about it (*ʿibāra*) in propositions that reach the heart without a veil, and the shifting, within a single meaning (maʿnā), from one expression to another, so that the meaning itself becomes the opposite of the expression, changing its exterior appearance and, while remaining one, it is as if was, in itself, different.

The process described by al-Murtaḍā can thus be understood as a thematic displacement: a progressive bending of a given poetic thought through shifting expressions that alter its original meaning and transform it into something else. The process is obtained by a continuous changing in expressions (for want of a better term, let us call this 'signifier variation') within the same poetic thought. Signifier variation displaces the original meaning of the section or theme and transforms it into something else — as when, for instance, the poet, in describing a greying lock, evokes the image of lightning, then of a thunderstorm, and so on.

It will be helpful at this point to recall Michael Sells's seminal article 'Guises of the Ghūl', in which, departing from Jakobson, he examined the process of semantic overflow in the *nasīb*. Sells demonstrates how the metaphorical vehicle that carries the description of the beloved is underpinned by a net of metonymical associations that, especially through synecdoche, shape the mythopoetic lost garden.[56] The convergence of the metonymical and the metaphorical axis creates semantic overflow: just like the shape-shifting Ghūl of pre-Islamic lore, the description of the beloved dissembles in an endless succession of images, each taking an independent life and contributing to shaping a parallel narrative within the *nasīb*. The association with al-Murtaḍā's theory of thematic displacement jumps to the eye: whereas the description of the beloved, with its net of metonymic associations of natural elements — the reed, the branch, the sand-dune etc. — is in fact evoking the mythopoetic world of the lost garden, signifier variation in the *al-shayb wa-l-shabāb* section

[55] Al-Murtaḍā, *al-Shihāb*, p. 3.

[56] Sells, *Guises of the Ghūl*, p. 131.

transform the original object, namely white hair, into something that has 'changed within itself' (*mukhtalif fī nafsi-hi*). As for this poem, the device of 'thematic displacement' is obtained through the variation in imagery on each of the three sections, that transport the *nasīb*, the *khamriyya*, and the *rawḍiyya* towards the *al-shayb wa-l-shabāb*. Ibn Ḥamdīs interweaves the theme of *al-shayb wa-l-shabāb* almost seamlessly within each section. The motif acts as the wider canvas against which the *nasīb*, *khamriyya*, and *rawḍiyya* are deployed. It is this canvas that shapes for the audience the poetic persona of an ageing man. But while *al-shayb wa-l-shabāb* is typically dominated by the description of the poet's own white hair and ageing body, the poetic persona that the poet draws here is less stark: the persona of a man transitioning — in line with the poem's own protean guises — from youth to maturity. If we assemble the transitional segments on *al-shayb wa-l-shabāb*, we have a sort of short piece, the portrayal of such a persona:

9. I have been madly in love with young girls: if I were youth itself I would never cease to chase them

10. I now avert my white hair from them, leaving with words of peace, or scars of war

11. Distract thy soul with basil and wine, obey the cupbearer and rebel against thirst!

16. Let me squander my youth in debauchery, you cannot force the foal to forbearance

17. A young man will thrive in this world only by banning all seriousness and embracing amusement

18. So pour me a drink, as the Sultan of Passion commands! For only a cup of good wine can heal my soul

19. And wait for restraint to return when I'm gone! how often debauchery is followed by restraint

33. Oh, will you not take advantage of a pleasant life, whose days and its nights have been numbered

34. considering that when you leave the flower of youth behind, nights will be stingy in granting your desires?

The extrapolation holds: it shapes the persona of a man at the turning point between youth and maturity. Such a man is noticing the unsettling effects of his hair turning grey: he is shunned by young ladies, and meets his beloved only in reveries. At the same time, within the brigade of boon companions, he is in a position to behave as the voice of experience, which indeed he does in lines nine, thirty-three and thirty-four which close the poem. Introducing such a narrating persona by means of transitional lines allows for signifier variation and, thereby, thematic displacement of the poem's main themes. It thus ensures its cohesion and it also allows for a sophisticated layering of meanings (*maʿānī*) which enrich the ode at the metatextual level. This semantic layering, or thematic polysemy, is a trademark of Ibn Ḥamdīs's own poetics, as it has been argued elsewhere.[57] It very likely lies at the heart of the 'magic' for which al-Muʿtamid ibn ʿAbbād lavished praises on him, as seen above:

وانت ابن حمديس الدي كنتَ مهدياً لنا السحر إذا لم يأت في زمان السحر[58]

> You are Ibn Ḥamdīs, who brought us the magic, when it eluded us in times of magic.

Even after his long journeys, his felicitous encounter with al-Muʿtamid, his success as a panegyrist at the Zirid court, and his reaching old age, Ibn Ḥamdīs never forgot his beloved Sicily, and was to remain emotionally attached to the memory of his native island throughout his life. In many a poem penned away from 'home', the poet remembered Sicily with verses filled with nostalgia and regret. These poems are by far the most studied and best known of the overall production of Ibn Ḥamdīs. Structurally, they display some of the qualities already analysed above. As Granara pointed out, the Sicilian poems (*ṣiqilliyāt*) are typically built on sets of oppositions: light/darkness, youth/old age, bodily health/weakness.[59] Interestingly, in the majority of these Sicilian poems Ibn Ḥamdīs explicitly contrasts his exile and his old age with his youth in Sicily. One of these Sicilian odes exemplifies this binary construction:

[57] See Carpentieri, *Towards a Poetics of Ageing*, pp. 120–32.

[58] Ibn Ḥamdīs, *Dīwān*, 153: Ibn Ḥamdīs, *Dīwān*, ed. by Iḥsān ʿAbbās, p. 270

[59] Granara, *Remaking Muslim Sicily*, p. 172.

Ibn Ḥamdīs, no. 2[60]

١. نفى همُّ شيبي سرورَ الشبابِ   لقد أظلمَ الشيبُ لمّ أضاءَ
٢. قضيتُ لظلّ الصبا بالزوا   لِ لمّا تحوّلَ عنّي وفاءَ
٣. أتعرفُ لي عن شبابي سُلُوّاً   ومن يجدِ الداءَ يَبْغِ الدواء
٤. أأكسو المشيبَ سوادَ الخضاب   فأجعلَ للصبح ليلاً غطاء
٥. وكيفَ أُرَجّي وفاءَ الخضاب   إذا لم أجِدْ لشبابي وفاء

1. The cares of white hair have dispelled the mirth of youth. When white hair is lit, it is the darkest of nights
2. I spent the noon (of my life) under the shade of youth, when it left me declining
3. Do you know how to comfort me for the loss of youth? For one who finds illness must seek a remedy.
4. Will I dye my white hair black, trying to cover up the morning with the night?
5. How can I trust a dye, when I found no trust in my own youth!

The theme of ageing dominates the poem's incipit (ll. 1–5): youth has vanished and the poet is left seeking a remedy for its loss, but, the poet declares, the loss cannot be mended, and no dye or word of comfort will suffice to compensate it. In line 1 the poet muses over his ageing, with puns on the terms cares (*hamm*), mirth (*surūr*), light, and darkness (*aẓlama ash-shayb lammā aḍā'a*). The brightness of white hair is opposed to the metaphorical darkness of the poet's gloom over the loss of his youth. This opposition is replicated in line 2, as the poet employs the metaphor of the noon (*bi-zawāl*) to describe the prime of his life, which he spent in the comfort of 'youth's shade' (*li-ẓill aṣ-ṣibā*). Too suddenly, the poet laments, the noon has declined into life's evening (*lamma taḥawwala ʿannī wafā'a*). With the *iltifāt* in line 3 the poet addresses his audience/interlocutor, requesting a remedy for his sorrows. The rhetorical shift leads to the next line 4, where the poet conjectures the use of dye (*al-khiḍāb*) as a remedy to repair the damage of white hair. The opposition of darkness and light resurfaces in the second hemistich: resisting the onset of old age with the use of dye is as feasible

[60] Ibn Ḥamdīs, *Dīwān*, ed. by Iḥsān ʿAbbās, pp. 3–4. An English version of this poem also appears in Granara, 'Remaking Muslim Sicily', p. 174.

a task as attempting to bring back the night upon the onset of morning. Line 5, which concludes the poem's first section, insists on the concept of trust and hope disappointed (*lam ajid li-shabābī wafā'a*). The intimate, longing tone is maintained in the subsequent sections of the ode, as the poet remembers the painful separation from his homeland in the central *raḥīl* (ll. 6–10), formulates a heart-rending invocation for rain over the ruins of his home (ll. 11–15) and expresses his longing for an impossible return (ll. 16–23). The central part of the poem consists of a desert-journey (ll. 6–10) and an invocation for rain (ll. 11–15):

٦. وريحٍ خفيفةِ رَوحِ النّسيمِ   أطّتْ بليلاً وهبّت رُخاء
٧. سرت وحياها شقيقُ الحياةِ   على مَيّتِ الأرضِ تُبكي السماء
٧. فمن صَوْتِ رَعدٍ يسوق السحابَ   كما يسمعُ الفحلُ شولاً رغاء
٩. وتُشعِلُ في جانبَيها البروقُ   بريقَ السيوف تُهَزّ انتضاء
١٠. فبِتّ من الليل في ظلمةٍ   فيا غُرّةَ الصبح هاتي الضياء

6. A light wind, the whisper of zephyr, was murmuring softly, blowing gently
7. I set out to travel, while its rain, giver of life, shed tears from the sky over the dead ground
8. Roaring, the thunder was chasing the clouds, like a young horse groaning for the mare
9. And on the clouds' sides, lightning flashed like swords drawn in battle.
10. I spent the night enveloped in its darkness: come morning! bringer of light!

In these lines, the poet describes his departure for a night-journey. Given the many references to Sicily within the poem, it is natural to read into this section a representation of Ibn Ḥamdīs' departure from the island. This departure takes place under promising auspices: a light wind (l. 6), a reviving rain (l. 7), then a thunderstorm (ll. 8–10). Line 11, however, reverses the positive imagery of this section, introducing a section of nostalgia for the homeland, which is dominated by images of drought and desolation:

١١. ويا ريحُ إمّا مَرَيْتِ الحيا   ورَوّيْتِ منه الربوعَ الظلماء
٢١. فسوقي إليَّ جهامَ السحابِ   لأملأهنّ من الدمعِ ماء
١٣. ويسقي بكائيَ ربعَ الصبا   فما زالَ في المحل يسقي البكاء

١٤. ولا تُعْطِشي طللاً بالحمى تَدَانى على مُزْنَةٍ أو تناءى
١٥. وإن تَجْهَلِيهِ فَعيدانُهُ لظى الشمس تلذَعُ منها الكباء
١٦. ولا تعجبي فمغاني الهوى يطيّب طيبُ ثراها الهواءَ
١٧. ولي بينها مهجةٌ صبّةٌ تزودتُ في الجسم منها ذماء
١٨. ديارٌ تمشّتْ إليها الخطوبُ كما تتمشى الذئابُ الضراء
١٩. صحبتُ بها في الغياض الأسودَ وزرتُ بها في الكناس الظباء

11. And you, oh wind, who melt the clouds into rain, and quench the thirst of the encampments
12. Bring me the dry clouds, so that I may fill them with the water of my tears
13. And may my crying wash the abode of my youth that even in time of drought never ceased to be washed by crying.
14. Let the ruins of the abode of my homeland never be thirsty, whether rain clouds approach it or abandon it
15. If you don't know it, it is a place where branches the sun distills the perfume of aloe
16. Let this not marvel you, for in chambers of love the soil's perfume fills the air
17. In those 'chambers' my loving heart dwells, from them I draw my last breaths
18. Rooms to which my desires run, like wolves run to the forest
19. There I have been a companion to lions in battles, there I visited gazelles in their alcoves.

This section brings the audience from the desert journey back to the present, as the poet formulates a dismal invocation for rain over his homeland, now deserted. Line fourteen concludes the invocation for rain, evoking the pre-Islamic motif of the abandoned encampment (*ṭalalān*), and the proverbial sacred ground of *al-ḥimā*.[61] From these lines, we can appraise the poet's reworking of pre-Islamic and *muḥdath* motifs and rhetorics into a poem that encapsulates his personal experience of ageing and exile. We read in these lines

[61] Granara, 'Remaking Muslim Sicily', p. 174.

the poet's dismay as he contemplates the many hopes of his youth which never came to fruition: first and foremost, his hope of returning home. This implicit statement is rendered explicitly in the ending of the poem:

٢٠. وراءك يا بحرُ لي جَنّةٌ لبستُ النّعيم بها لا الشقاء
٢١. إذا أنا حاولت منها صباحاً تعرضتَ من دونها لي مساء
٢٢. فلو أنّني كنتُ أُعطى المنى إذا مَنَعَ البحرُ منها اللّقاء
٢٣. ركبتُ الهلالَ به زورقاً إلى أن أعانقَ فيها ذُكاء

20. Beyond you, O sea, I have a paradise in which I wore delight and not misfortune
21. When I was waiting the dawn to rise from it, you have interposed the night instead.
22. Would that I had my wishes granted, when the Sea thwarted their attainment,
23. I would have crossed it with the arched moon for a ship, so to embrace a sun there!

It is easily observed that this last section of the ode closely resembles its opening in imagery. Line 20 builds upon on the same sets of oppositions between dawn (*ṣabāḥ*) and evening (*masā'*), delight (*an-na'īm*) and misfortune (*ash-shaqā'*). Line 21, in particular, parallels line 2, with the image of the noon sun declining into the sunset, a metaphor of life's prime fading into old age. The poet is waiting for the morning to rise from the sea, addressed (*warā'uka yā baḥr*) in the previous line 20, an explicit reference to Sicily. This image represents the poet, a young man away from his homeland who is hoping for a return home and a fulfilment of his wishes, symbolized by the rising dawn. However, the night has fallen instead, and with night, old age. The poet voices his sorrow over the failing of his wishes in a dismal invocation in line 22 (*fa-law annī kuntu u'ṭā al-munā*). In the last line 23, Ibn Ḥamdīṣ reiterates, in a hyperbole, his longing for a return home. He hints towards his wish to embrace one more time, in Sicily, a sun (*dhukā'*), a common metaphor for a revered or beloved person. The line may make reference to the poet's father, who died in Sicily while he was in Seville.[62]

[62] Ibn Ḥamdīs mentions his father's passing in a panegyric to al-Mu'tamid: see *Dīwān*, 170: Ibn Ḥamdīs, *Dīwān*, ed. by Iḥsān 'Abbās, p. 287.

A comprehensive glance at the sections analysed above reveals how the motifs of *al-shayb wa-l-shabāb*, the desert-journey, the invocation for rain and the nostalgia for the homeland converge to shape the poet's articulation of his feeling of having grown old away from his rightful place on earth. The highly stylized forms of the classical *qaṣīda*, to which he adhered, represent the preferential channels through which Ibn Ḥamdīs was capable of sharing these more private and personal concerns with his audiences. Old age also inspired the poet with *ad hoc* poems, occasional pieces centred solely on the many facets of growing old. The following is one example, about a walking stick, which tampers, with subtle irony, with the uncertain boundaries between praise and blame of old age. This short poem (*qiṭʿa*) may have been set to music, as the introductory remark seems to point at.

Ibn Ḥamdīs, no. 300[63]

وقال في العصا او انشد فيها

١. ولي عصا من طريق الذم أحمدها   بها أقدم في تأخيرها قدمي

٢. كأنما وهي في كفي أهشُّ بها   على الثمانين عاماً لا على غنمي

٣. كأنني قوسُ رامٍ وهي لي وتر   أرمي عليها رميّ الشيب والهرم

He said, or sang, about his walking stick

1. I have a stick which I praise in blame, I use it to go forward, while my leg falls behind
2. It is as if, with it, I tried to chase away my eighty years, instead of chasing sheep
3. I am like the bow of an archer and she is the string, on which I place the arrows of white hair and old age

[63] Ibn Ḥamdīs, *Dīwān*, ed. by Iḥsān ʿAbbās, p. 482.

Chapter Three

A Poetics of Loss: The Elegies

In the previous chapters, we have seen how ageing had an impact on both Abū Isḥāq's and Ibn Ḥamdīs's responses to the political turmoil that affected the western Mediterranean and how the two poets were capable of appropriating the motif of *al-shayb wa-l-shabāb* to confront their own ageing. As they witnessed the deterioration of political structures in their homelands, the poets commemorated the worlds of their youth by tapping into the motif of *al-shayb wa-l-shabāb*, mourning at once the loss of their youth and the loss of the familiar worlds they had been a part of. This chapter focuses on a different aspect of mourning over a loss: elegies to persons and places. Helen Small considers the processes of ageing and decline as:

> not simply biological facts...but highly responsive to a person's perception of their ability to go on possessing certain goods crucial to their sense of themselves as themselves — including favorable historical, political and intellectual environments.[1]

Such favourable historical, political, and intellectual conditions, that had allowed Abū Isḥāq and Ibn Ḥamdīs to acquire the intellectual and social capital through which they flourished professionally, began crumbling as they aged. It was especially through the medium of the elegy that the two poets documented and mourned the demise of key places and persons in their lives that went hand in hand with their growing old.

This chapter focuses on the two poets' elegies, seeking their own voices as they face personal losses, the end of their own lives, and their apprehension in view of the afterlife. The chapter revolves around the poetic theme of the Arabic elegy (*rithāʾ/marthiyya*), a poetic thought by which the two poets expressed the loss of beloved family members or places and faced the enigma of dying while examining their many regrets and mistakes. These poems of mourning provide us with a compelling document of how both poets appropriated the universal experience of growing old, facing personal losses and mortality, in personal and creative ways, while remaining loyal to the canonical images of the Arabic *mar-*

[1] Small, *The Long Life*, p. 21.

thiyya. These poems are naturally more personal and intimate in tone, when compared to the public poems analysed for instance in the first chapter of this book. Yet, I find it interesting to examine how these more intimate lines complement, rather than contrasting with, the public personae of the two poets. In my reading — and this is the central idea that this book articulates — Abū Isḥāq and Ibn Ḥamdīs thought and expressed their growing old as part and parcel of the political decline in their homelands. The two poets appropriated a specific code, a poetic language which crossed and defied the strict constrictions of Arabic manuals of poetics in their classifications of aims, and types (see Chapter Two), and allowed them to document their psychological and physical deterioration and the collapse of their societies. In other words, the poets crafted, as their verse evolved with their ageing, a form of 'vernacular of loss' capable of incapsulating private and collective demise, personal apprehension over the decline of old age, and collective apprehension in the face of collapsing political structures.

In evoking their youth they looked back at an idealized age of Islamic majesty and glory; as they faced the reality of death, they considered the changing tides of history that were washing away the world as they knew it. Cognisant of these changes, Abū Isḥāq and Ibn Ḥamdīs adopted similar strategies to articulate, bear witness to, and survive them. On the one hand, both poets clung obstinately to idealized representations of an 'orthodox' Islam which they celebrated in panegyrics, invectives and war-poems. I here use the term 'orthodox' — in quotation marks — to describe a certain narrative of Dār al-Islām as a politically and doctrinally united front resisting outer aggressions, even when such a narrative stood in stark contrast to the reality of sectarian divisions and internecine struggles which were shaking Dār al-Islām during the poets' lifetimes. On the other hand, both poets inscribed the decline of their worlds, their personal losses, and their mortality into their own late poetics. They did so by appropriating a codified poetics which re-proposed and redeployed the classical motifs of the *qaṣīda,* both in the Pre-Islamic and *muḥdath* tradition, while it tampered with such motifs through close association with the poetic thought of *al-shayb wa-l-shabāb*, as seen in the previous chapter. In their elegies, the focus of the present chapter, the two poets immortalized family members, lovers, and friends as foundational elements of their interior worlds. In these interior worlds, the deceased take their place besides the poets' lost homelands, their false hopes, disappointments, and defeats.

I. *Abū Isḥāq: The Elegy to his Wife*

The Arabic elegy (*marthiyya*) needs but a short introduction: it is the genre of funerary dirges by which poets mourned and praised the deceased. It dates back to the early history of Arabic poetry, when mourning lamentations at funerals were performed in *sājʿ* (rhymed speech) and later in verse, traditionally by women.[2] Arabic critics often associated it with praise poetry (*madīḥ*), but the theme has, of course, a purpose of its own: commemorating the dead and expressing mourning publicly. As it developed into a proper poetic thought, the *marthiyya* acquired some recurring structural features. In the customary opening, the poet muses over the transience of life, the frailty of material things, and the vicissitudes of Time (*al-dahr*). The only remedy to grief is patience (*ṣabr*), resignation to the order of things, and reliance upon God (*al-tawakkul bi-Llah*). The elegy is thus typically structured as follows: a gnomic introduction (*muqaddima ḥikamiyya*), followed by the praise of the deceased person, where his/her typical manly (generosity, valour, strength) or womanly (piety, modesty, loyalty) qualities are extolled. Beyond its commemorative aim the *marthiyya* carried out the obvious function of reinforcing, through communal mourning, social bonds among the members of the immediate circle of the deceased. This function was evolved, as is to be expected, through the various ages of the *qaṣīda*. Pre-Islamic Arabia had as its fundamental social structure the tribe; thus, the customary subjects of an elegy were kinsmen and family members. With the rise of the Islamicate court, from the Umayyad age onward, the *marthiyya* was incorporated into the social framework of this institution, and thus prominent political figures became the subjects publicly mourned by professional poets. This evolution of the *marthiyya* mirrors, obviously, that of the *madīḥ*: in an era in which poetry became a lucrative occupation, even the elegy became an instrument tied to political patronage and propaganda. Finally, since no formal rule forbade the dirge for an object or animal, poets also wrote elegies to their homelands, when these fell to invaders, and even to their beloved pets — in at least one case, to their own garments!

As we have seen in chapter two, Abū Isḥāq's 'Elegy to Elvira' is best read within the Andalusian tradition of elegies to Andalusian cities fallen to the Christian conquest. In Chapter Two we have also seen the some examples of Ibn Ḥamdīs's elegies to Sicily much in the same style. The elegies to places and the elegies to persons can be read as complementary: the elegiac production of both poets compounds the loss of the homeland with that of family members.

[2] Gaudefroy-Demombynes, *Ibn Qutaiba*, pp. 17–18.

For Abū Isḥāq we have only one example, but it is a quite long and significant *qaṣīda*, which the poet dedicated to his own wife. The poem is striking in the originality of its imagery, in the unpredictable mixture of poetic thoughts, and in the lyricism of some of its lines that read as heartfelt and personal, showing us a sensitive side to the generally bitter and angry *faqīh*. The poem contains six general segments: lines one to six proffer the imagery and tropes of the pre-Islamic *nasīb*, lines nine to fifteen constitute the elegy proper, in which the deceased is mentioned, lines sixteen to twenty-seven contain a lament over lost youth and old age. The middle and final sections bring the poem back to the elegy proper: lines twenty-eight to thirty-five are a gnomic interlude in which the poet articulates existential and universal themes; lines thirty-six to fifty-six can be read as personal reminiscences imbued with the imagery of the *raḥīl*, and it is especially in this segment that we most clearly detect the autobiographical voice of the poet. Lines fifty-seven to sixty end the poem with the stereotypical *duʿāʾ*, or prayer to God, for forgiveness. Let us see the poem in detail:

Abū Isḥāq, no. 21[3]

١. عـج بالمَطـيّ علـى اليبـابِ الغامِـرِ واربَـعْ عَلـى قَبـرٍ تَضَمَّـنَ ناظـري
٢. فستَتَسْـتَبِينُ مكانَـهُ بضَجِيعِـهِ ويَنِـمُّ منـه إليـك عَـرفُ العاطـر
٣. فلكَـم تضمَّـنَ مـن تُقـىً وتعفُّـفٍ وكريـمِ أعـراقٍ وعِـرضٍ طاهِـرِ
٤. واقْـرَ السَّـلامَ عليـه مـن ذي لَوعَـةٍ صَدعَتـهُ صدعـاً مالَـهُ مـن جابِـرِ
٥. فَعَسـاهُ يسـمحُ لـي بوَصـلٍ فـي الكَرى متعاهـداً لـي بالخيـال الزَّائـرِ
٦. فأُعَلِّـل القلـبَ العليـلَ بطيفِـهِ عَلِّـي أوافيـه ولسـتُ بغـادر
٧. إنـي لأسـتحييه وهـو مُغَيَّـبٌ فـي لحَـدِه فكأنّـه كالحاضـر
٨. أرعـى أذمّتَـهُ وأحفـظُ عهـدَهُ وعنـدي فمـا يَجـري سـواه بخاطـري

1. Halt your mount on the barren wasteland, and lean over a tomb which my eyes embrace
2. You will see a sepulchre, and its bed-companion. Her fragrant perfume will reveal it to you.
3. There you will see piety, modesty, a noble lineage, an immaculate reputation.

[3] Abū Isḥāq, *Dīwān*, ed. by Muḥammad Riḍwān al-Dāya, pp. 89–94.

4. Send it my greetings, the greetings of one who is tormented by grief over the one whom he loved.
5. So that perhaps I be granted sleep, and be visited by the *khayāl*!
6. And thus I will distract my afflicted heart with a phantom, whose faithful visits keep my mind occupied, for I am not faithless!
7. For I keep it alive while he is absent, in its grave, as if he resided there
8. I watch over it, I keep the promise it made to me, and this all happens but in my mind!

We see how Abū Isḥāq reworks into his elegy the traditional imagery of the pre-Islamic ode: the apostrophe to the travelling companion, the stopping over the abandoned ruins (*aṭlāl*), and the appearance of the phantom of the beloved (*ṭayf al-khayāl*) in lines one to five. But the poet does not express his longing for his wife only through this set of traditional imagery. He also pledges his promise of eternal love to her and his faithfulness to her memory (ll. 7–9), and he stakes a claim to his marital union through the permanent memorial of his own poetry (ll. 10–11). This first section, centred on imagery drawn from the *nasīb* and on the voice of the poet, is followed by an exquisitely crafted transition to the elegy, in which Abū Isḥāq praises his deceased wife. This transitional segment insists on the effacing of the wife's physical presence, and evokes images of the wife's tomb and of her corpse, mirroring the poem's opening:

٩. إن كان يَدثُر جسمُه في رسمه   فَهَواي فيه الدَّهرَ ليس بداثِرِ
١٠. قَطَعَ الزمان معي بأكرمِ عِشرَةٍ   لهَفي عليه من أبَرِّ مُعاشر
١١. ما كان إلا ندرةً لا أرتجي   عوضاً بها فرثيتهُ بنوادر
١٣. وشققتُ في خلب الفؤادِ بكونه   وسقيته أبداً بماءِ محاجري

9. Though the traces of its material body may have been effaced, my love for her will never cease
10. Time has cut my bond with the most noble of companions, now my grief is my companion, the most pious one!
11. She was but a rarity for whom there is no hope for return, whom I bewail with poetic rarities
13. Inside the shell of my heart, I break her tombstone and water [her corpse] with the water of my eyes

Line thirteen reinforces the shift from a *nasīb* to an elegy, creating the effect of *ḥusn al-takhalluṣ* through a subtle transition from the emotional, intangible sphere to the sensorial and tangible one, and through the deployment of the images of stone and water. In subsequent lines we see Abū Isḥāq bemoaning the loss of a wife not just as an exemplar of piety and devotion, as he had done in lines three and four, but also as an attractive woman, whom he depicts through the use of the elegiac lexicon of the *ghazal* (ll. 16–17).

١٦. أخلِـقْ بمثلـي أن يُـرى متطلّبـاً   حَـوراءَ ذات غدائـر وأسـوار
١٧. مقصـورةً فـي قُبَّـةٍ مـن لؤلـؤ   ذخـرت ثوابـاً للمصـاب الصابـر

16. Is it fitting for one like me to be seen in need of black eyes, long-tresses, arms adorned with bracelets
17. [black eyes] enclosed in a chapel made of pearls, which hold a reward for the patient, ill-stricken?

In the third segment of the poem, as anticipated above, Abū Isḥāq redeploys the by now familiar tropes of old age poetry in the Arabic tradition; what he adds to such familiar tropes, however, is a subtle but poignant contrast between his expressions of undying love as an old man, to the passions of other men, young and old, who pursue amorous adventures. Following this segment, (ll. 16–27) the poet further expands upon the theme of old age using the more universal religious themes of sin and salvation. What we see is the shift from the universal poet-lover to the private persona of Abū Isḥāq as a bereaved husband: in this section of the poem, Abū Isḥāq shifts the attention from the subject of the elegy to his own persona. In particular, this next section is compelling for the autobiographical voice of the old poet: we see him looking back at his long life, examining his faults, his aspirations, his merits and his many sorrows:

٢٠. مـن جـاوز السـتين لـم يجمـل بـه   شـغلٌ بجمـل والربـاب وغـادر
٢١. بـلْ شـغله فـي زاده لمعـاده   فالـزاد آكـدُ شـغل كل مسـافر
٢٢. والشـيخ ليـس قَصـارُه إلا التقـى   لا أنْ يهيـمَ صبابَـةً بجـآذرِ
٢٧. حسـبي كتـابُ الله فهـو تنعّمـي   وتأنُّسـي فـي وحشـتي بدفاتـري
٢٨. أفتـضُّ أبـكاراً بهـا يغسـلن مـن   يفتضّهـنَّ بـكل معنـى طاهـر
٢٩. وإذا أردت نزاهـةً طالعتهـا   فأجـولُ منهـا فـي أنيـق زاهـر
٣٠. وأرى بهـا نحـج الهدايـة واضحـا   ينجـو بـه مـن ليـس عنـه بجائـر

٣١. قد آن لي أن أستفيق وأرعوي   لو أنني ممن تصحُّ بصائري
٣٢. فلكم أروح واغتدي في غمرة   متردداً فيها كمثل الحائر
٣٣. وأرى شبابي ظاعناً في عسكر   عني وشيبي وافداً بعساكر
٣٤. فغدت مظفّرة عليّ ولم تزل   قدماً معلاةً قداح الظافر
٣٥. ولقد رأيت من الزمان عجائباً   جرّبتها بمواردي و مصادري
٣٦. فوجدت إخوان الصفاء بزعمهم   يلقاك أمحضهم بعرض سابري
٣٧. ولربّما قد شذّ منهم نادرٌ   وأَصولنا: أن لا قياس بنادر
٣٨. وإذا نبا لي منزلٌ أو رابني   صفّقتُ عنه كالعقاب الكاسر
٣٩. فأجوبُ أرضاً سهلها كحزونها   عندي وأوّل قطرها كالآخر

20. It does not befit a man who has passed his sixties to entertain himself with beauties and lutes, for he is leaving [the world].

21. His preoccupation, instead, should be devoted to preparing for his journey of return; provisions are the first worry of every traveller.

22. The best an old man can accomplish is to be pious, and not to be preoccupied with passionate love affairs

27. For me, it suffices the book of God; it is my comfort and ease in my loneliness along with my notebooks

28. With them, I open new meanings that will cleanse the one who opens them with all pure meanings

29. If I want to be unblemished, I look into them, and I depart from them pure and glowing

30. In them I see clearly the best of gifts, it will save the one who is not unfair towards it.

31. The time has come for me to regain conscience and to restrain myself, if I am to be among those endowed with clear vision

32. So, to you I come, evening and morning in time of trouble, going back over and over like one who is restless

33. And I see my youth abandoning me like a [vanquished] army, and my white hair coming to me in numerous, [victorious] armies

34. It dawned on me victorious and it does not cease to bring ailments like piercing arrows
35. Yet, I have seen all sorts of marvels from Time, I have tried them in my arrivals and in my departures
36. I have found the brethren of purity with their claim that will light upon you as the most genuine, with a clear demonstration
37. And perhaps a rarity has come out of them, and I here accuse all of us: isn't true reason a rarity?
38. And when it became impossible for me to remain in my abode or if suspicion had risen over me, I flew away from it like the wild eagle
39. So I roamed the earth in good and evil, its first region like its last

In the verses above, we see Abū Isḥāq articulating a poetics of ageing which emanates from powerful autobiographical references: the painful loss of his beloved wife, his advanced old age, professional and political disappointments, which the poet compensates for with a heartfelt religiosity. The first lines of this section appear as Abū Isḥāq's quasi-formulaic return to his forte: the ascetic poem. Old men should abstain from the pleasures reserved for the youth and prepare themselves for the final journey by pursuing a pious life. These musings lead the poet to an autobiographical digression, which emerges more strongly in the poet's recalling of his leaving home to seek refuge in the hermitage of *al-ʿuqāb* (ll. 38–39). This word translates into English as 'eagle', and the toponym of *al-ʿUqāb* echoes in the poet's comparison of himself to an eagle. We also see the old Abū Isḥāq seeking consolation for his many sorrows such as exile, the loss of his beloved, and the loss of his youth in his faith, as well — perhaps — in his studies and in his own verses (notebooks, *dafatīr*), to which, he says, he returns over and over (ll. 27–30). Lines 30 to 39 are a most compelling testament to Abū Isḥāq's reflections upon his ageing as they touch upon the challenges he had to face during his lifetime. Particularly compelling is his reference to the *Ikhwān aṣ-Ṣafāʾ* (The Brethren of Purity) in lines thirty-six and thirty-seven. The *Ikhwān* is a collection of epistles afferent to Ismāʿilī doctrines which espoused much of Greek scientific learning, as well as Neoplatonist doctrines.[4] Abū Isḥāq lines seem to express a degree of admira-

[4] The bibliogaphy on the Ikhwān al-Ṣafāʾ is extensive. The Institute for Ismaili Studies in London has recently undertaken the task of compiling a new edition and English translation for Oxford University Press, featuring leading orientalists. Secondary literature on this work

tion for this work, and my reading of line thirty-seven, in particular, opens new fascinating perspectives on this poet, dubbed by previous studies — see Chapter One — as a 'reactionary'. If my reading is correct — and I must admit that this verse is rather obscure, to me at least — then Abū Isḥāq is casting an accusing finger against those members of his own entourage who, moved by a certain dogmatic obtusity, were all too quick in dismissing the allure of a work such as the *Ikhwān*, whose arguments they, as *Mālikī sunnī fuqahā'*, would consider suspicious if not altogether blasphemous. In other words, in these two lines Abū Isḥāq numbers the epistles of the *Ikhwān aṣ-Ṣafā'* among the many challenges that Maghribī Islam found itself facing during his lifetime: the epistles, with their 'genuine' claims and 'clear demonstration' stood in dark contrast with the 'lack of reasoning' that the poet attributes to his own people ('us' in *asūlu-nā* — a pronoun which I read as a reference to the Andalusian *Mālikī* community — the orthodox Muslims). Let us recall here that Abū Isḥāq was probably born not long after the Fatimid takeover in North Africa (909), and that, during his lifetime, the threat of a spread of Ismāʿīlism was very tangible. Line thirty-eight is yet another reference to the poet's many disappointments, and to his exile in al-ʿUqab, which, the poet says, he had to pursue when 'suspicion arose' over him. Was this suspicion perhaps bound to the poet's admitted admiration for the doctrines contained in the epistles of the Brethren of Purity, which he mentioned in the immediately preceding lines?

A compelling mixture of themes pervades this poem: the loss of a beloved one, the end of youth and the approach of old age, the loss of homeland and patronage, hardship and poverty, withdrawal from public life, refuge in religion and books, substantial challenges to Islamic 'orthodoxy', but also a sense pride in facing these hardships, and pious reliance upon God. All these life experiences and emotions, both public and private, universal and local come together to form what we can read as an encompassing 'poetics of ageing'.

includes: Adīwān, *al-Ṣawt bayna al-naẓarayn al-falsafī wa-al-lisānī ʿinda Ikhwān al-Ṣafā'*; Baffioni, 'Ikhwān al-Ṣafā''; Callataÿ, *Ikhwan al-Safa'*; Krinis, 'Cyclical Time in the Ismāʿīlī Circle of Ikhwān al-ṣafā''; Mattila, 'The Ikhwān al-Ṣafā' on Religious Diversity'; Sallām, *al-Sulṭah wa-al-dawlah bayna al-Muʿtazilah wa-Ikhwān al-Ṣafā'*; Vaulx d'Arcy, *Les Épîtres des Frères en pureté*. For the *Ikhwān* in al-Andalus see for instance: Ebstein, *Mysticism and Philosophy in al-Andalus*; Kacimi, 'La relación de Maslama al-Mayriti con las obras Rasa'il Ijwan al-Safa'; Treiger, *The Longer Theology of Aristotle in al-Andalus*; Cordonnier, 'Influences directes et indirectes'; Callataÿ, and Moureau, 'De nuevo sobre Maslama Ibn Qāsim al-Qurṭubī, los Ijwān al-Ṣafā' e Ibn Jaldūn'; Stroumsa, *Andalus and Sefarad*.

II. Ibn Ḥamdīs: The Elegy to his Wife

Throughout his long life, Ibn Ḥamdīs had to face the passing of many a loved one: partners, friends, and relatives. He commemorated them in his elegies, using — once again — the medium of the *qaṣīda* to face this other challenge of growing old. In what follows, I will focus on four subjects of Ibn Ḥamdīs's elegies: his own wife whom he eulogized in the voice of one his children; Jawhara, an enslaved young woman, who perished at sea upon the poet's second exile from Seville in 1091, after the fall of al-Muʿtamid Ibn ʿAbbād at the hands of the Almoravids; a compatriot, al-Fihrī, who was killed in a failed attempt to assassinate the Zirid prince Yaḥyā whom Ibn Ḥamdīs served as a court panegyrist; and his beloved daughter, Kifāḥ, who died upon receiving false news of the poet's death.

Ibn Ḥamdīs, like Abū Isḥāq, also wrote an elegy for his wife, which he composed in the voice of his son ʿUmar. This choice may be informed by a customary reticence on behalf of Arabic poets to write verse for their wives, although, as we have seen, Abū Isḥāq's only elegy also broke with this custom; this may lead to further studies for a reappraisal of this trend. Another possibility for this choice is that Ibn Ḥamdīs, in writing an elegy for his wife, was in fact lamenting the loss of a person he had grown estranged from, during the many years that followed his exile: he chose to mourn her in the voice of his younger son, the closest relative, physically and emotionally, to the deceased woman. The poem opens with a gnomic section, a customary opening which remains very much within the typical themes of the elegy: death is inescapable, *ubi sunt*, humans are subjected to never-ending calamities and patience is the only course of action. It is towards the centre of the poem that this elegy acquires a more personal character. Here, Ibn Ḥamdīs imagines the voice of his younger son ʿUmar as he addresses his elder brother Abū Bakr, remembering and mourning their mother:

Ibn Ḥamdīs, no. 297[5]

قال يرثى زوجته التي كانت أم ولديه أبي بكر وعمر، وصنعها على لسان عمر الله رحمهم تعالى

٢٤. يـا ابـن أمـي إنـي بحكمـك أبكـي   فقـد أمـي الغـداة فابـك بحكمـي

٢٥. قسـم الحـزن بيننـا فثبيـر   لـك قسـم ويدبـل منـه قسـمي

[5] Ibn Ḥamdīs, *Dīwān*, ed. by Iḥsān ʿAbbās, pp. 477–80.

٢٦. لم أقل والأسى يصدق قولي   جمدت عبرتي فلذت بحلمي
٢٧. ولو آني كففت دمعي عليها   عقتني برها فأصبح خصمي
٢٨. أمتا هل سمعتني من قريب   حيث لي في النياح صرخة قرم
٢٩. كنت أخشى عليك ما أنت فيه   لو تخيلت في مصابك همّي
٣٠. كم خيال يبيت يمسح عطفي   لك يا أمتا ويهتف باسمي

He said, mourning his wife, who was the mother of his two sons Abu Bakr and ʿUmar, and he made this poem in the voice of ʿUmar, may God have mercy on them all.

24. O brother, today I cry for you the loss of my mother, so cry for me as well
25. Sorrow is split between us: yours is mount Thabir and mine mount Yadbul
26. I do not speak, but sorrow is the truest speech: she would forebear my tears, and she would rejoice in my forbearance
27. And if I was to hide my tears for her, my filial piety would haunt me like an enemy
28. Oh mum, did you not hear me — not long ago — as I wailed like a young foal?
29. I feared what was ailing you, if only you had fathomed, in your ordeal, my worries!
30. And how many a ghost — your ghost — spends the night by my side, mum, calling me by my name

What transpires from this section of the elegy is the unique pathos that the voice of ʿUmar — a young boy at the time of his mother's passing, as revealed by line twenty-eight,- allows to convey. The poet, by adopting the child's voice, strips himself of the gravity, forbearance, and restraint that adulthood, and particularly male adulthood, imposed. We know that in Arabic poetry, the funerary lamentation was traditionally reserved for women poets — and one immediately summons the name of al-Kansāʾ. The tradition conveys a neat demarcation of roles: women as public and even professional mourners (a tradition observable until recently in Southern Italy, as in my father's hometown of Taranto, and reminiscent of Roman *praeficae* — professional mourners), men as keepers of restraint and gravity. By impersonating his young son, he can give free rein to his sorrow over the loss of a life companion: the mother of his children. He mourns her in accordance with the traditional canons: with gnomic themes and stereotypical formulas of praise (her virtue, her generosity) but also in a more personal, intimate way: as a tender mother who raised her children with care and affection. In lines twenty-six and twenty-seven, in particular, the voice of ʿUmar raises a lament that undos the stale formulas of a praise: only tears outpoured can truly commemorate his dead mother. The ghost of the beloved (*al-khayāl*) appears in line thirty, outside his traditional *locus*, in the *nasīb*: if the poet will eschew mourning his wife as a lover openly, he will do so covertly by having her visiting his young child. And yet this totemic figure of the Arabic ode gives away the poet's longing for his deceased wife as a lover.

If we compare the above fragment with Abū Isḥāq's own elegy for his wife we find a common trait in these two elegies: both poets have found ways to go beyond the ritual formulas of mourning, crafting heartfelt odes to their life-companions. Against a tradition that made of wives a poetic taboo, Abū Isḥāq unabashedly declares her wife to have been his best and only companion; having lost her, he relies solely on the book of God. Abū Isḥāq also inscribes his elegy in the wider framework of his ascetic poetry, which he intertwines in the traditional framework of the dirge. Ibn Ḥamdīs, more subtly, bypasses this tradition, by articulating his elegy in the voice of his young son ʿUmar, through whom he expresses his sorrow and love, even by redeploying the elegiac lexicon of the *nasīb* within the dirge. The theme of ageing, so dominant in Abū Isḥāq's own poem, is instead entirely absent in Ibn Ḥamdīs's. The poet is here entirely effaced, replaced by the poetic persona of a child crying for his dead mother, a child through whose voice, however, we detect the sorrow of the adult man contemplating the dismemberment of his own family. His bewilderment and apprehension are perhaps more apparent at the beginning of the fragment quoted above, in lines twenty-four and twenty-five, where ʿUmar seeks to renew a bond of brotherhood with Abū Bakr in facing their common loss. It is in these lines that Ibn Ḥamdīs, an exile who, willingly or not, was continuously buffeted by fate and separated from family, protectors and friends, delivers a message to his family members: to stay close in the face of life's sorrows and adversities.

III. The Cycle of Jawhara

Ibn Ḥamdīs composed three heart-wrenching poems for Jawhara, who was his travelling companion on a perilous sea crossing from al-Andalus to North Africa. The poems range from fully fledged *qaṣīdas*, to short occasional pieces. One poem, for instance, consists of only four lines: the poet improvises it upon seeing a young boy playing in the water. The boy pretends to be drowning evoking — in Ibn Ḥamdīs's mind — the terrible image of Jawhara disappearing under water. A second poem, longer and more elaborate, was probably written later in the poet's life, after long contemplation over the loss of the enslaved young woman. This poem best resonates with Abū Isḥāq's elegy in its shared expression of reclaiming a physical bond with the past. Just like Abū Isḥāq, Ibn Ḥamdīs laments the loss of his beloved adopting a lexicon which bears largely upon the realm of the senses. Let us see in detail.

Ibn Ḥamdīs, no. 131[6]

وقال يرثي جارية له ماتت غريقة في المركب الذي عطب به في خروجه من الأندلس إلى إفريرية

١. أيا رشاقة غصن البان ما هصرك   ويا تألُّفَ نظم الشمل من نثرك
٢. ويا شؤوني وسأني كله حزن   فُضّي يواقيتَ دمعي واحبسي دررك
٣. ما خلت قلبي و تبريحي يُقلّبه   إلا جناح قطاة في اعتقال شرك
٤. لا صبر عنك و كيف الصبر عنكِ وقد   طواك عن عيني الموجُ الذي نشرك
٥. هلا وروضة ذاك الحسن ناضرة   لا تلحظ العين فيها ذابلا زهرك
٦. أماتك البحر ذو التيار من حسد   لما درى الدرُّ منه حاسداً ثغرك
٧. وقعت الدمع إذ أغرقت في لجج   قد كاد يغمرني منه الذي غمرك
٨. أي الثلاثة أبكي فقدَهُ بدم   عميم خلقك أم معناج أم صغرك
٩. من أين يقبح أن أفنى عليك أسى   والحسن في كل من يقتفي أثرك
١٠. كنت الشبيبة إذ ولّت ولا عوضٌ   منها ولو ربح الدنيا الذي خسرك
١١. ما كنت عنك مطيلا بالهوى سفري   وقد أطلت لحيني في البلى سفرك

He mourns a slave of his, who died drowning in a shipwreck on his journey from al-Andalus to North Africa.

1. Tender willow branch, what snapped you? Perfect necklace of pearls, who ripped you apart?
2. Oh my tears, I am but sadness, so shed your rubies, and spare your pearls.

[6] Ibn Ḥamdīs, *Dīwān*, ed. by Iḥsān ʿAbbās, pp. 212–13.

3. I can't describe my heart's agitation other than as the wings of a qata' bird trapped in a net.
4. There is no bearing this. How can I bear that the sea embraced you, hiding you from my eyes?
5. Am I wrong? Yours was a garden in bloom, the eye could not find a withered flower.
6. The raging sea took your life out of envy, when its pearls became jealous of your front teeth.
7. I am left in tears since you drowned in the abyss; that which submerged you has almost submerged me.
8. Which of these three will I cry with blood-filled tears: your perfect figure? Your qualities? your youth?
9. How can I be blamed for wasting away in sadness, while the beauty of all art has drowned in your wake?
10. You were youth. Now that it is gone, nothing can ransom it, not this entire world that has lost you!
11. For your love, never did I prolong my journeys, and you, in spite of me, have made your journey eternal.

As he mourns the death of Jawhara in this poem, Ibn Ḥamdīs looks back at a moment of profound shock and uncertainty in his life. Jawhara's drowning took place during the time when the poet was forced out of Seville. A host of sorrowful thoughts must have been haunting him as he embarked from al-Andalus bound for North Africa: dramatic political upturns were forcing him to abandon his safe haven of Seville, the city in which he had lived for thirteen years. He had also lost his protector and friend al-Muʿtamid, imprisoned and deported to North Africa along with his family by the Almoravids. He had to witness the slaying of al-Muʿtamid male heirs, killed before their father's very eyes. Adding to all this, news may have reached him about how his homeland, Sicily, had fallen to the invading armies of the Normans.

This host of traumatic setbacks echoes throughout the poem, in particular in images of fracture, violence, and bloodshed which pervade the poem's opening lines. The poet's address to Jawhara in line one relies largely on the realm of the tactile, with images of the physical act of rupture: the snapping of a branch and the breaking of a necklace. Then, through the metaphor of ruby and pearls, line two describes the poet's blood-filled tears (also making allusion to the name Jawhara, which means 'Jewel') while line three conveys the poet draws upon imagery borrowed from the pre-Islamic *qaṣīda* (the sand grouse flapping his wings against a net for the troubled heart, from Imrū al-Qays) to convey his restlessness and sorrow. Contrary to the customary opening of the elegy, centred on religious and metaphysical themes (*al-dahr*) and maxims (*ḥikam*), the opening of this poem makes constant reference to the sensorial, the immanent and the physical: abstraction, universal and eschatological themes are kept to a minimum throughout the poem. This trend continues for instance in the following lines, where Ibn Ḥamdīs recalls Jawhara through the physical imagery of the *nasīb*, summoning, through the process of synecdoche, an image of the lost garden. This process, obtained through relations of contiguity, is the dominant trait of the *nasīb* since its inception in pre-Islamic times, as explained by Sells:[7] Jawhara's body is a garden in full bloom (line 5), her front teeth, pearls (line 6) her slender waist a willow branch (line 1). Grief over the loss of physical proximity to Jawhara's body, and over its being consumed by the sea, haunts the poet and surfaces in multiple lines (ll. 4, 8, 10, 11, 12, 13, 14). In response to, contrast with or in revenge over the impossibility of physical reunion with Jawhara, Ibn Ḥamdīs builds each line of his poem relying on the senses to evoke the dead. Jawhara, in this poem, is a physical, tangible presence. In fact, the whole poem can be read as an attempt to revive, through the highly sensorial language of the *nasīb*, the body of Jawhara. Much in keeping with the conventions of the *nasīb,* after evoking the body of Jawhara, Ibn Ḥamdīs addresses her phantom in subsequent lines. This evocation of the *ṭayf al-khayāl* also resembles that of Abū Isḥāq in the elegy to his wife. In both cases the evocation of the phantom of the beloved is followed by the image of the poet visiting her tomb:

١٢. هل أصلي منك إلا طيف ميتة   تهدي لعيني من ذاك السكون حرك

١٣. أعانق القبر شوقاً وهو مشتملٌ   عليك لو كنتُ فيه عالما خبرك

12. What else is left for me of you but the ghost of a dead woman, whose stillness brings me agitation?
13. Carried by burning desire, I embrace that grave that contains you. If only I had known your news!

Again very similarly to Abū Isḥāq, who imagined breaking the tombstone of his wife's grave and watering her corpse with his tears, Ibn Ḥamdīs makes reference to his desire to be reunited to Jawhara, whose sepulchre he embraces.

[7] Sells, 'Guises of the Ghūl', pp. 130–44.

He wishes to see his beloved once again, to share one more loving gesture with her body, repelling the soil and pebbles that have adhered to her skin:

وددت يا نور عيني لو وقى بصري   جنادلاً وتراباً لاسقا بشرك

14. Light of my eyes! How I wish I could see you now, to ward off the pebbles and soil that stick to your skin

Throughout this *nasīb*-like section of the elegy, Ibn Ḥamdīs sketches the archetypical persona of the pre-Islamic poet/lover. While the poetic voice thus immortalizes Jawhara through her physical, tangible attributes, Ibn Ḥamdīs, the man, voices his desperation before the loss of Jawhara's body, with his desire to shelter a buried corpse from water and soil. Both the physical evocation of the beloved and the poet's wish to reunite with her, be it with her phantom or with her corpse, resonate once again with Abū Isḥāq's elegy. But the two poems also display important differences. Abū Isḥāq's poem sketched, albeit summarily and in a stereotypical fashion, a psychological and moral portrait of the deceased. Ibn Ḥamdīs's poem, on the other hand, appears a highly gendered appropriation of the elegy: a male master regrets the loss of an enslaved female. It is her physicality, rather than her psychological and emotional world, that the poet mourns first and foremost. A host of questions arises from this comparison: who were these two women and who exactly is Jawhara? Where did she hail from? Was she a Christian captured in Castile, Galicia, or Asturias during one of the many incursions of the Muslim Iberian armies in Norther Spain? Was she an African woman sold into slavery in the markets at Ceuta, Malaga, or Seville? Was she a 'present' in payment for a felicitous poem? What was her age at the time of her drowning? What was her role in Ibn Ḥamdīs' family, a family that we know was composed of at least one wife and children? Why would Ibn Ḥamdīs, contrary to Abū Isḥāq, mourn Jawhara in three poems, and yet, no poem is devoted to the mother of his children, is this simply in keeping with a poetic convention or can we read more into this display of affection to this young woman? These fascinating questions deserve a thorough investigation, which, however, lies beyond the scope of this book.

Ibn Ḥamdīs's use of sensorial images in the elegy to Jawhara is much reminiscent of his poetic forte, namely his *ṣiqilliyyāt*, poems describing his youth in Sicily that also rely heavily on imagery bearing upon sensorial faculties. Strikingly, the same holds true for Abū Isḥāq, who also remembered both his wife and his hometown, Elvira, very much in physical terms. Both Ibn Ḥamdīs's Sicilian poems and Abū Isḥāq's elegy to Elvira attempt to revive these places through a sensorial reconstruction. Abū Isḥāq's elegy to his wife and Ibn Ḥamdīs's poem to Jawhara also deploy imagery that celebrates the deceased through the senses and through the re-evocation of certain qualities: youth, beauty, and virtue. In sum, as old men, both Abū Isḥāq and Ibn Ḥamdīs opted to evoke the past not relying upon an ostensibly failing memory, but rather through more immediate means, and one cannot but think of Proust's *Recherche*, of the use of sensorial experience to summon up the past. Through the senses, the two poets bridge a distance, both temporal and physical, with their past. The *qaṣīda*, with its array of canonical motifs, provided both poets with ready venues for their own quests to retrieve the past: they evoked youth as the *nasīb*'s beloved, the *ḥanīn ilā al-waṭan*'s homeland, or the *bukā' ʿalā faqd al-shabāb*. Both poets appropriated these modes in inventive ways, to mould them and adapt them to their own story. One ingenious example of this personal, creative reworking of the classical Arabic literary canon is found in Ibn Ḥamdīs's representation of the sea as the great divider in his life. Similar images of the sea as such recur in both his elegies to Jawhara, as they do in many of his *ṣiqilliyyāt*.

١٥. أقول البحر إذ أغشيته نظري   ما كدّر العيش إلا شربها كدرك
١٦. هلا كففت أجاجاً منك عن أشر   من ثغر لمياء لولا ضعفها أسرك
١٧. هلا نظرت إلى تفتير مقلتها   إني لأعجب منه كيف ما سحرك
١٨. يا وجه جوهرة المحبوبَ عن بصري   من ذا يقيك كسوفاً قد علا قمرك
١٩. يا جسمها كيف أخلو من جوى حزني   وأنت خال من الروح الذي عمرك

15. When I gaze at the sea I say to it: 'Nothing has troubled me more than her drinking your impure water'.
16. Why did you not keep apart your salt water from her perfect teeth, from her red lips! But alas, her weakness made you strong!
17. Did you not see her eyes? Did they not charm you?
18. O beloved countenance of Jawhara, who is eclipsing you from my sight?
19. O her body! How can I be free from the madness of my sorrow, while you are deprived of the soul that gave you life?

The sea, in these lines, becomes a rival in love to the poet. The paronomasia of line fifteen (*kaddara* — to trouble, spoil and *kadar* — turbidity, muddiness) conveys the image of the sea violating Jawhara's purity, which is readily associated with ritual purity: the image of impure water contrasts with that of ablutional water and the sea's bitter waters find an immediate opposite in fresh drinking water. This imagery contributes to morphing the drowning of Jawhara into an act of violence, specifically sexual violence: the sea becomes a rapist of the helpless young woman. The personification of the sea continues in following lines: the image of a physical violation of Jawhara by the sea is fortified in line sixteen, whence the sea actively forces its impure water into the woman's mouth. The physicality of the imagery of these lines extends onto the following lines, where the poet returns once again to Jawhara's physical attributes, fusing the *nasīb*'s lexicon with the elegiac theme of sorrow and loss, particularly in line nineteen. It is remarkable that throughout this section the sea continues to be addressed as the poet's rival in love: the sea is personified, confronted, accused, and reprimanded by the poet. For Ibn Ḥamdīs, born on an island and fleeing war and devastation through many a sea-journey, the sea would prove an enemy to confront, an obstacle to cross, a boundary that prevented him to reach his goal. It is predictable that the sea would have a long-term significance in his overall poetics. The image of the sea as rival, as found in the elegy to Jawhara, recurs in Ibn Ḥamdīs' *ṣiqilliyyāt*, as seen above.

Ibn Ḥamdīs, no. 2[8]

٢٠. وراءك يا بحرُ لي جنّةٌ   لبست النعيم بها لا الشقاء
٢١. إذا أنا حاولت منها صباحاً   تعرضتَ من دونها لي مساء
٢٢. فلو أنّني كنتُ أعطى المنى   إذا منعَ البحرُ منها اللّقاء
٢٣. ركبتُ الهلال به زورقاً   ألى أن أعانقَ فيها ذكاء

20. Beyond you, O sea, I have a paradise in which I donned the robe of joy and not that of trouble.
21. When I was waiting for the dawn to rise from it, you interposed the night instead.
22. Oh! Would that I had had my hopes fulfilled! When the sea stood between us,
23. I would have crossed it with the arched moon for a ship, so to embrace the sun there!

[8] Ibn Ḥamdīs, *Dīwān*, ed. by Iḥsān ʿAbbās, p. 4.

The parallel representation of the sea in Jawhara's elegy and in the poem to Sicily brings me back to my appraisal of the shared lyric quality, and the imagery, of Ibn Ḥamdīs' elegies to persons and places. A nuanced, conjunctive reading of the two allows us to appreciate their shared emotional dimension, as the poet confronts the boundaries of physical separation, death, and distance. The trauma of the loss of homeland, the death family of members, and the turmoil within Islam's political and cultural worlds are conflated in Ibn Ḥamdīs's elegies, to the point that the boundary between various type of losses — i.e. losses of persons, places, youth — become blurred. A case in point is another elegy that Ibn Ḥamdīs penned in North Africa, a decade or so after the death of Jawhara.

IV. The Elegy to al-Fihrī

Having returned and resettled in Ifrīqiya, the ancestral home of many Sicilian Muslims, Ibn Ḥamdīs was jolted back by the waves of refugees who left the island in turbulent times and sought refuge in the lands of their ancestors. The memory of Sicily hit him with the island's tangible presence, only a day's journey away by boat, and with the imminent catastrophe for Sicilian Islam. The poet became reacquainted with former compatriots who were resettling in North Africa who brought with them the painful and shared experience of exile. Having spent the last thirteen years in al-Andalus Ibn Ḥamdīs undoubtedly was shielded by spatial distance, and his return to Ifrīqiya, close to Sicily and now full of his compatriots escaping the Norman avalanche, turned an abstract nostalgia into a more immediate, perhaps shocking encounter with Sicily's reality. To one of these Sicilian compatriots, Ibn Ḥamdīs devoted an elegy upon his death, happened in a foreign country as he shielded, with his own body, a foreign ruler from an attempted assassination.

Alī Aḥmad al-Sharīf al-Fihrī al-Ṣiqillī served as prime minister at the court of Zirid prince Yaḥyā b. Tamīm (1108–1131) in al-Mahdiyya. As his *nisba* 'al-Ṣiqillī ' indicates, he was of Sicilian origin. It is likely that the Sicilian-born al-Fihrī was a member of the Sicilian *khāṣṣa* (aristocracy) that re-settled in North Africa after the Norman invasion.[9] In 1131, Yaḥyā b. Tamīm suffered an assassination attempt, al-Fihrī, who was with the prince at the moment of the attack, defended his patron by shielding him from the attackers with his own

[9] On the *khāṣṣa*/ *'āmma* divide see for example Beg, 'al-khāṣṣa wa-l-ʿāmma', *Encyclopaedia of Islam,* 2nd edition.

body. He managed to save Yaḥyā, but took the fatal wound in his stead and died shortly thereafter.

The fact that Ibn Ḥamdīs composed an elegy on this occasion strongly suggests some kind of professional or personal relation between the poet and al-Fihrī. The language and tone of the poem adhere to the conventions of the Arabic elegy; however, between the lines we detect the personal utterances and asides of Ibn Ḥamdīs as a Sicilian émigré crying over the tragic end of a fellow Sicilian exile. In addition to the poet's lament over a fellow Sicilian Muslim, and quite possibly a personal friend, we read two other important factors in the context of this poem. In the elegy, Ibn Ḥamdīs characterizes the attempted assassination of Yaḥyā b. Tamīm as a challenge to the Zirid dynasty, and adding a more personal stance to the poem, to their position of potential defenders of Muslim Sicily. Since the formal break between the Zirids and their Fatimid patrons, following the Fatimid move to Cairo, the Zirid princes had assumed in fact the role of Muslim Sicily's benefactors and protectors. A murdered Zirid prince, to Ibn Ḥamdīs, would add to the political uncertainty that plagues western Islam at this time. Secondly, the fact that the attack on Yaḥyā and the murder of al-Fihrī was carried out by court insiders — that is to say, it was violence carried out by Muslims against Muslims — points to yet another painful reminder that Muslim unity was tenuous at best. The attempted murder uncovered all the dangerous rifts that were threatening Muslim unity in the Maghrib, rifts that, not long before, had torn Muslim Sicily apart and made it subject to the Hauteville. The poem is a rather long one, (fifty-seven lines) and it comprises four thematic segments: a brief gnomic introduction on the vicissitudes of Time (ll. 1–2); the news of the death (*al-naʿya*) of al-Fihrī, grief over his demise (ll. 3–14); a long section in his praise, the elegy proper, (ll. 15–47); and a concluding segment on the poet's own expression of sorrow and affection for al-Fihrī (ll. 48–57). Let us see it in detail:

Ibn Ḥamdīs, no. 96[10]

١. إذا البدر يطوى ربوع البلى لحدا   أم الطود حطوّا في ثرى القبر إذ هدّا
٢. كسوف وهد تحسب الدهر منهما   لعين وأذن ظلمة ملئت رعدا
٣. تولّى عن الدنيا علي بن أحمد   أبقي لها من ذكره الفخر
٤. حملنا على التكذيب تصديق نعيه   وسدت له الأسماع وانصرف صدا

[10] Ibn Ḥamdīs, *Dīwān*, ed. by Iḥsān ʿAbbās, pp. 163–66.

٥. وقال لمن أدّى المصاب معنف   فظيع من الأنباء جئت به إذّا

٦. إلى أن نعاه الدهر ملء لسانه   ومن ذا الذي يخفي من الرزاء ما أبدى

٧. هناك خضنا في العويل ولم نجد   على الكره من تصديق ما قاله بداً

1. When the full moon is enwrapped in the abodes of havoc, it is like a tomb; and when a mountain is crushed it becomes the turf of a tomb
2. Eclipses and ruination, to both the eye and the ear, you think [the work of] Time, a darkness full of thunder
3. Ali Ibn Ahmad has departed from this world, and his memory bequeaths to it pride and glory
4. We accused the truthful news of his passing as being a lie; all ears were blocked to it, and they turned away in denial
5. One by whom the sad report was afflicted said in rebuke: How dreadful that you disturb us with such sorrow.
6. But alas! It is Time that announces his death with its full tongue, and who among us can conceal what tragedy Time exposes.
7. It was then that we sank into wailing, and grudgingly, we found no way other than to accept the truth of what was said.

The poem's dramatic opening (ll. 1–2) sets the sombre tone of the elegy: al-Fihrī is likened to a full moon which is now eclipsed, or a mountain which has crumbled down. Subsequently, the poem moves into the scene of the reception of the news of al-Fihrī's assassination. The announcement of the news of a death (*naʿya*) is a customary passage of the Arabic elegy: in this occasion, the choral image of an assembly of men responding in shock to the news of the death of al-Fihrī situates his assassination in the context of the Zirid court and the role that Sicilian exiles played in it (ll. 3–7): Ibn Ḥamdīs voices his grief on the personal and the collective level at once: his own, as a personal friend to al-Fihrī, the grief of the entire Zirid court at the loss of a public officer, and perhaps especially the grief of the community of Sicilian Muslims in Mahdiyya, at the loss of a compatriot and fellow exile. Following the récit around the *naʿya*,the bulk of the poem (ll. 8 to 52) provides the space for the elegy proper, in which al-Fihrī is extolled for his many — and heavily stereotyped — qualities: generosity, liberality, determination, and courage. This segment is standard in its content, giving little personal depth to the figure of al-Fihrī or to the relationship between him and the poet. On the other hand, Ibn Ḥamdīs's own voice in addressing his fellow-countryman is best heard in the last segment of the *qaṣīda*.

٥٣. رثيتــك حزنــاً بالقوافــي التــي بهــا   مدحتــك ودّاً فاعتقــدت لــي الــودّا
٥٦. أدرنــا لــك الدنيــا القليــل بقاؤهــا   وربّك فـي الأخـرى أراد لك الخلدا
٥٧. فـلا برحـت مـن رحمـة الله دائبـاً تزور   نــدى كفّيــك فــي قبــرك الأنــدا

53. I recite my elegy to you with rhymes of sorrow; I praise you with affection to which you would have responded favourably.
56. We wished you a long life, which now has endured but a short time, and God has willed for you the hereafter which will last an eternity
57. May the moistures of the morning dew, by God's mercy, never cease, and the generosity of your hand will be visited in the grave.

The poem concludes with the poet's expression of his personal affection for al-Fihrī (ll. 53, 56) and with the customary invocation of rain (l. 57): that is, an appeal to God to have mercy on his soul. At a glance, the poem's structure can be summarized as follows: *muqaddima ḥikamiyya* (lines 1 to 3) *naʿya* (4 to 7), *rithāʾ* (8 to 52) *istisqāʾ* (53 to 57). This structure delineates the character of an official, public elegy: the poet's own feelings stand in the background while the eulogized and his accomplishments stand out. This elegy points to the late years of the poet's life as a moment of political crisis that disturbs his hopes for a return to his homeland: Ibn Ḥamdīs wrote this long elegy in his old age, and when he was closer than he had been in a long time to Sicily; he wrote it for a fellow countryman, murdered by fellow Muslims who were attempting to take the life of the Zirid emir himself. Like the poet, al-Fihrī was an expatriate; also like the poet, he probably enjoyed a privileged upbringing in Sicily; thirdly, and also like Ibn Ḥamdīs, al-Fihrī left Sicily to pursue a career at the court outside of his homeland.

For Ibn Ḥamdīs, who in many a poem addresses his fellow countrymen as 'sons of the frontier', and extols Sicily as Islam's bulwark against the Christians, the killing of al-Fihrī at the hands of Muslim political rivals contradicts and disturbs the poetic fantasy he so often evoked in his *ḥarbiyyāt*, of Muslim unity against the Christian enemy. Ibn Ḥamdīs would have seen, in the assassination of the Sicilian minister, the repetition of an act of Muslim-to-Muslim betrayal which some decades earlier had caused Sicily to fall to the Normans. This was also the case with the fall of al-Muʿtamid's Seville court at the hands of the Almoravids in 1091. Ibn Ḥamdīs did not customarily compose invectives (*hijā'*), yet he nevertheless denounced, with unforgiving vehemence, acts of betrayal (*al-khīyāna*) on the part of Muslims. The theme of betrayal resounds strongly in several verses of Ibn Ḥamdīs. These may be read against the elegy to al-Fihrī, in that the minister was the victim of such a treasonous act. In another poem (*dīwān* 12) Ibn Ḥamdīs warns again his coreligionists against breaking ranks.

Ibn Ḥamdīs, no. 12[11]

١٨. وقـد بدّلـت بعـد سـراة قومـي   ذئابـاً فـي الصحابـة لا صحابـا
١٩. وألفيتُ الجليس علـى خلافـي   فلسـت مجالسـاً إلّا كتابـا
٢٠. وما العنقاء أعوزُ من صديقٍ إذا خَبُثَ   الزمـان عليـك طابـا

18. After the departure of my people, I was given wolves instead of companions.
19. I found my friend turning against me, and I found my only company in my books.
20. how many loyal friends this calamity has thrown into misery! Friends that, when fortune was propitious, were generous ones!

In these three lines, which follow verses on old age (not cited here), Ibn Ḥamdīs once again inscribes his own life-experiences against the musings of the reversals of history and the theme of the treason of time (*al-dahr*). Internecine struggle, treason, and the progressive shrinking of Muslim territory resound strongly in lines eighteen and nineteen, where Ibn Ḥamdīs voices his dismay in observing the Muslims as disunited and treacherous towards each other. The expression 'after the departure of my people' of line eighteen can be read, for example, as a reference to the first migration of Sicilian Muslims out of the island at the time of the *fitna* and subsequent beginning of the Norman invasion. With the departure of the Sicilian elite (the first to leave were presumably those who could afford to), the island, and the poet, were left in the company of 'wolves', who had little scruples in tearing Sicily apart or selling it out to the Normans (is the spectre of Ibn al-Thumna, the great traitor of Muslim Sicily, echoing in these lines?). Also in these lines, Ibn Ḥamdīs links Sicilian Islam's general disunity, expressed by the word *qawmī* — my people — to the treason of his own

[11] Ibn Ḥamdīs, *Dīwān*, ed. by Iḥsān ʿAbbās, pp. 14–16.

friends (*al-jalīs* — the boon-companion). The macro-narrative of the decline of Maghribī Islam of line eighteen finds a counterpart in the micro-narrative of the treason of the poet's own friends, expressed in lines nineteen and twenty.

V. The Elegy to his Daughter

The combination of personal and political loss is the focus of more than one elegy by Ibn Ḥamdīs. Of these, one stands out as being among Ibn Ḥamdīs' most touching poems, a poem he composed for his daughter, Kifāḥ, who died upon receiving false news of her father's death. The poet refers to himself in the poem as a man of eighty years, separated in distance from his daughter and his kin. Throughout the verses of this long poem (forty lines) we learn that his daughter was residing in the hometown of his ancestors in Sfax, while the poet was then at the court of Mahdiyya or Bijāya. The lyric quality of this poem is much higher in emotion than the one composed for al-Fihrī, for obvious reasons. The death of his beloved daughter, the mother of small children herself, the long separation from her, and the poet's guilty feeling for this long separation, make this poem particularly poignant, especially from an elderly man facing his own mortality.

The elegy to Kifāḥ can be broadly divided in two sections: a gnomic introduction (ll. 1–19) and the elegy proper (ll. 20–34). In the gnomic introduction, Ibn Ḥamdīs articulates in a highly reflective mood the grief he feels over this loss while making allusions to the many setbacks of his long, unpredictable and unstable life.

Ibn Ḥamdīs, no. 245[12]

٩. ثمانون عاما عشتها ووجدتها　　تهدم ما تبني وخفض من تعلي
١٠. وإني لحيّ القول في الأمل الذي　　إذا رمته ألفيته ميّتَ الفعل
١١. إذا الله لم يمنحك خيراً ، منعتَهُ　　على ما تعانيه من الحذقِ والنبل

9. I have lived eighty years, and I see them destroying what they had built and debasing those whom they had honoured.
10. How will I say 'I still hope to live', when I find all my hope dead indeed?
11. When God does not grant you a blessing you will be devoid of it, no matter your skill or your intellect.

[12] Ibn Ḥamdīs, *Dīwān*, ed. by Iḥsān ʿAbbās, pp. 364–67.

In expressing his bereavement for his beloved child, Ibn Ḥamdīs once again fuses the emotions of his private sorrow with the political and existential angst he has been carrying throughout his life. The poet's grief is conveyed with particular poignancy in line nine, in which Ibn Ḥamdīs muses upon the tragic circumstances of receiving the news of his daughter's death while he himself is on the verge of dying. In the same line, he is reminding his audience of the many ups and downs that he and his contemporaries experienced in political and personal life: once again we observe Ibn Ḥamdīs fashioning a 'poetics of ageing' by bringing in the various facets of his public and private life. In the following line, line ten, we hear the voice of an elderly father grieving the loss of a daughter for whom he hoped to nourish and protect; yet another of the many hopes in his life that never came to fruition. In a subsequent section (ll. 11–12), Ibn Ḥamdīs adopts once again the motifs of ageing, this time tainted by a misanthropical note, to increase the pathos of his lines.

١٢. فيا سائلي عن اهل ذا العصر دعهم   فبالفرع منهم يُستدل على الأصل
١٣. إذا خلل في الحال منك وجدته   فإياك والتعويل منهم على خل
١٤. تأملت في عقلي وضعفي فقل إذا   سئلتَ رأيت الشيخ في عمر الطفل
١٥. وهم له حمل على الهم ثقله   فيا ليته منه على كاهل الكهل
١٦. رجعت إلى ذكر الحمام فأنه   له زمن ملآن بالغدر والختل

12. O you who inquire about the people of this time, leave them! From their branches you can judge their root.
13. If you are in trouble, beware of asking their help!
14. I was hoping that my mind would have never weakened; if you are asked about me you can tell them: I see that old man has turned a child again!
15. My sorrows have a weight, it crushes my back. Would that they were weighing upon my first white hair instead!
16. I often long for death, for my time was full of treasons and illusions.

The shift from the first to the second person (*iltifāt*) of line twelve marks a movement from the personal dimension of the poet's private grief to a communal grief for the loss of unity among Muslims. The expression of 'the people of this time', for example, in conjunction with the image of branches and roots, connects a collective loss with an individual loss. The poet's own feelings of guilt for abandoning his daughter are synonymous with his compatriots' abandonment of their homeland. The psychological and emotional trauma over the loss of Sicily, the fall of Seville and other *taifas*, the sectarian divisions in North Africa, Arab/Berber rivalries, and the political intrigues that compromised Muslim unity, resonate powerfully with the trauma of losing his own daughter. Once again, we see how the poet is able to manipulate the conventions of Arabic poetry to convey the most immediate political and emotional sentiments. Above all in these lines, we see Ibn Ḥamdīs once again compounding the fear of growing old on top of other devastations: in this case, the decline of his political world and the loss of his daughter. These aspects inform the background of Ibn Ḥamdīs' late poems, much more than the kind of religious zeal that Gabrieli argued for in discussing these poems.[13] In this instance, rather than religious rhetoric, the imagery, language, and meaning of the above lines encompass the two principal rubrics of the 'poetics of ageing': the rupture of social ties along with political decline (ll. 12–13), and the poet's own mental and physical deterioration (ll. 14–15). We see surfacing, in this brief section, all the principal themes that have been thus far discussed in commenting upon selected lines: the poet's exile, his separation from his family, his painful ageing, his loss of agency and the heart-rendering news of his own daughter's death.

The poem continues, in keeping with tradition, with the poet's praise for the deceased. But more powerful than customary formulas of praise, we hear the distressed voice of a father and learn of his affection towards his daughter, whom he describes as a branch cut off from his own trunk, and whose death deprives him of his fruit. From line twenty-eight onwards, the poet mentions his advanced age, his sorrow at facing the loss of hope, his perpetual exile, and an overpowering sense of disappointment:

٢٠. فيا غرسة للأجر كنت نقلتها   إلى كنفي صوني وألحفتها ظلي
٢١. وأنكحتها من بعد صدقٍ حمدته   كريما فلم تذمم معاشرة البعل
٢٢. أتاني نعي عنك أذكى جوى الأسى   عليّ اشتعال النار في الحطب الجزل
٢٣. وجاءك عني نعي حي فلم يجز   لك الكحل فيه ما لبست من الكحل
٢٤. على أنّ أسماع البلاد تسامعت   به وهو يجري بين ألسنة السبل
٢٥. فنحت على حيٍ أمات شبابه   زمان مشيب لا يجدّد ما يبلي

[13] Gabrieli, *Ibn Ḥamdīs*, pp. 284–85: 'l'animo del poeta torno' a vibrare, oltre che per zelo sentenzioso morale, per la speranza nella riconquista araba della Sicilia' (the poet's soul vibrated once more with sententious moral zeal and with the hope of an Arab reconquest of Sicily).

٢٦. فمتّ بما شاء الإلهُ ولم أمت   ليكتب عمري من حياتي الذي يملي
٢٧. وفارقت روحاً كان منك انتزاعه   أدقّ دبيباً في الجسوم من النمل
٢٨. أراني غريباً قد بكيتُ غريبة   كلانا مشوقٌ للمواطن والأهل
٢٩. بكتني وظنت أنني متّ قبلها   فعشتُ وماتت وهي محزونة قبلي
٣٠. أقامت على موتي الذي قيل مأتماً   وأبكت عيون الناس بالطل والوبل
٣١. وكل على مقدار حسرته بكى   عليّ ولاقى ما اقتضاه من الشكل
٣٢. أساكنة القبر الذي ضمّ قطره   على البرّ منها والديانة والفضل
٣٣. أصابك حزن من مصابي قاتل   فهل أجل لاقاك قد كان من أجلي

20. O branch, hoping in your fruit I took you under my cares and under my shadow

21. and married you to a noble man, whose sincerity I had praised, you who never objected to the company of your husband!

22. I have received the news of your death. Now the flames of sorrow are stalked within me. They're ablaze, they devour me like dry wood.

23. and you...you had received the news of the death of someone who was alive....

24. That news spread in our country on all ears, and still it wanders on the tongues of men.

25. The time of white hair clutches man and kills his youth, and does not renew what he consumes.

26. I am dead. As God pleases, but I am not dead, and my age is writing now what He dictates to me.

27. I am forsaking my soul for your sake. My steps are smaller than an ant's.

28. I feel like a stranger mourning a stranger. We both wished only for homeland and family.

29. She cried for me, thinking I had died before her. I lived and she died, bringing grim sorrow upon me.

30. She performed the mourning wails, causing all eyes to shed a rain thin and perpetual.

31. Each cried according to his grief, each affected in his own way.

32. O you, who lie in a tomb which now encloses your piety, your religion, your virtue,

33. you were overcome by grief over my misfortune. Is it that death took you because of me?

The tragic circumstances of the poet's daughter's death, evoked in lines twenty-three and twenty-nine, are compounded by the poet's sorrow in contemplating two lives — his and that of his daughter — spent in separation and exile (l. 28). It is in these lines (in particular ll. 25–28) that the private voice of Ibn Ḥamdīs as an old man surfaces most clearly. We see the old man considering, through the aesthetics of the motif of *al-ḥanīn ilā al-waṭan*, the many sorrows of his long life: his perpetual exile, the loss of his homeland, his estrangement (*al-ghurba*) in the changing face of Islam in the Maghrib, and finally the loss of his own daughter. The poem reaches a unique pathos in the poet's description of his own funeral and the traditional mourning chants performed by his daughter, who is to die shortly thereafter (ll. 30–31). As he contemplates the sepulchre of his daughter and praises her virtues, the old poet is left with the daunting accusation that he levels against himself: of being unwittingly responsible for her death (ll. 32–33). There is much more than we can read in this last line: regret, helplessness and guilt. As an old man, the poet looks back at his life considering his losses, thinking back about his self-imposed exile, the end of youth's hopes, and a feeling of having been responsible for many of the calamities that befell him.

All these reflections complement what we have seen before in the political poems of Ibn Ḥamdīs, in which the glories of Sicily are represented in conjunction with the golden years of the poet's youth, while the decline of Islam is associated with the poet's grim old age. Here, such decline is also bound to the deaths during his own lifetime of his family members, adding to his sense of fatigue and frustration. Both Abū Isḥāq and Ibn Ḥamdīs, as old men, we may recall, remembered and commemorated their most valuable affects: i.e. family members, lovers, homeland, and a host of favourable political and professional successes they enjoyed in their younger days. As they aged, the departure of significant individuals came to symbolize the demise of their worlds, and a harbinger of the end of their lives. Given what we know of their biographies, we can appreciate how in their elegies both poets reflected on their personal losses in the wider context of political setbacks, cultural decline, and their own mortality. For bothAbū Isḥāq and for Ibn Ḥamdīs, political defeat as well personal grief compelled the poets to seek a more intimate, withdrawn, and spiritually charged poetics at the end of their lives. Once again, the Classical poetic canon provides a venue for this: ascetic poetry, in Arabic, *zuhdiyya*.

Chapter Four

The Poetics of Withdrawal: Ascetic Verse

Ascetic poetry emerged as a poetic motif in the ʿAbbasid age, in the ninth and tenth centuries. As a poetic *maʿnā*, it was consecrated as a canonical theme of the *qaṣīda* thanks in particular to the ʿAbbāsid poet Abū-l-ʿAtāhiya (748–828), whose production focused largely on ascetic themes, after repenting a life of wantonness and profligacy, Abū Nūwās style (he was in fact a friend of Abū Nūwās, with whom he competed in dissipation, before turning to asceticism — as it happens — and making his name in this domain of poetry). Ascetic poetry is referred to in Arabic as *zuhdiyya*, from the verb *zahada,* meaning 'to renounce' or 'to voluntarily abstain from something'. The verbal noun *zuhd* can be rendered through a range of terms which span modesty, piety, renunciation, and asceticism. In the literary context, poems defined as *zuhdiyyāt* generally focus on the idea of decay, old age, mortality, and the afterlife. A customary beginning of the *zuhdiyya* has the poet reflecting on the rapid passing of earthly glory, typically symbolized by the remains of once-grand palaces and cities, now in ruins. Very often the poet confronts the signs of ageing in himself, white hair in particular, reading them as harbingers of the approach of death. The poet thus muses upon his many sins, his shameless desires as an old man, and also ponders the unworthiness of honour and wealth, and the vanity of sensual pleasures. Worldly gratifications, often acquired at the expense of spiritual integrity, appear now, in old age, as deceiving allurements and deceptions.

The *zuhdiyya* is often formulated in the form of an admonition: the poet addresses his audience warning them against the temptations of the material world (*al-dunyā*) and inciting them to abandon their worldly desires in favour of piety and religion. Old men in particular should abandon pleasure-seeking and flee the deceptive temptations of *al-dunyā:* given the approximation of the fatal hour, they should focus on prayer and repentance if they are to escape hellfire.

It goes without saying that asceticism, both as a literary motif and as a spiritual and social phenomenon, is not specifically Islamic. Jewish and Christian

Andalusian poets also cultivated the genre. Also, the broad themes of the *zuhdiyya*, such as renouncing honours, wealth, and ambitions, are universally present in various tradition of gnomic literature from Stoicism onwards. This notwithstanding, within the canon of classical Arabic poetry, the *zuhdiyya* is eminently a product of Islam, as it draws heavily on the corpus of religious writings for its imagery and conceptual frame. But even this mainly Islamic genre borrows from the pre-Islamic canon and, although the *zuhdiyya* as a poetic thought makes its appearance in the Islamic period, many of its concepts and stock-phrases can be retraced to pre-Islamic poetry. Consistent examples from the *jāhilī* poetic tradition have been classified by authors of medieval literary studies as pertaining to *zuhd*. Those *jāhilī* verses, however, differ from the *zuhdiyya* as they lack a significant connection to established religious beliefs. They usually address the more universal aspects of the *zuhdiyya*: mortality, inevitability of decay, the succession of old age after youth, the annihilation of the great civilizations of the past, and the precariousness of human glory. Secondly, the *jāhilī* poet does not characterize the world as intrinsically evil, as later Muslim poets of *zuhd* would do. Old age, the loss of beloved ones and family members, death, and the hardships of everyday life in the desert are simply part of the human condition, to be endured by the individual as well as is possible.

Thirdly, the afterlife, which assumes a central role in the Islamic *zuhdiyya*, is not a preoccupation of the *jāhilī* poet: death should spur one to live life to the fullest here and now, according to the *jāhilī* ethos. As Hamori has remarked: 'a man should take what pleasures he could, and stand his ground in battle, for only a good name escaped the general ruin: this was, in the pagan view, the sensible conclusion from the premise of mortality.'[1] Lastly, another pillar of *zuhd* poetry, namely the question of salvation, does not appear in the spiritual and moral world of the *jāhilī* man. However, in the period of Islam these *zuhdiyyāt* contain the poet's warnings for sinners to repent and renounce worldly temptations, striving to save themselves from hellfire all in accordance with Muslim tenets of faith. It is particularly through the development of the *zuhdiyya* in the Islamic period that we see how Islam co-opted (and we may even say domesticated) Arabic poetry.

Before Islam another tradition, namely the homiletic tradition of the Eastern Church, had a strong influence on the Arabic *zuhdiyya*. The Christian Arab poet of the sixth century, ʿAdī ibn Zayd (d. *c.* AD 600) of al-Ḥīra wrote verses about the vanity of life and human endeavours, characterizing the world

[1] Hamori, 'Ascetic Poetry', p. 265.

as fundamentally evil and proclaiming that worldly passions should be sacrificed to a pious life. ʿAdī ibn Zayd's poems are dominated by the *ubi sunt* motif, another pillar of the *zuhdiyya*: the poet recalls the glory and majesty of bygone civilizations, he questions the real nature of such glory, to conclude with musings over the vanity of worldly possessions. The *ubi sunt* motif that inspired Christian poets such as ʿAdī ibn Zayd plays a major role in the Islamic *zuhdiyyāt*; likewise, the cardinal virtue of temperance resonates most clearly with the Islamic concept of *zuhd*.

As stated above, ascetic poetry became a distinct poetic *maʿnā* in the golden age of the ʿAbbāsid Caliphate (eighth–ninth century) particularly thanks to the oeuvre of Abū-l-ʿAtāhiya, who set the foundations of this poetic motif. For the *zuhdiyya* in this period, the Qurʾān itself constitutes a primary source for inspiration: 'Then seest thou such a one as takes as his god his own vain desire? Allah has, knowing, left him astray, and sealed his hearing and his heart, and put a cover on his sight. Who, then, will guide him after Allah? Will ye not then receive admonition?' (45:23) And, in 3:14: 'Fair in the eyes of men is the love of things they covet: women and sons; heaped-up hoards of gold and silver; horses branded; and cattle and well-tilled land. Such are the possessions of this world's life; but in nearness to Allah is the best of goals.' The Qurʾān teaches that greed for worldly goods corrupts morality and leads to a bad end: 'As for those who wish for the life of this world and its glitter, We will give them in this life the wages of their works in full, and they shall not be shortchanged in it. These are the ones who in the next world will have nothing but fire' (9:16–17)

The reflection on mortality that characterizes the *zuhdiyya* finds its literary and aesthetic inspiration in the *ḥadīth* according to which Muḥammad, upon being asked who most truly renounces the world, replied: 'He who is ever mindful of decay in the tomb, who prizes the enduring above the transitory, and who numbers himself among the dead.'[2] But, as already underscored by Hamori, the *zuhdiyya* tends to emphasize the evil nature of the world in a fashion that is not common in the Qurʾān:

> despite the stress on the transitory nature of this life, despite the ascetic mood of many passages, the Qur'an, so the Muslim could feel, did not represent the world as an altogether evil place. The bloom, to be sure, withers...nevertheless it is bloom... the *zuhdiyya*, as it emerges in the early Islamic age, tends to see in the bloom of this world only evil, a baited snare.[3]

[2] Hamori, 'Ascetic Poetry', p. 266.

[3] Hamori, 'Ascetic Poetry', p. 267.

Hamori has also effectively classified the genre's themes as follows:

Ubi Sunt: The living should contemplate the dead. Here the poet often recalls the glory of past kingdoms whose annihilation has rendered ephemeral.

Tawakkul (trust in God): man's striving is laughable and implies distrust in God. To a certain extent (ḥadīth literature censures extremes in tawakkul) men should content themselves with God's decree and rely totally on His will.

Heedlessness of humankind: love of this world is incurable. The *zuhdiyya* insists on the reiteration of sin on behalf of men. The author most often reproaches himself for his obstinacy in sin, reaching, in his confession, a lyrical depth that breaks through the genre's quasi-formulaic tone.

Fear of God's punishment and hope in His mercy: the *zuhdiyya* deals with the emotions with which man looks at the final judgment. Fear predominates, but hope is not abandoned.

Questioning the author's steadiness of purpose: the poet ponders the nature of his repentance and his perseverance in it. He recognizes his own weakness in renouncing the world.[4]

II. Withdrawal or Engagement?

What did it mean for Abū Isḥāq and Ibn Ḥamdīs to write ascetic verses, while remaining obsessively engaged in politics up to the end to their lives? In their ascetic poems, Abū Isḥāq and Ibn Ḥamdīs reflected upon the fragility of worldly glory and advocated a withdrawal from material pursuits. How can we read such stances, considering the fact that these men would not or could not withdraw completely from their worlds? And if in fact Abū Isḥāq and Ibn Ḥamdīs did advocate a withdrawal from the world in their ascetic poems, what exactly were they withdrawing from?

These questions can be addressed by elaborating on what has been suggested by Iḥsān ʿAbbas and Muḥammad Riḍwān al-Dāya, who both related the success of *zuhd* in the *taifa* period of al-Andalus to the political uncertainty and social disruption of this period.[5] It is my contention that both Abū Isḥāq and Ibn Ḥamdīs used ascetic poetry as a way to reflect upon the collapse of al-Andalus and of Muslim Sicily. They reworked the *zuhdiyya* to voice their personal angst

[4] Hamori, 'Ascetic Poetry', pp. 265–73.

[5] ʿAbbās, *Tārīkh*, p. 105; Abu Isḥāq, *Dīwān*, ed. by Muḥammad Riḍwān al-Dāya, p. 17.

as well as that of their societies: two germane cultures which, after an abrupt fall, looked back at their apogees with dismay, nostalgia, and longing. Political and personal trauma played a fundamental part in the ascetic bend of Abū Isḥāq and Ibn Ḥamdīs's old age verses. When read in conjunction with their political poems, elegies, and their reworking of the motif of *al-shayb wa-l-shabāb*, these ascetic verses acquire new meanings, conveying the poet's late reflections on their many losses: that of homeland, that of dear ones and family members, and that of their own lives. What informs this ascetic poetry, both for Abū Isḥāq and Ibn Ḥamdīs, is the reality of all these losses, personal and communal. It is this combination of all of the above factors — political defeat, private and public loss, and apprehension over the afterlife — which moulds a 'poetics of ageing' shared by both poets.

As mentioned in the previous chapter, Francesco Gabrieli, in his monograph on Ibn Ḥamdīs, briefly addressed the Sicilian's late production as being informed by a warrior-like nationalism, and by a form of moral zeal.

> l'animo del poeta torno' a vibrare, oltre che per zelo sentenzioso morale, per la speranza nella riconquista araba della Sicilia.[6]

> (the poet's soul quivered once more with moral zeal, as well as with the hope for an Arab reconquest of Sicily.)

Gabrieli has thus summarized two of the main binaries along which the Ibn Ḥamdīs's (as well as Abū Isḥāq's) late production revolved. But we can nuance the two poets' late production further to include their grappling with their own physical decline, their own mortality, the loss of loved ones and friends, and the many setbacks suffered by Maghribī Islam during their old age. These instances all informed their poetics of ageing, pushing the two poets to tap into a variety of religious discourses that ranged from a physical *jihād* on the one hand to the traditional Islamic *zuhdiyya* on the other. Far from being a form of withdrawal, *zuhd* poetry was for both Ibn Ḥamdīs and Abū Isḥāq much informed by the immediate time and place which they were occupying. The two poets' obsessive concern with their physical demise in the *zuhdiyya* is particularly telling in this sense: asceticism, both for Abū Isḥāq and Ibn Ḥamdīs, emanates from the fatigue of old age, the loss of agency on both a physical and mental level as well as their sorrow over the loss of family, friends and patrons, and the demise of the political world around them. These factors merge in the late verses of both poets, as they appropriate the traditional themes of the appearance of white

[6] Gabrieli, *Ibn Ḥamdīs*, pp. 284–85.

hair, the passing of the poets' youth (and, by extension, the nostalgia for the past), the phantom of the beloved, the crossing of endless deserts, and, as we will see in what follows, in their ascetic poems.

II. Abū Isḥāq's Zuhd: A Late Poetics of Contrasts

The themes summarized by Hamori, and sketched in this chapter's introduction, resurface consistently in both Abū Isḥāq's and Ibn Ḥamdīs's *zuhdiyyāt*. These poems may thus appear, at a first glance, as heavily standardized, yet perhaps the most striking feature shared by their ascetic poems is an insistence on the discrepancy between their growing old and their lack in spiritual contentment. As for Abū Isḥāq, this is indeed a leitmotif in his overall poetics, as underscored by Scheindlin.[7] In his *zuhdiyyāt* Abū Isḥāq denounces, almost obsessively, his own pathetic attempts to obtain sexual gratification as an old man. Let us consider the following example:

Abū Isḥāq, no. 8[8]

١. الشيب نبّهَ ذا النُّهى فتنبّها   ونهى الجهولَ فما استفاق ولا انتهى
٢. بل زاد نفسي رغبةً فتهافَتتْ   تَبغي اللُّهى وكأنْ بها بين اللّها
٣. فإلى متى ألهو وأفرَحُ بالمُنى   والشَّيخُ أقبَحُ ما يَكونُ إذ لها
٤. ما حسنُهُ إلا التُّقى لا أن يُرى   صبّاً بألْحاظِ الجآذرِ والمها
٥. أنى يقاتل وهو مفلولُ الظُّبا   كابي الجوادِ إذا استقلَّ تأوَّها
٦. محقَ الزمانُ هلالَه فكأنما   أبقى له منه على قدر السُها

1. White hair warns the sensible ones, and they obey; it is forbidding for the ignorant one, he does not awake and he does not refrain
2. Indeed, my soul increased its cravings, they come in crowds! It seeks pleasure, while it is about to be swallowed
3. Until when will I amuse myself and rejoice in my desires? How ugly is an old man given to pleasures!
4. There is nothing more laudable than fearing God, and not being seen casting covetous glances at young girls!

[7] Scheindlin, 'Old Age in Hebrew and Arabic "Zuhd" Poetry', pp. 85–104.

[8] Abū Isḥāq, *Dīwān*, ed. by Muḥammad Riḍwān al-Dāya, pp. 53–55.

5. How will he fight with a blunted sword, and a stumbling horse that pants and moans when he rises?
6. Time has shrunken his crescent, there remains nothing of it but a fading star.

In the first verse, the *dramatis persona* of white hair appears in its traditional role of admonisher and censor. Line two introduces the voice of the poet through the use of the first-person possessive suffix pronoun attached to *nafs*. From this line on, the focus is on the poet which the poem casts as the epitome of the ageing man who is incapable of withdrawing: while his hair gone white, he still is unable to renounce material pleasures. In line four, the poet reminds himself that, as an old man, he should devote himself entirely to religion, instead of casting lewd glances at young girls. Adding fuel to the fire, he insists on old men's sexual impotence through graphic imagery which parodies the martial tone of the *ḥarbiyya*, and elegiac lexicon of the *nasīb*. Consider, for example, the phallic symbolism of the blunted sword in line five, or of the crescent now shrunken and barely visible in line six. The rhythm of the poem flows through a liberal use of alliteration and paronomasia (*tajnīs*). Abū Isḥāq's choice of alliteration for this poem on old age and mortality appears to be highly symbolic: the final letters of the Arabic alphabet. In line one, for example, the root *nahā* is pervasive, as are the letters *hā'*, *wāw*, and *yā'*. These letters, the last three of the Arabic alphabet, recur in the majority of the poem's lines. The poem's rhyme is in *hā'*, the antepenultimate letter of the Arabic alphabet. Consider the alliteration in the following lines:

٧. فغدا حسيراً يشتهي أن يشتهي   ولكم جرى طلقَ الجموحِ كما اشتهى
٨. إن أنّ أوّاهٌ وأجهشَ في   البكا لذنوبه ضحك الظلوم وقهقها
٩. ليستْ تُنهنِهُهُ العظاتُ   ومثلُهُ في سنّهِ قد آنَ أن يتنتنها
١٠. فقد اللدات وزاد غيا بعدهم   هلّا تيقّظَ بعدهم وتنبّها؟
١١. يا ويحهُ ما بالهُ لا ينتهي   عن غيّه والعمرُ منه قد انتهى

7. He has grown tired of craving to crave, and how often does the toiling of a headstrong man result as he had wished?
8. If he laments and weeps for his sins, darkness laughs and guffaws
9. Sermons do not restrain him, while it is time for the like of him, at his age, to restrain!

10. His peers in age are less and less, he multiplies his transgressions after them. Will he not be vigilant after them, and be aware?
11. Woe unto him, what is it with him that he will not stop his transgressions, while his time is running out?

It is easily observed that the rhyming letter *hāʾ* is not confined to the end of each line, but rather pervades the entire poem. Line seven, for instance, is built around the verb *ishtahā*, to desire, which recurs three times. The subsequent line complements this one by depicting the result of men's stubborn desires: wailing and lamentations (both containing the letter *hāʾ*). To these, the darkness of the tomb responds with chilling laughter (*qahqahā*). Line nine is centred on yet another quadrilateral verb *nahnaha*, to restrain, also dominated by *hāʾ*. Line eleven is played out on the verb *intahā*, to end, and half the total words of this line contain *hāʾ*. Through the alliteration in *hāʾ*, and *tajnīs* of the alphabet's final letters, the sense of impending end and termination is conveyed both in form and meaning. The poem's message, like other *zuhdiyyāt* by Abū Isḥāq, is surprising: the poet casts appeals to abandon the pursuit pleasure (particularly sexual pleasure), which is now unattainable, but he appears to do so regretfully. As Scheindlin has has it: 'no more women for me — not only it is disgusting for an old man to lust after them, but they are revolted by him; so I take comfort in religion'.[9] We have also seen how Abū Isḥāq's *zuhdiyya* is enlivened by self-irony and satire. The use of an elegiac and martial lexicon (the crescent and the fading star of line six, the sword and horse of line five) to describe the pedestrian subject of an impotent penis results in the comical effect which, just as it strikes today's reader, would not have been lost on Abū Isḥāq's audience. Thus Abū Isḥāq's ascetic verse, while surprisingly accessible and direct in lexicon, is subtly built on the revisitation of ancient models; first and foremost, the pre-Islamic *nasīb* and secondly the war poem, the *ḥarbiyya*. It is a singular revisitation, that of Abū Isḥāq, in that the motif is subverted and parodied. The poet's borrowing from genres antithetical to the *zuhdiyya*, such as the *nasīb* and the *ḥarbiyya*, enriches his poetry by allowing for the important interplay between the audience's expectation and the delivered message, this was precisely the metatextual effect sought by professional and dilettante poets, aptly underscored by Gruendler, which attests to the quality of Abū Isḥāq's *zuhd* poetry.[10]

[9] Scheindlin, 'Old Age in Hebrew and Arabic "Zuhd" Poetry', p. 95.

[10] Gruendler, *Praise Poetry*, p. 6.

The withdrawal from human society upon which *zuhd* is centred took, at times, singular turns that led Abū Isḥāq to seek the company of animals. In fact, Abū Isḥāq's misanthropic rants are at times compensated for by an inclination to empathize with animals. In a short poem, (*qiṭʿa*), already seen above, Abū Isḥāq describes the wolves that roam around his monastery. These are, in his words, 'meeker than the *faqīḥ*' the latter word being a possible allusion not only to professional rivals but also to the poet himself. In an appeal somehow reminiscent of Ṣuʿlūk poetry, the poet chooses to forsake the company of his hypocritical colleagues, and to associate with wild animals, which he finds less dangerous than men:

Abū Isḥāq, no. 19[11]

١. الله حـــي العُقـــاب وقاطنيــه   وقــل اهــلاً بــه وبزائريــه
٢. حللـتُ بـه فنفّـسَ مـا بنفســي   وأنَّسَــني فمــا استوحشــتُ فيــه
٣. وكــم ذِيــبٍ يجــاوره ولكــن   رأيــت الذئــب أسـلم مــن الفقيــه
٤. ولــم اجــزع لفقــد أخ لأنّــي   رأيــتُ المــراء يؤتــي مــن أخيــه

1. May God bless al-'Uqab and its inhabitants, welcome to its visitors!
2. I have been absolved in it, and alleviated of what was in my soul and tamed of my bestial inclinations.
3. How many a wolf wanders around it, but I have found that the wolf is more submissive than the faqīh!
4. And I don't worry about the absence of a brother, because I found that man is ruined by his own brother!

In this other poem, Abū Isḥāq evokes the familiar character of the dove, to whom he confesses his sins:

Abū Isḥāq, no. 3[12]

١. أحمامــةَ البيــداء أطلــتِ بُــكاكِ   فبِحسـنِ صوتـكِ مـا الـذي أبـاكِ؟
٢. إن كان حقـاً مـا ظننـتُ فـإنّ بـي   فـوق الـذي بـكِ مـن شـديد جـواكِ

[11] Abū Isḥāq, *Dīwān*, ed. by Muḥammad Riḍwān al-Dāya, pp. 83–84.

[12] Abū Isḥāq, *Dīwān*, ed. by Muḥammad Riḍwān al-Dāya, pp. 38–39.

٣. إنـــي أظنّـــكِ قــد دهيــتِ بفرقــةٍ   مـن مؤنـسٍ لـكِ فارتمضـتِ لـذاكِ
٤. لكـنَّ مـا أشـكوهُ مـن فَـرطِ الجوى   بخـلافِ مـا تجديـنَ مـن شـكاوكِ
٥. أنـا إنمـا أبكـي الذنـوبَ وأسـرَها   وهنـــايَ الشـــكوك منـــالُ فـــكاكِ
٦. إذا بكيــتُ ســألتُ ربــي رحمـــةً   وتجـــاوُزاً فبـــكاي غيـــر بـــكاكِ

1. Oh dove of the deserts, long is your weeping; what is it you cry with your beautiful verse?
2. Yet, if I am right, what ails me is more painful than your sorrow
3. For I think you have been struck by the loss of a friend and are tormented by grief.
4. The overflowing grief I lament is far different from what ails thee!
5. For I cry over my sins and their fetters, and my wish, as I cry, is to obtain deliverance,
6. as I weep, I ask my Lord to have mercy and forgive...my crying is not your crying.

The poetic persona that Abū Isḥāq crafts in his ascetic poems gives us an interesting perspective on the *zuhdiyya*. This persona is built upon the dialectic opposition of the inherently human — evident in explicit representations of carnality and conceptualizations of desire — and the unattained transcendent, which is hoped and yearned for, but is reserved for God's mercy in the afterlife. The poet's choice of lexicon and register is straightforward, stripped bare of any preciosity and syntactical complexity: Abū Isḥāq aims to deliver an immediate message. He succeeds by adopting swift metrical choices and straightforward wording. Some verses are pervaded by tenderness and convey the private regret of this medieval man who seeks an intimate communion with his audience through his verse. Abū Isḥāq's *zuhdiyyāt* articulate a personal poetics which encompasses stylistic norms, shared existential concerns, and the crafting of an exaggerated, almost caricatured, ageing poetic persona. Reading this persona literally as a representation of the historical poet, as Dozy or Nykl have done, is misleading. It is important instead to contextualize Abū Isḥāq's ascetic poems within the poetic *maʿnā* to which they belong: a *maʿnā* which foregrounds the question of ageing. Only then can we appreciate the distinctive traits of Abū Isḥāq's *zuhd*. These traits, which are vehemently depicted, are unforgiving towards the poet's own persona, his poetic avatar, his literary self. And precisely the 'self', in Arabic *nafs*, is the natural opposite to *zuhd*. Hence its debasement, first and foremost, in the very persona that is satirized time after time in Abū Isḥāq's *zuhdiyyāt*.

Abū Isḥāq would not forsake his ascetic poetry and his persona of a moral censor to the very end of his life. The poem that follows, according to the compiler of the *dīwān*, the last one he ever proffered.[13] In this poem, the old *faqīh* comes back as a kind of preacher. From his deathbed, he rebukes a member of the Grenadine *khāṣṣa* (loosely translatable as aristocracy). Having learned that Abū Isḥāq was gravely ill in bed, Ibn Abī Rajā', a minister whom the poet had previously criticized for his ostentatious clothing, went to visit him. When Ibn Abī Rajā' made a remark about the poet's modest dwelling, Abū Isḥāq rebuked him once again, improvising the following verses:

Abū Isḥāq, no. 13[14]

١. قالوا ألا تستجدّ بيتاً	تعجب من حسنه البيوت
٢. فقلت ما ذلكم صواب	حفشٌ كثيرٌ لمن يموت
٣. لولا شتاءٌ ولفحُ قيظٍ	وخوفُ لصٍ وحفظ قوت
٤. ونسوة يبتغين ستراً	بنيتُ بنيان عنكبوت
٥. وأيّ معنى لحُسنِ مغنى	ليسَ لأربابه ثبوت
٦. ما أوعظ القبر لو قبلنا	موعظة الناطق الصموت

1. They told me: would you not renovate a house, so that other houses may admire its beauty?
2. I replied: don't you think a small hut is very appropriate for one who is dying?
3. If it weren't for the winter, for the scorching heat of summer, for the fear of thieves, for preserving my sustenance
4. and for preserving the honour of women, I would build a house like the spider's web.
5. What is the meaning of a beautiful abode, when its masters are bound to pass away?
6. No speech is more eloquent than the grave, if only we accepted the sermon of a silent preacher!

[13] Abū Isḥāq, *Dīwān*, ed. by Muḥammad Riḍwān al-Dāya, pp. 69–70.

[14] Abū Isḥāq, *Dīwān*, ed. by Muḥammad Riḍwān al-Dāya, pp. 69–71.

The poem reiterates the message of *zuhd* poetry in a dialogue form: worldly pursuits are worthless, death is impending and the afterlife awaits; mankind should be contented with little. On the other hand, another facet of Abū Isḥāq's character surfaces from this poem: his passion for invectives and rebukes. Most of the ascetic poems of Abū Isḥāq (and of Ibn Ḥamdīs) open with a section on the loss of youth, old age, and physical decline, generally followed by another section on the poet's lack of self-restraint and preoccupation with salvation and punishment. This sequence is part of a strategic articulation of the message of ascetic poetry, for once the poet has gained the audience's attention by raising the motifs of old age, he is free to ponder his life experiences, enumerating his faults and mistakes and expressing his feelings of guilt in the face of mortality. Abū Isḥāq drew in many a poem upon the theme of his own aging in order to warn his audience against sin (both in youth and in old age). The poet's appeals to moral reform, restraint, and fear of God's punishment consistently follow his lamentations on withering youth and the transience of earthly life. If *zuhd* defines 'a voluntary abstention from the world', then we are at odds with Abū Isḥāq's persona of a *zāhid* — an ascetic individual — as drawn in the lines above. His *zuhdiyya*, quite on the opposite, constructs a persona that does not withdraw, a situation that does not resolve, attachment that will not subside. Carnality is not replaced by contemplation. It is recreated in the many evocations of the beloved's physical attributes. This beloved is elusive but corporeal: not the mystic's beloved of *taṣawwuf*, but the sensorially charged subject of the *nasīb*. Repentance is wished for but not achieved, solace in death is overshadowed by apprehension.

III. Ibn Ḥamdīs: Withdrawal and Nostalgia

Abū Isḥāq's laments of his sins and the allure of the flesh resonate, as already anticipated, with the ascetic poems of Ibn Ḥamdīs, which generally start out with the poet's musing over his lost youth. Below is an example, the opening of one of his poems, a *zuhdiyya* of ten lines.

Ibn Ḥamdīs, no. 30[15]

١. وُعظـت بلمتـك الشـائبة وفقـد شـبيبتك الذاهبـة
٢. وسبشـين عامـاً تـرى شمسـها بعينـك طالعـةً غاربـة

[15] Ibn Ḥamdīs, *Dīwān*, ed. by Iḥsān ʿAbbās, pp. 40–41.

٣. فويحك هل عبرت ساعةٌ   ونفسك عن زلة راغبة
٤. فرغت لصنعك ما لا يقيل   كأنك عاملة ناصبة
٥. وغرّتك دنياك إذ فوّضت   إليك أمانيّها الكاذبه
٦. أصاحبةً خلتها ؟ إنها   باحداثها بئستْ الصاحبة
٧. أما سلبت بُردَ الشبابِ؟   فهل يُستردّ من الشالبة
٨. وإنّ دقائق ساعاتها   لعُمركَ آكلةٌ شاربه

1. You have been warned by the greying of your side curls and by the loss of your fading youth
2. At seventy years you behold its sun rising and setting with your eyes
3. So woe unto you! Has one hour passed without your soul desiring sin?
4. You devoted yourself to actions that will not preserve you, as if you were an industrious bawd
5. Your world has enticed you when it entrusted you with its deceiving desires
6. Did you think of it as a companion? Indeed with its fornication, it has been a sad companion!
7. Has not it stripped you of the garment of youth? And how do you claim (it) back from the very thief?
8. Indeed, each minute of its hour devours and drinks your life

In line one, we make note of Ibn Ḥamdīs's reference to the trope of *al-shayb wa-l-shabāb* as a warning about repentance. This opening sets the tone for the rest of the *qaṣīda*: the poet, an old man of seventy, examines his life-experience finding regrets, guilt, and a sense of non-achievement which haunts these eight lines. In lines two to four, the voice of the ageing poet echoes with a bitter, sombre tone, as he considers how he has grown old with scant preoccupation for his salvation. The opening section, however, focuses less on the ageing poetic persona in itself than on the personification of the world (*al-dunyā*), as a robber of the poet's life, who finds himself duped by false hopes and futile desires. Ibn Ḥamdīs's biographical voice fares prominently in these lines. As a professional poet, he achieved success and was admitted to the principal Islamic courts of the West, and yet, his occupation, and his very success, caused him to a series of setback that poisoned the good outcomes in his life: he left Sicily to pursue his dream to become a court poet, but lost his homeland irremediably; he was a court panegyrist to al-Muʿtamid, whom he praised (begrudgingly?) on the day when his and the Almoravid's forces won at Zallāqa, only to see al-Muʿtamid driven away in chains by his very former allies; he managed to live the sophisticated life of the courtier, but lost his most immediate affects in the process. As an old man, Ibn Ḥamdīs would look back at these many setbacks, and his regret would be sharpened by his apprehension over death and the afterlife. Looking back as a Muslim who examined his life, Ibn Ḥamdīs found sins and mistakes, and a dismal inability to let go of the material world (*al-dunyā*), that very world that had so bitterly disappointed him. This concept echoes in lines five to eight, in which the poet reflects on his own incapacity to abandon his worldly desires and aspirations, considering that his time is running short. The section articulates the idea that the experience of ageing is a process of learning to let go, to strip ourselves of desire, ambition, and the need for gratification. Time (*al-dahr*), after all, will ultimately deprive us of these things. Furthermore, in the pursuit of these desires, men get caught in a net of sin and faulty behaviour. For a Muslim man approaching death, this is but a dangerous slope towards hellfire. The preoccupation with sin and heedlessness, as already stated, is another central theme of the *zuhdiyya*: while the customary opening of the *zuhdiyyāt* usually contemplates old age and the passing of youth, the recurrent motif in its central section is that of men's sinning and heedlessness to the warning of white hair. In the second chapter of this book, I focused on how the theme of white hair allowed poets to capture the audience's attention by creating an emotional bond between them and the persona of the ageing poet. This bond operates both horizontally and vertically: horizontally in that the poet addresses other ageing men, who share and participate in his description of life's multiple trials; vertically, in that the poet is also addressing a young audience, and a patron who may be younger than himself. As he addresses a younger audience, the poet positions himself as the voice of elderly wisdom and advice. The *zuhdiyya* reinforces this aspect of the ageing persona: it casts the poet as both preacher and admonisher. The fact that this advice comes from an old man and that it is based on his own life experiences, which the poet takes pains to illustrate, reinforces the message of the *zuhdiyya*: the mention of the poet's many sins and many sorrows and his apprehension in the face of death resonate with an audience that would receive these poems as a sort of *vademecum* for growing old: a collection of advice from one who has been there and done that, and now directs them toward the righteous path. The reiterative structural composition of these *zuhdiyyāt* is not random: the poet first describes his painful ageing, establishing the aforementioned bond with his audience. Secondly, he enumerates his sins and the sorrows of his life, providing a solid background for his advice. Thirdly, he voices his own fear of damnation, inviting his audience to repent. Lastly, he concludes with a supplication to God as a way of ending the poem. In the final section of yet another *zuhdiyya* by Ibn Ḥamdīs as a representative example of how the above structure recurs in the Sicilian's ascetic poems:

Ibn Ḥamdīs, no. 34[16]

٩. وإنّ المنية من نحوها　　عليك بأظفرها واثبه
١٠. ألم ترها بحصاةِ الردى　　لكلِّ حميم لها حاصبه
١١. كأنّ لنفسك مغنيطياً　　غدت للذنوب به جاذبه
٢١. فيا حاضراً أبداً ذنبهُ　　وتوبتهُ أبداً غائبه
١٣. أذِب منك قلباً تُجاري به　　سوابقَ عبرتك الساكبه
١٤. على كلّ ذنبٍ مضى في الصبا　　وأتعبَ إثباتُه كاتبه
١٥. عسى الله يدرأ عنك العقابَ　　وإلا فقد ذُمّت العاقبه

9. And surely death from it will jump on you with its long claws
10. Don't you see it throwing down stones; for each hot season there is a tempest that scatters stones away
11. It is as if your soul had a magnet with which it became attached to sin
12. Oh you, whose sin is always present and whose repentance is always far
13. Let your heart melt, let it weep with gushing tears
14. over the sins that happened during youth, which registration tired who wrote them
15. May God draw far from your punishment, otherwise the consequences will be terrible

We see how the lines above also reflect the thematic arrangement of Abū Isḥāq's poem: the question of time and the end of life (ll. 9–10), sin and repentance (ll. 11 to 14), and the final supplication to God for mercy (l. 15). A further example of this structure is a short *zuhdiyya*, of only five lines: poem n. 228 from the *dīwān* of Ibn Ḥamdīs.

[16] Ibn Ḥamdīs, *Dīwān*, ed. by Iḥsān ʿAbbās, pp. 50–53.

Ibn Ḥamdīs, no. 228[17]

١. إن الليالي والأيام يدركها   شيبٌ ويعقبها من بعده هلك
٢. فشيب ليلك من إصباحة يقق   وشيبُ يومك من إمسائه حلك
٣. والعيشُ والموت بين الخلق في شغلٍ   حتى يُسكَّنَ من تحريكه الفلك
٤. ويبعثَ الله من جوفِ الثرى أُمماً   كانت عظامُهم تبلى وتنتهك
٥. في موقفٍ ما لحلق عنه من حولٍ   ولا يحقّرُ فيه سوقةً ملك

1. White hair reaches the nights and the days and after it death takes over them
2. The white hair in your night is brightly white in the rising of (its) day and the white hair in your day is deeply black in the falling of (its) night
3. Life and death will govern creatures, until the sky will be stopped in its movement
4. Allah will raise from the bowels of the earth all peoples, whose bones are dried and consumed
5. Into a residence that for creatures will be impossible to leave, and in which a King will not diminish his people.

These similar structures, which move from the theme of white hair towards supplication to God, construct a sort of teleological narrative of life as a quest towards redemption. Youth is depicted as the time of foolishness and error, while old age is the time allotted to men for withdrawal, introspection, repentance, and cleansing. Yet, the *zuhdiyya* is not a straightforward narrative: 'sin-repent-be saved.' On the contrary, this type of poetry is fuelled by an internal contrast, a tension between the appeal to withdrawal and reform, and the admission to an incapacity to withdraw. This contrast is observed both in the ascetic poems that made Abū Isḥāq famous (as Scheindlin has observed)[18] and in Ibn Ḥamdīs's *zuhdiyyāt*. The ascetic mood, with its obsessive contemplation of mortality, decay, and the ravages of time, dominates these poems. And yet, it is interesting that even in this state of mind both poets, while worrying for their personal salvation, still address youth with longing and nostalgia as a time

17 Ibn Ḥamdīs, *Dīwān*, ed. by Iḥsān ʿAbbās, p. 347.

18 Scheindlin, 'Old Age in Hebrew and Arabic "Zuhd" Poetry', pp. 85–104.

of happiness which cannot be revived in old age. Even in these ascetic poems, which traditionally focus on old age and the afterlife, the two poets perform a mental revisitation of the abodes of their youth, both as concrete physical places and as metaphors of a time of bygone splendour. The *zuhdiyyāt* by Ibn Ḥamdīs seem to conflate the ascetic theme and the loss of homeland and family members, drawing close — in both imagery and mood — his *zuhdiyyāt* and his *ṣiqilliyyāt*. Abū Isḥāq's *zuhdiyyāt* are also highly reminiscent of his two elegies, the elegy to Elvira and the elegy to his wife: the poet's withdrawal is hampered by his need to relive and revive what is lost. The binding concept between these three elements — i.e., death of family members together with loss of homeland and ascetic withdrawal — is most often illustrated in the classical poetic tradition by the way of the motif of *ubi sunt*. Such a motif recurs in the context of ascetic poems, political poems, and elegies. As the theme crosses from one genre to another, it also unites them as a conceptual unit. This is exemplified, in the poetry of Ibn Ḥamdīs, in yet another poem, that clusters, in its opening, the main motifs of the *zuhdiyya*:

Ibn Ḥamdīs, no. 229[19]

وقال أيضاً في الزهد

١. بيتك فيه مصرعك   وفي الضريح مضجعك
٢. غرتك دنياك التي   لها شراب يخدعك
٣. همت بحب فارك   وقلما تمتعك
٤. يضرك الحرص بها   والزهدُ فيها يفعك

He also said, on asceticism

1. Your home is your battlefield and the tomb your resting place
2. Your world has deceived you, in which a draught led you into error
3. You have been duped in love by a woman who hates her husband, and who pleases you hardly at all.
4. Your craving for her destroys you, and abstinence in it would benefit you

The poem revolves around the poet's usage of *ṭibāq* (antithesis), at the level of the single line. Line one, for instance, contrasts the temporary security of 'home' with the eternal abode of death (the tomb). The term for home (*bayt*)

[19] Ibn Ḥamdīs, *Dīwān*, ed. by Iḥsān ʿAbbās, p. 348.

in this line is charged with a host of meanings which are worth exploring. First, *bayt* can be read in the abstract, in the sense of the residence of earthly life. However, keeping in mind Ibn Ḥamdīs's involvement with the Sicilian cause, we cannot overlook the concrete reference to the actual homeland of the poet, a battlefield between Christianity and Islam. Secondly, *bayt* in Arabic is unequivocally read as a line of poetry. Hence, the line can be read as: in your lines of poetry is your battlefield, while your final destination is death. Ibn Ḥamdīs thus portrays his poetic craft as an act of war, and, we may say, of political resistance to the Christian reconquest. Yet the poem continues by stressing the vanity of all human endeavours. It is significant to point out, in particular, how the poet stresses the failure of his hopes in line two, and the deceptive nature of the material world in lines three and four. In these images we hear the echo of the poet's worldly experiences following his departure from Sicily (read, the powerful autobiographical voice): the loss of his patron in Seville, the loss of Muslim Sicily, and the loss of beloved ones and family members. The final verse, in which Ibn Ḥamdīs invites himself to become pious and withdrawal is built upon his sombre statement that all of his life's hopes, and all of his world, have passed.

٥. لا تأمنن منية   إنّ عصاها تقرعك
٦. مغربك القبر الذي   يكون منه مطلعك
٧. إنْ فرقتك تربة   فالله سوف يجمعك
٨. وللحساب موقف   أهواله تروّعك
٩. كم جرّ ما أشفقت من   لمسك منه إصبعك
١٠. فكيف بالنار التي   من كل وجه تلذعك
١١. يراك ذو العرش إذا   ناديته ويسمعك
٢١. فثق به ولايكن   لغيره تضرعك

5. Do not feel safe from death, indeed her stick will hit you
6. Your twilight is in the grave, and from it you will rise again
7. If the soil will undo you, God Almighty will resurrect you
8. The is a place set for the final reckoning, whose horrors will terrify you
9. How many things your fingers have clasped, things that you were aware should not be touched!

10. So what will you do with the fire, burning you from every side?
11. Only the One on the Throne will see you, and hear you when you call His name
12. So trust in Him, and do not humble yourself before others.

I should like to start from the 'twilight' in line six: the life of a man as a journey to the West, the sunset, the sun's resting place after its hyperbolic celestial journey (*maghribuka*) and then off to a new sunrise (*maṭlaʿuka*): the resurrection of the flesh in the final judgement. How well these lines condense Ibn Ḥamdīs's own odyssey, his exhausting, perpetual exile in the West, his quest for a return, both physical and spiritual, to a 'resting place', a 'home' that would not prove a new battlefield. In this poem, Ibn Ḥamdīs pushes himself before the void of death: as he looks behind, the old man sees the challenges of human existence: his choice between sin and piety. As he looks ahead, he stares at the frightening prospect, for a Muslim, of facing divine judgment. The poem draws upon religious imagery to evoke the soul's ordeal after death: the resurrection of the flesh, divine judgement, hellfire. We now see what kind of battlefield the world is, for the old poet (line one): a trial for the soul, a *locus*, perhaps, of greater *jihād*, (*jihād al-nafs* or *jihad of the self/soul*), where humans must make choices. Looking back, Ibn Ḥamdīs would contemplate the long road that led him, as a young man, out of Syracuse, across the sea to North Africa, and then again onwards to Seville, were he reached maturity and was exalted as a prized court poet, but then cast in the dust again, following his deposed patron in prison and exile, and then again, wandering the Mediterranean to the safe but precarious port of Majorca, and finally back to the motherland, North Africa, from which his ancestor Ḥamdīs once sough refuge in Sicily and where the poet would grow old and die. In this *zuhdiyya*, Ibn Ḥamdīs ponders his many disappointments (line two), how the material world (*al-dunya*) duped him and deceived his most intimate hopes (lines three, four). Yes, the young refugee from the Sicilian backwaters did become a great court poet...but at what price? How many losses did he have to endure, the estrangement from family, kin, and homeland, how long a trial to attain peace? And did Ibn Ḥamdīs ever attain such peace? It is in these lines, informed by life's many disappointments, that the poet formulates his uncertain answer. We perceive his apprehension, his desire to abandon 'craving the world' (line five) and to finally leave behind life's concerns. The real concerns, at the twilight of this medieval man's life, are different: the imminent judgement (line eight), repenting his many sins (line nine), and a very tangible threat: scorching hellfire (line ten). The poem builds up tension up to this cathartic point, in a journey from the materiality and contingency of existence to the eternal destination of the soul. The tension resolves in the poem's closure: an invocation to Allah for salvation. Here, the old poet surrenders and withdraws: no more pleading before kings and princes, fickle rewards, false hopes; as the twilight approaches, a new dawn is promised solely to the one who surrenders.

IV. Abū Isḥāq's zuhd and Ibn Ḥamdīs's zuhd

The ascetic poems of Ibn Ḥamdīs and Abū Isḥāq share two fundamental characteristics. On the one hand, they address the loss of youth and of physical strength with longing and dismay, on the other, they return obsessively to the question of man's heedlessness to the warning of old age, and his incapacity to withdraw from the material world, its allurements and its challenges. It is remarkable that this obsessive insistence on the motif of heedlessness problematizes the nature of the *zuhdiyya* as simply ascetic. I should like to address once again Gabrieli's argument about the late production of Ibn Ḥamdīs, a production that, through a comparison with Abū Isḥāq, emerges as more nuanced and complex. Francesco Gabrieli, in his monograph on Ibn Ḥamdīs, briefly addressed the Sicilian's late production as being informed by a warrior-like nationalism, and by a sort of moralizing zeal. This reading, although not wrong in principle, fails, in my opinion, to capture the complexity that lay at the heart of Ibn Ḥamdīs's (and, in an analogous way, Abū Isḥāq's) later verses. The two poets' grappling with their physical decline, and by extension their own mortality, along with the loss of loved ones, friends, and of their own homelands — the city of Elvira for Abū Isḥāq, Sicily for Ibn Ḥamdīs, prompted them to tap into a variety of religious discourses that ranged from a physical *jihād* on the one hand to the traditional Islamic *zuhdiyya* on the other. If we read *zuhd* poetry as a form of religious zealotry, we overlook the most compelling aspect of the *zuhdiyyāt* in both Ibn Ḥamdīs and Abū Isḥāq, that is, their concern with the immediate time and place which they occupied. In particular, the two poets' obsessive concern with their physical demise and the loss of their youth make their *zuhdiyyāt* particularly compelling for a reading of a poetics of ageing. The uses of asceticism for Abū Isḥāq and Ibn Ḥamdīs emanate from the fatigue of old age, the sorrow over the loss of one's loved ones and homeland, and the demise of the political world around them. These three factors cohere in the late verses of these two men in various ways: through the re-working of the traditional themes of the appearance of white hair, the passing of the poets' youth (and, by extension, the nostalgia for the past), the phantom of the beloved, the crossing of endless deserts, and other conventional poetic tropes.

The ascetic poems written by Abū Isḥāq and Ibn Ḥamdīs also share an almost obsessive concern with the discrepancy between appeals to withdrawal to religion and a lack in spiritual contentment. While this discrepancy is in fact one of the main theme of the *zuhdiyya*, in the ascetic poems penned by Abū Isḥāq (underscored by Scheindlin)[20] and Ibn Ḥamdīs this discrepancy is a salient feature. The ascetic poems, both in Abū Isḥāq and Ibn Ḥamdīs, sketch two poetic personae of old men who are not at ease with renouncing the world, and who have by no means withdrawn from it. Instead, these ascetic poems are filled with a sense of nostalgia over the loss of a material world — not the renunciation of it per se — a world that the two poets recall, recreate, regret. We can sense this attitude in many of Abū Isḥāq's *zuhdiyyāt*, some of which have been quoted above, in which he expresses preoccupation over his own incapacity to abandon the pursuit of pleasure even in his old age. His proclaimed withdrawal from the world, even when it happens, find its deeper motivation in the unattainable character of human desires rather than in a form of religious zeal. This concept is also found in the verses of Ibn Ḥamdīs. As a final example of the poetics of ageing, the following poem encapsulates his thoughts as an old man. Firstly looking back at his life and conflating the vanishing world of his youth and recounting his many sins, and finally looking forward at the void of death and the afterlife. The poem is a short piece of five lines:

Ibn Ḥamdīs, no. 149[21]

١. خلتْ منك أيّام الشبيبة فاعمرها   وماتت لياليها من العُمرِ فانشُرها
٢. وهذا لعمري كلّهُ غيرُ كائِنٍ   فأخْراكَ واصلْها ودنياكَ فاجرها
٣. أرى لك نفساً في هواكَ مُقيمةً   وقد طال ذا منها لك الويلُ فاقصرها
٤. وكَمْ سيّئاتٍ أُحصِيَتْ فَنَسيتَها   وأنتَ مَتى تُقْرأ كِتابُكَ تذكورْها
٥. فَيا رَبِّ إني في الخضوعِ لَقائلٌ   ذنوبي عيوبي يومَ ألقاكَ فاخستُرْها

1. The days of your youth have become empty, now repopulate them;
   its nights died away with the passing of life, now resuscitate them

[20] Scheindlin, 'Old Age in Hebrew and Arabic "Zuhd" Poetry'.

[21] Ibn Ḥamdīs, *Dīwān*, ed. by Iḥsān ʿAbbās, p. 265.

2. By my life! Nothing of this exists anymore, so strive towards your afterlife and leave your material world.
3. I see your soul plunged in vain passion, this calamity has dragged on too long! Cut it short!
4. How many a sin have been counted, which you have forgotten, and you, when your book will be read, will remember them!
5. Oh Lord, prostrated before you I will say: my sins are my shame, please draw a veil upon them.

This chapter focussed on the ascetic poems of Abū Isḥāq and Ibn Ḥamdīs, in an attempt to show the many similarities between the poetics of these two men who lived in different times and places but whose life experiences ran along parallel lines. Both men lived at the western edges of the Islamic empire in a time and place in which Christian offensives and Muslim disunity were chipping away at the worlds they had once known. Among the similarities shared by these two poets were a longing for the past, deep frustration over political and professional setbacks, the loss of loved ones who preceded them in death, and their own physical decline.

What distinguishes the verses of these two poets, particularly in their writing of *zuhdiyyāt,* is that, will voicing appeals for a withdrawal from worldly pursuits, neither one ever totally withdrew from the world around them: their writing of *zuhd* verse was predicated on literary and aesthetic choices as much as on religious sentiments, and it was informed by the many setbacks and losses, both personal and collective that the two poets experienced during their lifetimes. It is true that they looked back at their lives and reflected on their own mistakes and sin, and it is true that they sought forgiveness from God with their supplications; however, their consciousness of the political world around them, i.e. their allusions to political and military events in their public poems, and their admonitions to co-religionists to refrain from disunity reinforce the idea that these poems were not written by men who had withdrawn from their societies, and even their poetic personae of a 'frustrated *zāhid*' attest to this. The ascetic poems of Abū Isḥāq and Ibn Ḥamdīs did not emanate solely from a late-life turn towards religion. Rather, these two poets appropriated the *zuhdiyya* to express at once the loss of Islam's political sovereignty in al-Andalus and Sicily, their own personal losses, and their fear in the face of mortality.

Conclusion

There is something deeply personal and at the same time shared and universal in the 'poetics of ageing' of the Andalusian Abū Isḥāq al-Ilbīrī and of the Sicilian ʿAbd al-Jabbār Ibn Ḥamdīs. On the personal side, the historical circumstances and the places in which they lived deeply influenced their poems of old age. On the shared, universal side, these poems are animated by the contrast between the *amālī*, the most intimate hopes of an individual, on the one hand, and, on the others, the treason of Time — *al-dahr* — the blows and reversals that life forces us to bear: the loss of loved ones and of our own health and agency, as well as political, social, and professional setbacks. In this book, I selected verses spanning a variety of poetic thoughts arguing that they all concurred in informing a personal 'poetics of ageing' for these two poets. I have argued that their 'poetics of ageing' was informed by multiple factors, as follows:

1. An active engagement with Maghribī politics in their late life, which led both poets to quixotic quests for reviving, in their verses, a world order which was rapidly fading around them. Such an engagement is attested by their use of the panegyric (*madīḥ*), the public exhortation (*taḥrīḍ*), the elegy to a fallen homeland (*rithāʾ al-mudun*), the invective (*hijāʾ*).

2. An inventive, personal redeployment of the motif of *al-shayb wa-l-shabāb*. Abū Isḥāq reworked the motif to the shape a prominent, unique poetic voice in the *zuhdiyya*, his poetic forte. Ibn Ḥamdīs, on the other hand, deployed the motif in close contact, and contrast, with the many poetic thoughts of the *qaṣīda* which, as a professional poet, he mastered. Through relations of contiguity among contrasting imagery, themes, and poetic thoughts, Ibn Ḥamdīs obtained a much-sought-after effect which I have called 'thematic displacement'.

3. The rise of the two poets' autobiographical voice in their elegies for family members (as in the case of Abū Isḥāq's wife), friends, colleagues and beloved ones. I have argued, in particular, that these poems compound, on the personal level, the many collective losses — political defeat, social

dismemberment — that the poets witnessed as they grew old. In this sense, the private elegies were a concurrent factor in shaping their 'poetics of ageing': through this medium, the poets voiced their angst at contemplating the demise of their personal world, and the decline of their immediate social entourage.

4. An unresolved contrast between late life appeals to withdrawal from the public arena, and an urge to cling to the material world, especially the worlds of their youth. This aspect of Abū Isḥāq's and Ibn Ḥamdīs's own 'poetics of ageing' is encapsulated in their ascetic poems (*zuhdiyyāt*), which I explored in the fourth and final chapter of this book.

I have argued that understanding a 'poetics of ageing' as informed by these many factors and poetic themes, helps us understand the intersections between culture and politics as they played out in the history of al-Andalus and Muslim Sicily at the time of their decline. In their political twilight, a long one for al-Andalus, a quicker and more abrupt one for Sicily, both al-Andalus and Muslim Sicily fell victim to civil and confessional strife. The political decline in al-Andalus is best represented by the fall of the Caliphate in Córdoba at the end of the tenth century, and the subsequent partition of the country into petty fiefdoms which were most often at war with each other. These partitions were to facilitate the interference of foreign powers in local Andalusian politics, and ultimately condemned al-Andalus to be repeatedly invaded and colonized by rival forces, whether Muslim or Christian. The decline in Muslim Sicily is best represented by the fall of the Kalbid dynasty in the early decades of the eleventh century. This decline originated from a similar process of disintegration, which eventually made way for the conquest of the island by the Normans. Many of these events are articulated, explicitly or implicitly, throughout the many verses of both Abū Isḥāq and Ibn Ḥamdīs which have been the subject of this book. The first chapter of this book mapped out the interplay between these traumatic political events and the lives and oeuvres of Abū Isḥāq and Ibn Ḥamdīs. I have focused on the two poets' political verses (panegyrics and invectives), as sources for reconstructing their biographies, alongside with the many setbacks that Islam suffered in the tenth, eleventh, and twelfth centuries in both al-Andalus and Sicily. As the two poets aged, political conditions deteriorated rapidly in their homelands. Their verses provide insights into political decline and the unpredictability of Abū Isḥāq's and Ibn Ḥamdīs lives in al-Andalus, North Africa, and Sicily. On many an occasion, for instance, the two poets directed heartfelt poems of exhortation (*taḥrīḍ*) towards their countrymen, against the breaking of political ranks and of social cohesion: Abū Isḥāq's invective against the Jews of Granada and Ibn Ḥamdīs's vituperations of the Normans are more often than not accompanied by references to Muslim divisiveness, weakness, and greed.

Chapter Two focused on the trope '*al-shayb wa-l-shabāb*'. I surveyed selected critical sources towards a definition of the motif within Arabic poetics, using as my sources selected medieval works of poetic criticism, with a special focus on two Maghribī authors. The chapter also examined how Abū Isḥāq and Ibn Ḥamdīs appropriated the motif of old age within their own poems. While the two poets fought quixotic battles against the many life challenges they faced, they also felt the fatigue of their own ageing, which they voiced in many a poem, elaborating on the motif of white hair and the loss of youth. Both poets not only adopted traditional, codified tropes and images, but they also infused the motif with personal, autobiographical insights that are intertwined with the precariousness and uncertainty — political, social, and existential — in which they both grew old.

Chapter Three focused more closely on the autobiographical voice of the two poets, showing, by examining elegies to friends and family members, how they elaborated the trauma of personal loss. The chapter attempted to contextualize these losses and their significance in the overall poetics of Abū Isḥāq and Ibn Ḥamdīs, and to examine the interplay between their desire to celebrate the deceased and to reflect upon and commemorate, at once, the demise of the world of their youth and maturity. With their late verse, the two poets were capable of drawing a richly layered picture of these worlds: physical places, people (patrons, friends, family members, rivals), as well as a spiritual relationship to places explored through the gaze of youth vs. the gaze of old age.

Chapter Four focused on Ibn Ḥamdīs's and Abū Isḥāq's ascetic poems, questioning their meaning against the wider scope of their poetic production, and the significance of their advocated withdrawal from the material world in their old age. Their choice of ascetic motifs and images, I have argued, allowed them to convey a wide range of sentiments, including the examination of their consciences, their regret over their own human faults, and their supplication to God as they faced their own mortality. It also allowed them to mourn, in a more intimate way, the loss of an idealized social and political arrangement that they felt was waning along with their own lifeblood.

Throughout their careers as public poets, both Abū Isḥāq and Ibn Ḥamdīs addressed the political events of their lives as they mourned their homelands, while calling for a resurgence of Maghribī Islam. Rather than joining in and profiting from the newly shaping cultural milieu as was the case with later poets and scholars — exemplary cases are, for instance the Andalusian poet of revelry Ibn Quzmān (died 1060?) and the Sicilian Muslim geographer al-Idrīsī (d. 1165) — Ibn Ḥamdīs and Abū Isḥāq chose to adhere to a traditional poetics, and a traditional world-view — to lament the loss of their homelands, their beloved ones, and their own agency. Precisely due to their liminality as individuals, which was historical and geographical but not cultural, they felt uncomfortable with the new status quo of *Taifa* al-Andalus and of Norman Sicily. The two poets never admitted to the marginality of al-Andalus and Sicily within the Muslim *umma*, instead, they purported to be heirs and defenders of a Maghribī Islam, which they felt was being threatened by the sudden social and political changes around them. Abū Isḥāq did this brandishing religious rhetoric in his ascetic poems, in his panegyrics and in his famous invective against the Jews of Granada. Ibn Ḥamdīs did this through his revival of the classical Arabic ode, in the whole array — exception made for the invective — of poetic thoughts and meaning that this medium provided him with. With their verses, both poets strove to bring the literary and cultural faces of al-Andalus and Sicily into the quasi-sacred code of the *qaṣīda*.

As they faced the decline in their countries and the decline in their bodies, both poets resorted to religion and piety in an effort to seek refuge and consolation from the chaos and constant strife around them. In an age of political instability, relentless violence, invasions and, to be sure, poverty and uncertainty, these individuals sought in religion a safe pillar to cling to. Iḥsān ʿAbbās notes in his *Tārīkh al-Adab al-Andalusī*:

> عرف الأندلسي الاتجاه الزهدي في العصر السابق على يد ابن أبي زمنين، وكان حينئذ يلتبس كثيرا بالشعر التعليمي أو يصدر عن دواعي الشيخوخة وما تحدثه من خوف الموت وما بعده. أما في هذا العصر فكانت بواعثه مختلفة بعض الاختلاف، فقد شحذته فوضى الحياة السياسية، وزادت في حب الخلاص لدى الفرد من غوائل الحياة، وشجعته على طلب النجاة لنفسه حين كان يرى الاوضاع الاجتماعية تزداد سوءاً، وأصبح الزهد لدى بعض أصحابه مذهباً أدبياً أخلاقياً معاً[1]

Andalusians became acquainted with the ascetic mood during the previous age at the hand of Ibn Abī Zamanīn; it was therefore mixed up with edifying poetry or emanated from the vicissitudes of old age, fear of death, and so on. As for this age (the Taifa period), its motives were entirely different, for it was fuelled by the political chaos, which increased the propensity of the individual towards religion as a way out of the hor-

[1] ʿAbbās, *Tārīkh*, p. 13.

> rors of daily life and pushed them to seek their own salvation when faced with increasingly dire social circumstances. Asceticism thus became for some of its practitioners both a literary and a moral discipline.

Abū Isḥāq and Ibn Ḥamdīs, as they looked back at their youth, were both conscious that the political, cultural, and social apogee of Maghribī Islam had passed, and that the cause of reviving political Islam in Iberia and Sicily — the cause that they brandished as a political weapon in their public poems — was in fact a lost one. Both poets were painfully aware that Islam's political and cultural hegemony in the Maghrib was declining. We as modern readers can read their 'poetics of ageing' beyond the mere conventions of the poetic motif of *al-shayb wa-l-shabāb,* as the testament of a personal and collective twilight. The 'poetics of ageing' articulates the anxiety of two poets in contemplating the demise of their own civilizational glory through metaphorical use of tropes of bodily decay. The two poets' use of language and their appropriation of the *qaṣīda*'s many registers create a poetics that finesses the tension between accepting or surrendering to loss on the one hand, and on the other, struggling to keep alive affects, ideals, persons, and societies. For these two poets, the standardized tropes of the Arabic poetry of old age, such as the image of the ageing man incapable of accepting his own decline, are in fact preferential modes of writing a precise historical phase: the dissolution of Islam's political sovereignty in the West in the eleventh and twelfth centuries.

Bibliography

ʿAbbās, Iḥsān, *Al-ʿArab fī Ṣiqillīya: Dirasāt fī al-Tāʾrīkh wa al-Adab* (Cairo: Dār al-Maʿārif, 1959)

——, *Muʿjam al-ʿulamāʾ wa al-shuʿarāʾ al-ṣiqillīyīn* (Beirut: Dār al-Gharb al-Islāmī, 1994)

——, *Tārikh al-Adab al-Andalusī* (Beirut: Dār al-Thaqāfa, 1964)

Abū al-Fidāʾ, *Al-Mukhtaṣar fī Akhbār al-Bashar* ed. by Maḥmūd Dayyūb (Beirut: Dār al-kutub al-ʿilmīyah, 1997)

Abū Isḥāq al-Ilbīrī, *Dīwān*, ed. by Muḥammad Riḍwān al-Dāya (Beirut: Dār al-Fikr, 1991)

Abulafia, David, 'The End of Muslim Sicily', in *Muslims under Latin Rule 1100–1300*, ed. by James M. Powell (Princeton: Princeton University Press, 1990), pp. 103–33

——, 'The Norman Kingdom of Africa and the Norman Expedition to Majorca and the Muslim Mediterranean', *Anglo-Norman Studies* VII/7 (1986), 26–49

——, *Italy, Sicily and the Mediterranean 1100–1400* (London: Variorum Reprints, 1987)

Abū Tammām, Ḥabīb b. Aws al-Ṭāʾī, *Dīwān*, ed. by Muḥyī al-Dīn Khayyāṭ (Cairo: Muḥammad Jamāl, 1875)

Adīwān, Muḥammad, *al-Ṣawt bayna al-naẓarayn al-falsafī wa-al-lisānī ʿinda Ikhwān al-Ṣafāʾ* (Rabat: Dār al-Amān lil-Ṭibāʿah wa-al-Nashr wa-al-Tawzīʿ, 2006)

Akasoy, Anna A., 'Al-Andalus in Exile: Identity and Diversity in Islamic Intellectual History', in *Christlicher Norden-Muslimischer Süden. Ansprüche und Wirklichkeiten von Christen, Juden und Muslimen auf der iberischen Halbinsel im Hoch- und Spätmittelalter*, ed. by Matthias M. Tischler and Alexander Fidora (Münster: Aschendorff, 2001), pp. 329–43

Al-Idrīsī, *L'Italia descritta nel Libro del Re Ruggero,* trans. by Michele Amari and Celestino Schiaparelli (Rome: Salviucci, 1883)

Al-Jāḥiz, *Salwa al-Kharīf in al-Sharīf al-Murtaḍā al-Shihāb fī al-shayb wa-al-shabāb* (Constantine: Maṭbaʿat al-Jawāʾib, 1884)

Al-Maqqarī, Aḥmad ibn Muḥammad, *Nafḥ al-ṭīb min ghuṣn al-Andālus al-raṭīb wa-dhikr wazīrihā Lisān al-Dīn ibn al-Khaṭīb* (Beirut: Dār Ṣādir, 1968)

Al-Nuwayrī, *Nihāyat al-arab fī funūn al-adab* (Tehran: Amīr Kabīr, 1985)

Al-Qarṭājannī, Ibn Ḥāzim, *Minhāj al-Bulaghāʾ wa-Sirāj al-Udabāʾ* (Tunis: Dār al-Kutub al-Sharqīyah, 1966)

Al-Saraqusṭī Ibn al-Ashtarkūnī, Muḥammad ibn Yūsuf, *Al-Maqāmāt al-Luzūmīyah*, trans. James Monroe (Leiden: Brill, 2002)

Al-Sharīf al-Murtaḍā, ʿAlam al-Hudá ʿAlī ibn al-Ḥusayn, *Al-Shihāb fī al-shayb wa-al-shabāb* (Constantine: Maṭbaʿat al-Jawāʾib, 1884)

Al-Zbūn, Raghda, 'al-Shabāb wa-l-Shayb fī al-Shiʿr al-Andalusī, Dirāsa Mawḍūʿiyya Nafsiyya', *Dirāsāt al-ʿUlūm al-Insāniyya wa-l-Ijtimāʿiyya*, 42.1 (2015), 211–32

Amari, Michele, *Biblioteca Arabo-Sicula* (Turin: Ermanno Loescher, 1880–1881)

——, *Le epigrafi arabiche di Sicilia,* ed. Francesco Gabrieli (Palermo: Flaccovio, 1971)

——, *Storia dei Musulmani in Sicilia* (Catania: Prampolini 1933)

Arazi, Albert, 'al-Shayb wa-l-Shabāb', *Encyclopaedia of Islam*, 2nd edn (Leiden: Brill, 1954–2005)

Arcifa, Lucia, Nef, Annliese, and Prigent, Vivien, 'Sicily in a Mediterranean Context: Imperiality, Mediterranean Polycentrism and Internal Diversity (6th–10th century)', in *Mélanges de l'Ecole Française de Rome. Moyen âge* 133.2 (Rome: École française de Rome, 2021), 339–74

Arnesano, Daniele and others, *Multilingual and Multigraphic Documents and Manuscripts of East and West*, ed. by Giuseppe Mandalà, and Inmaculada Pèrez Martin (Piscataway: Gorgias Press, 2018)

Baffioni, Carmela, 'Ikhwān al-Ṣafā'', *Encyclopedia of Medieval Philosophy* (Berlin: Springer Dordrecht, 2011)

Benaboud, Mohamed, 'El papel político y social de los 'ulama en al-Andalus durante el período de los taifas', *Cuadernos de Historia del Islam*, 11 (1984), 7–32

Borruso, Antonino, 'Poésie arabe en sicile', *Al-Masaq*, 4.1 (1991), 17–34

——, 'Una poesia di Ibn Ḥamdīs ad al-Muʿtamid', *Quaderni di studi arabi*, 9 (1991), 177–82

Callataÿ, Godefroid De, *Ikhwan al-Safa': A Brotherhood of Idealists on the Fringe of Orthodox Islam* (New York: Simon and Schuster, 2012)

Callataÿ, Godefroid De, and Moureau, Sébastien, 'De nuevo sobre Maslama Ibn Qāsim al-Qurṭubī, los Ijwān al-Ṣafā' e Ibn Jaldūn: Nuevos datos de dos manuscritos de la Rutbat al-ḥakīm', *Al-Qantara*, 37.2 (2017), 329–72

Carpentieri, Nicola, 'Abū Isḥāq al-Ilbīrī: a Literary Revisitation', *Medievalia*, 19.1 (2016), 67–95

——, 'Adab as Social Currency: The Survival of the Qaṣīda in Medieval Sicily', *Mediterranea, International Journal on the Transfer of Knowledge*, 3 (2018), 1–18

——, 'At War with the Age: Ring Composition in Ibn Ḥamdīs no. 27', *Quaderni di Studi Arabi, Nuova Serie*, 10 (2015), 39–55

——, 'Towards a Poetics of Ageing. Private and Collective Loss in Ibn Ḥamdīs' Late Verse', *Journal of Transcultural Medieval Studies*, 3, 1–2 (2016), 119–43

Carpentieri, Nicola, and Symes, Carol, *Medieval Sicily, al-Andalus and the Maghrib: Writing in Times of Turmoil* (Amsterdam: Amsterdam University Press, 2020)

Carrillo, Alicia, 'Architectural Exchanges between North Africa and the Iberian Peninsula: Muqarnas in al-Andalus', *The Journal of North African Studies*, 19.1 (2014), 68–82

Chiarelli, Leonard, *A History of Muslim Sicily*, (Malta: Midsea Books, 2011)

Constable, Olivia, 'Cross-cultural Contacts: Sales of Land between Christians and Muslims in 12th-Century Palermo', *Studia Islamica*, 85 (1997), 67–84

——, *Housing the Stranger in the Mediterranean World*, (Cambridge: Cambridge University Press, 2003)

Cordonnier, Rémy, 'Influences directes et indirectes de l'encyclopédie des Ikhwân al-Safâ' dans l'Occident chrétien', *Le Muséon* (2012)

Corfis, Ivy, *Al-Andalus, Sepharad and Medieval Iberia:Cultural Contact and Diffusion* (Leiden: Brill, 2009)

Corrao, Francesca Maria, *Poeti arabi di Sicilia: nella versione di poeti italiani contemporanei*, 1st edn (Milano: Mondadori, 1987)

Denaro, Roberta, 'And God Dispersed their Unity: Historiographical Patterns in Recounting the End of Muslim Rule in Sicily and al-Andalus', in *Medieval Sicily, al-Andalus and the Maghrib: Writing in Times of Turmoil*, ed. by Nicola Carpentieri and Carol Symes, (Amsterdam: Amsterdam University Press, 2020), pp. 105–26

De Simone, Adalgisa, 'Palermo nei Geografi e Viaggiatori Arabi del Medioevo', in *Studi Maghrebini* 2, (1968), 89–129

De Simone, Adalgisa, and Mandalà, Giuseppe, *L'immagine araba di Roma: i geografi del Medioevo (secoli IX–XV)*, 1st edn (Bologna: Pàtron, 2002)

——, *Nella Sicilia Araba tra storia e filologia*, (Palermo: Luxograph, 1999)

De Stefano, Antonino, *La Cultura in Sicilia nel Periodo Normanno* (Bologna: Zanichelli 1954)

Dokmak, Ahmed, 'The Use of Groin Vault Sections in Islamic and Mudejar Architecture of Al-Andalus, North Africa and Sicily', *Anales de Historia Del Arte*, 19 (2010), 7–42

D'Ottone Rambach, Arianna, 'al-Ṣiqillī or al-Ṣaqalī / Sicily or Tunisia?', *Journal of Islamic Manuscripts*, 10.2 (2019), 171–89

Dozy, Reinhart, *Histoire des Musulmans d'Espagne* (Leiden: Brill, 1932)

——, *Recherches sur l'histoire et la littérature de l'Espagne pendant le moyen âge* (Leiden: Brill, 1881)

Ebstein, Michael, *Mysticism and Philosophy in al-Andalus: Ibn Masarra, Ibn al-ʾArabi and the Ismaʿili Tradition* (Leiden: Brill, 2014)

Elinson, Alexander, 'Loss Written in Stone: Ibn Shuhayd's Rithā' for Cordoba and its Place in the Arabic Elegiac Tradition', in *Transforming Loss into Beauty, Essays on Arabic Literature and Culture in Honor of Magda al-Nowaihi*, ed. by Marlé Hammond and Dana Sajdi (Cairo: American University in Cairo Press, 2008), pp. 79–114

Ferrando Fruyos, Ignacio, 'La Maqama Barbariyya', *Anaquel de Estudios Árabes*, 2 (1991), 119–29

Fierro, Maribel, 'Ulemas en las ciudades andalusíes: religión, política y prácticas sociales', *Congreso Internacional Escenarios Urbanos de al-Andalus y el Occidente musulmán*, 1 (2011), 137–67

Fletcher, Richard, *Moorish Spain* (Los Angeles: University of California Press, 1992)

Foulon, Brigitte and Tixier du Mesnil, Emmanuelle, 'Famille princière et poésie: le cas d'al-Muʿtamid Ibn ʿAbbād (1040–1095)', *Annales Islamologiques*, 47 (2014), 309–26

Frolov, Dimitri, *Classical Arabic Verse: History and Theory of ʿArūḍ* (Leiden: Brill, 2000)

Gabrieli, Francesco, 'Arabi di Sicilia e Arabi di Spagna' in *Dal mondo dell'Islàm: nuovi saggi di storia e civiltá musulmana* (Naples: Ricciardi, 1954), pp. 88–108

——, *Ibn Hamdis* (Mazara: SEI, 1948)

——, 'Sicilia e Spagna nella vita e nella poesia di Ibn Hamdis' in *Dal mondo dell'Islàm: nuovi saggi di storia e civiltá musulmana* (Naples: Ricciardi, 1954), pp. 109–26

García Gómez, Emilio, *Un alfaquí español, Abū Ishāq de Elvira. Texto árabe de su Dīwān, según el ms. Escur. 404, publicado por primera vez, con introducción, análisis, notas e indices* (Madrid: CSIC, 1944)

García Sanjuán, Alejandro, 'Violencia contra los Judíos: el pogromo de Granada del año 459H/1066', in *Estudios onomástico-biográficos de al-Andalus (EOBA)* XIV, ed. by Maribel Fierro (Madrid: CSIC, 2004), pp. 167–206

Garulo, Teresa, *La literatura Árabe de al-Andalus* (Madrid: Hiperión, 1998)

Gaudefroy-Demombynes, Maurice, *Ibn Qutaiba. Introduction au Livre de la poesie et des poetes* (Paris: Les Belles Lettres, 1947)

Gay, Jules, *L'Italie Meridionale et l'Empire Byzantin depuis l'avenement de Basile I jusqu'a la prise de Bari par les Normands 867–1071* (Paris: Fontemoing, 1904)

Gil, Moshe, *Jews in Islamic Countries in the Middle Ages* (Leiden: Brill, 2004)

Giuffrida, Romualdo, *Fonti per l'espulsione degli Ebrei di Sicilia* (Palermo: Accademia Nazionale di Scienze, Lettere e Arti, 1995)

Gobillot, Genevieve, 'Zuhd', *Encyclopaedia of Islam*, 2nd edn (Leiden: Brill, 1954–2005)

Goitein, Shlomo Dov, *Letters of Medieval Jewish Traders* (Princeton: Princeton University Press 1974)

Granara, William, 'The Battle of Zallaqa Between Mythos to Logos' in *Convivencia and Medieval Spain* ed. by Mark T. Abate (Cham: Palgrave McMillan, 2019), pp. 253–75

——, 'Ibn Ḥamdīs's al-Dīmās Qaṣida: Memorial to a Fallen Homeland' in *Poetry and History, the Value of Poetry in Reconstructing Arab History,* ed. by Balbaki, Ramzi Balbaki, and others (Beirut: American University of Beirut, 2011), pp. 248–62

——, *Ibn Hamdis the Sicilian: Eulogist for a Falling Homeland* (New York: Oneworld Publications, 2021)

——, 'Islamic Education and the Transmission of Knowledge in Medieval Sicily', in *Law and Education in Medieval Islam: Studies in Honor of George Makdisi*, ed. by Devin J. Stewart, Joseph Lowry, and Shawkat M. Toorawa (Cambridge, MA: E. J. W. Gibb Memorial Trust, 2004), pp. 150–73

——, *Narrating Muslim Sicily: War and Peace in the Medieval Mediterranean World* (London: I. B. Tauris, 2019)

——, 'Remaking Muslim Sicily: Ibn Ḥamdīs and the Poetics of Exile', *Edebiyat*, 9.2 (1998), 167–98

——, 'Rethinking Muslim Sicily's Golden Age: Poetry and Patronage at the Fatimid Kalbid Court of Palermo', *Alifba*, XXII/22 (2008), 95–108

——, 'Sicilian Poets in Seville: Literary Affinities across Political Boundaries' in *A Sea of Languages: Rethinking the Arabic Role in Medieval Literary History* ed. by Suzanne Akbari and Karla Mallette (Toronto: University of Toronto Press, 2013), pp. 199–216

Gruendler, Beatrice, *Medieval Arabic Praise Poetry, Ibn al-Rūmī and the Patron's Redemption* (London: Routledge, 2003)

Hamori, Andras, 'Ascetic poetry (Zuhdiyyāt)', in *The Cambridge History of Arabic Literature. ʿAbbasid Belles Lettres*, ed. by Julia Ashtiany and others (Cambridge: Cambridge University Press, 1990), pp. 265–74

——, 'Love Poetry (Ghazal)', in *The Cambridge History of Arabic Literature. ʿAbbasid Belles Lettres*, ed. by Julia Ashtiany and others (Cambridge: Cambridge University Press, 1990), pp. 202–18

Handler, Andrew, *The Zirids of Granada* (Miami: Miami University Press, 1974)

Haybah, 'Abd al-Raḥmān Muḥammad, *Shabāb wa-al-shayb fī al-shiʿr al-ʿArabī ḥattá nihāyat al-ʿaṣr al-ʿAbbāsī* (Alexandria: al-Hayʾah al-Miṣrīyah al-'Āmmah lil-Kitāb, Far' al-Iskandarīyah, 1981)

Heinrichs, Wolfhart, *The Hand of the Northwind: Opinions on Metaphor and the Early Meaning of Istiʿāra in Arabic poetics* (Wiesbaden: Steiner, 1977)

——, 'On the Genesis of the ḥaqîqa-majâz', *Studia Islamica*, 59 (1984), 111–40

——, 'Paired Metaphors in Muhdath Poetry', *Occasional Papers of the School of ʿAbbasid Studies at the University of St Andrews*, 1 (1986), 1–22

——, 'Ṭibāḳ', *Encyclopaedia of Islam*, 2nd edn (Leiden: Brill, 1954–2005)

Hodgson, Marshall G. S., *The Venture of Islam: Conscience and History in a World Civilization*, vol. 2 (Chicago, The University of Chicago Press, 1974)

The Holy Qur'an, trans. by Abdullah Yusuf Ali <https://quranyusufali.com/> [accessed 8 September 2022]

Ibn al-Athīr, *Al-Kāmil fī al-Tārīkh* in *Biblioteca Arabo-Sicula*, ed. by Michele Amari (Turin: Loescher, 1857), pp. 353–522

Ibn Bulukkīn, ʿAbd ʿAllah, *Kitāb al-Tibyān ʿan al-Ḥādithah al-Kāʾinah bi-Dawlat Banī Zīrī fī Gharnāṭa*, ed. by ʿAli ʿUmar (Cairo: Maktabat al-Thaqāfah al-Dīnīyah, 2006)

Ibn Ḥamdīs, 'Abd al-Jabbār, *Dīwān*, ed. by Iḥsān ʿAbbās (Beirut: Dār Ṣādir, 1960)

Ibn Jubayr, Muḥammad ibn Aḥmad, *Riḥla* (Beirut: Dār Ṣādir, 1964)

——, *The Travels of Ibn Jubayr*, trans. by Ronald J. C. Broadhurst (London: Jonathan Cape, 1952)

——, *Viaggio in Sicilia*, trans. G. Calasso (Rome: Adelphi, 2022)

Ibn Khāqān, al-Fatḥ ibn Muḥammad, *Maṭmaḥ al-anfus wa-masraḥ al-taʾannus fī mulaḥ ahl al-Andalus* (Cairo: IDEO, 2001)

Ibn Khaldūn, *Kitāb al-ʿIbar, wa-Dīwān al-Mubtadaʾ wa-l-Khabar, fī Taʾrīkh al-ʿArab wa-l-Barbar, wa-Man ʿĀṣarahum min Dhawī ash-Shaʾn al-Akbār*, ed. by Khalīl Shaḥāda, (Beirut: Dār al-Kutub al-'Ilmīyah, 2016)

Ibn al-Makkī, ʿUmar ibn Khalaf, *Tathqīf al-Lisān wa talqīḥ al-Jinān* (Cairo: Jumhūrīyah al-'Arabīyah al-Muttaḥidah. al-Majlis al-'Alá lil-Shuʾūn al-Islāmīyah. Lajnat Iḥyāʾ al-Turāth al-Islāmī, 1996)

Ibn al-Qaṭṭāʿ al-Ṣiqillī, *Al-Durra al-Khaṭīra fī shuʿarāʾ al-Jazīra*, ed. by Bashir Bakkush (Beirut: Dār al-Gharb al-Islāmī, 2005)

Ibn al-Qifṭī, *Inbah al-Ruwāt ʿalā Anbāh al-Nuḥāt* ed. by Muḥammad Ibrāhīm (Cairo: Dār al-Kutub al-Miṣrīyah, al-Qism al-Adabī 1950–1973)

Ibn Rashīq al-Qayrawānī, *al-ʿUmda fī Maḥāsin al-Shiʿr wa-naqdi-hi*, ed. by 'Aṭā, Muḥammad 'Abd al-Qādir al-Ḥasan (Beirut: Dār al-Kutub al-'Ilmīyah, 2001)

Idris, Hady Roger, *La Berbérie orientale sous les Zīrīdes, Xe-XIIe siècles* (Paris: Librairie d'Amérique et d'Orient, Adrien-Maisonneuve, 1962)

ʿIyād ibn Mūsā, *Tartīb al-Madārik wa Taqrīb al-Masālik* (Beirut: Dār al-Kutub al-ʻIlmīyah, 1998)

Ibn Ẓafar, *Ṣulwān al-Muṭāʿ ossiano Conforti politici*, trans. by Michele Amari (Palermo: Flaccovio, 1973)

Jacobi, Renate, 'The Khayāl Motif in Early Arabic Poetry', *Oriens*, 32 (1992), 50–64

Johns, Jeremy, *Arabic Administration in Norman Sicily* (Cambridge: Cambridge University Press, 2002)

Kacimi, Mourad, 'La relación de Maslama al-Mayriti con las obras Rasa'il Ijwan al-Safa', Risalat al-yami'a, Rutbat al-hakim y Gayat al-hakim1/The relation of Maslama al-Mayriti with the books Rasa'il Ijwan al-Safa', Risalat al-yami'a, Rutbat al-hakim and Gayat al-hakim', *Anaquel de estudios árabes*, 25 (2014), 29–44

Kennedy, Philip, 'Zuhdiyya', *Encyclopaedia of Islam*, 2nd edn (Leiden: Brill, 1954–2005)

Khalis, Salah, *La Vie Littéraire a Séville au XI Siécle* (Algiers: NED, 1966)

Khaṭrāwī, Muḥammd al-ʿId, *Kitāb al-shayb fī al-shiʿr al-ʿArabī al-qadīm*, 1st edn (Nādī al-Qaṣīm al-Adabī, 2007)

Kinberg, Leah, 'What is Meant by Zuhd?', *Studia Islamica*, 61 (1985), 27–44

Krinis, Ehud, 'Cyclical Time in the Ismāʿīlī Circle of Ikhwān al-ṣafāʾ (Tenth Century) and in Early Jewish Kabbalists Circles (Thirteenth and Fourteenth Centuries)', *Studia Islamica*, 111.1 (2016), 20–108

Ladha, Ally, 'From Bayt to Stanza: Arabic Khayāl and the Advent of Italian Vernacular Poetry', *Exemplaria*, 32.1 (2020), 1–31

Lewis, Bernard, *Islam in History* (Princeton: Princeton University Press, 1992)

Mallette, Karla, *The Kingdom of Sicily, 1100–1250: a Literary History* (Philadelphia: University of Pennsylvania Press, 2005)

——, 'Poetries of the Norman Courts', in *The Literature of Al-Andalus*. ed. by María Rosa Menocal, Raymond P. Scheindlin, and Michael Sells (Cambridge: Cambridge University Press, 2000), pp. 377–87

——, 'Translating Sicily' in *Medieval Encounters: Jewish, Christian, and Muslim Culture in Confluence and Dialogue*, 9.1 (Leiden: Brill, 2003), pp. 140–63

Mandalà, Giuseppe, 'An Arabic Codex In Hebrew Characters From Trapani Degli Abbate (Vat. ebr. 358)', *Sefarad*, 71.1 (2011), 7–24

——, 'Figlia d'al-Andalus! Due ǧazīra a confronto, Sicilia e al-Andalus, nelle fonti arabo-Islamiche del Medioevo', *Le forme e la storia*, 2 (2012), 43–54

——, 'L'incursione pisana contro Palermo musulmana in alcuni documenti della Genizah del Cairo (1064)', *Sefer Yuhasin*, 7 (2019), 65–84

——, 'The Martyrdom of Yūḥannā, Physician of Ibn Abī'l-Ḥusayn Ruler of the Island of Sicily. Editio Princeps and Historical Commentary', *Journal of Transcultural Medieval Studies*, 3.1 (2016), 33–118

——, 'Political Martyrdom and Religious Censorship in Islamic Sicily: a Case Study During the Age of Ibrāhīm II (261–89/875–902)', *Al-Qantara* 35.1 (2014), 151–86

——, 'The Sicilian Questions', *Journal of Transcultural Medieval Studies*, 3.1 (2016), 3–31

Manzano Moreno, Eduardo, *Conquistadores, emires y califas: los Omeyas y la formación de Al-Andalus* (Barcelona: Crítica, 2006)

Martin, James, D., 'The Religious Beliefs of Abū al-ʿAtāhiya according to the Zuhdiyyāt', *Glasgow Oriental Society Transactions*, XXIII/23 (1966), 56–67

Mattila, Janne, 'The Ikhwān al-Ṣafāʾ on Religious Diversity', *Journal of Islamic Studies*, 28.2 (2017), 178–92

Meisami, Julie S., *Structure and Meaning in Medieval Arabic and Persian Poetry* (London: Taylor and Francis, 2003)

Menocal, Maria Rosa, *The Ornament of the World: How Muslim, Jews and Christians Created a Culture of Tolerance in Medieval Spain* (New York: Little Brown & Company, 2002)

Metcalfe, Alex, *Muslims and Christians in Norman Sicily: Arabic Speakers and the End of Islam* (London: Routledge Curzon, 2003)

——, *The Muslims of Medieval Italy* (Edinburgh: Edinburgh University Press, 2009)

Monès, Hussain, 'The Role of Men of Religion in the History of Muslim Spain up to the End of the Caliphate', in *The Formation of al-Andalus Part Two,* ed. by Maribel Fierro and Julio Samsó (London: Taylor and Francis, 1998), pp. 51–84

Monroe, James, *Hispano-Arabic Poetry: An Anthology* (Berkeley: University of California Press, 1974)

Nef, Annliese, 'La Fitna Sicilienne: Une Fitna Inachevée?', *Médiévales*, 60 (2011), 103–16

Nef, Annliese, and Thom, Martin, *A Companion to Medieval Palermo: The History of a Mediterranean City from 600 to 1500* (Leiden: Brill, 2013)

Nykl, Alois Richard, *Hispano-Arabic Poetry and its Relations with the old Provencal Troubadours* (Baltimore: J. H. Furst Company 1946)

Orfali, Bilal, 'A Sketch Map of Arabic Poetry Anthologies up to the Fall of Baghdad', *Journal of Arabic Literature*, 43.1 (2012), 29–59

Pappalardo, Salvatore, 'From Ibn Ḥamdīs to Giufà: Leonardo Sciascia and the Writing of a Siculo-Arab Literary History', *Italian Culture*, 36.1 (2018), 32–47

Pellitteri, Antonino, *I Fatimiti e la Sicilia* (Palermo: Centro culturale Al-Farabi 1997)

Pérès, Henri, *La poésie andalouse en arabe classique au XIe siècle; ses aspects généraux, ses principaux thèmes et sa valeur documentaire,* (Paris: Adrienne-Maisonnneuve, 1953)

Ragep, Jamil, and Mimura, Taro, *Epistles of the Brethren of Purity. On astronomia: an Arabic critical edition and English translation of Epistle 3* (Oxford: Oxford University Press, 2015)

Reinhart, Kevin, 'Taḥsīn wa taqbīḥ', *Encyclopaedia of Islam*, 2nd edn (Leiden: Brill, 1954–2005)

Rizzitano, Umberto, 'Ibn Ḥamdīs', *Encyclopaedia of Islam*, 2nd edn (Leiden: Brill, 1954–2005)

——, *Storia e Cultura nella Sicilia Saracena* (Palermo: Flaccovio, 1975)

——, *Tārīkh al-Adab al-ʿArabī fī Ṣiqillīya* (ʿAmman: University of Jordan, 1965)

Robinson, Cynthia, 'Uḥud', *Encyclopaedia of Islam*, 2nd edn (Leiden: Brill, 1954–2005)

Safran, Janina, *The Second Umayyad Caliphate* (Cambridge: Cambridge University Press, 2000)

Said, Edward, *On Late Style* (New York: Pantheon Books, 2006)
Sallām, Sāmiya, *al-Sulṭah wa-al-dawlah bayna al-Muʿtazilah wa-Ikhwān al-Ṣafāʾ*, 1st edn (Cairo: Miṣr al-ʻArabīyah lil-Nashr wa-al-Tawzīʻ, 2015)
Samer, Ali, 'Reinterpreting al-Buḥturī's Īwān Kisrā Ode: Tears of Affection for the Cycles of History', *Journal of Arabic Lierature*, 37.1 (2006), 46–67
Sanūsī, Zayn Ad-ʿAbidīn, *ʿAbd al-Jabbār Ḥamdīs: ḥayātuhu wa-adabuh* (Tunis: Al-Dār al-Tūnisīyah lil-Nashr, 1983)
——, *Al-Waṭanīya fi shʿʿiʿr Ibn Ḥamdīs* (Tunis: Dār al-Maghrib al-ʻArabī, 1971)
Sanz Salvador, Ramira, *Almería en la guerra de Granada* (Almería: Universidad de Almería, 2007)
Scheindlin, Raymond, 'Old Age in Hebrew and Arabic "Zuhd" Poetry', in *Judíos y musulmanes en al-Andalus y el Magreb*, ed. by Maribel Fierro (Madrid: Casa de Velazquez, 2002), pp. 85–104
Sells, Michael A., 'Guises of the Ghūl, Dissembling Simile and Semantic Overflow in the Classical Arabic Nasīb', in *Reorientations/Arabic and Persian poetry*, ed. by Suzanne Stetkevych, (Bloomington: Indiana University Press, 1984), pp. 130–64
Schoeler, Gregor, 'Bashshar b. Burd, Abu al-Atahiya and Abu Nuwas', in *The Cambridge History of Arabic Literature. ʿAbbasid Belles Lettres*, ed. by Julia Ashtiany and others (Cambridge: Cambridge University Press, 1990), pp. 275–99
——, 'The Genres of Classical Arabic Poetry: Classifications of Poetic Themes and Poems by Pre-Modern Critics and Redactors of Dīwāns', *Quaderni di Studi Arabi Nuova Serie*, 5/6 (2010–2011), 1–48
Shammarī, Thāʾir Samīr Ḥasan, *al-Shayb fī al-shiʿr al-ʿAbbāsī ḥattá nihāyat al-qarn al-rābiʿ al-Hijrī* (الطبعة الأولى. ed.) (Dār Ṣafāʾ lil-Nashr wa-al-Tawzi, 2018)
Simonson, Shlomo, *The Jews in Sicily* (Leiden: Brill, 1997)
Small, Helen, *The Long Life* (Oxford: Oxford University Press, 2007)
Sperl, Stefan, *Mannerism in Arabic Poetry: A Structural Analysis of Selected Texts: (3rd century* AH*/9th century* AD*-5th Century AH/11th Century* AD*)* (Cambridge: Cambridge University Press, 1989)
Stetkevych, Jaroslav, 'Toward an Arabic Elegiac Lexicon: The Seven Words of the Nasīb', in *Reorientations/Arabic and Persian poetry*, ed. by Suzanne Stetkevych (Bloomington: Indiana University Press, 1984), pp. 58–129
——, *The Zephyrs of Najd* (Chicago: Chicago University Press, 1993)
Stetkevych, Suzanne P., *The Mute Immortals Speak: Pre-Islamic Poetry and the Poetics of Ritual*, Myth and Poetics Series (Ithaca, N.Y.: Cornell University Press, 1993)
——, *The Poetics of Islamic Legitimacy: Myth, Gender, and Ceremony in the Classical Arabic Ode* (Bloomington: Indiana University Press, 2022)
Stroumsa. Sarah, *Andalus and Sefarad: On Philosophy and Its History in Islamic Spain* (Princeton: Princeton University Press, 2019)
Torre, Salvo, *Di qua dal mare delle tenebre: geografi e viaggiatori della tradizione arabo-Islamica in Sicilia* (Catania: CUECM, 2007)
Tramontana, Salvatore, *L'Isola di Allah* (Turin: Einaudi, 2014)

Treiger, Alexander, 'The Longer Theology of Aristotle in al-Andalus', *Intellectual History of the Islamicate World*, 9.3 (2020), 338–63

Vaulx d'Arcy, Guillaume De, *Les Épîtres des Frères en pureté (Rasa'il ikhwan al-Safa): mathématique et philosophie* (Paris: Les Belles Lettres, 2019)

Wright, William, *A Grammar of the Arabic Language*, 3rd edn (Cambridge: Cambridge University Press, 1896–1898)

Weil, Gustav, ''Arūḍ', *Encyclopaedia of Islam*, 2nd edn (Leiden: Brill, 1954–2005)

Indices

Index of Poems

Abū Isḥāq

Poem no.	Page
1	83
2	87
3	155
5	89
6	91
8	152
9	85
13	157
16	30
19	31, 155
19	155
20	25
21	122
24	90
25	35
29	18
31	22

Ibn Ḥamdīs

Poem no.	Page
2	114, 136
12	141
28	56
30	158
34	161
56	105
95	95
96	138
98	46, 51
101	48
110	43
131	131
142	68
149	167
153	53
228	162
229	163
245	142
270	69
297	128
300	118

General Index

Abbasid(s): 2–4, 4 n. 3, 93, 106, 147, 149
Abū al-Fidā': 61 n. 116
Abū Tammām: 3, 23 n. 48, 50, 71, 80, 104
afterlife: 2–6, 15, 70, 91, 119, 147–67, 172 n. 1
agency: 26, 81, 144, 151, 169, 172
Al-Buḥturī: 71, 80, 104
Al-Idrīsī: 172
Al-Jāhiẓ: 3
Al-Murtaḍā, al-Sharīf: 3, 5–6, 73 n. 6, 79 n. 26, 80, 110–11, 111 n. 55
Al-Muʿtamid ibn ʿAbbād: 12, 47–55, 101, 113, 128, 132, 140, 160
Al-Mutanabbī: 50, 75
Al-Nuwayrī: 60
Al-Qarṭajānnī: 6, 76–78, 78 nn. 22 and 24
Amari, Michele: 12 n. 11, 41 nn. 85–87, 54 n. 106, 60 n. 114, 67 n. 129, 100, 102 nn. 49–50

Bādīs ibn Habbūs: 5, 31–40
Berbers: 5, 10, 13–14, 21, 29, 33–34, 39–40, 51, 57–58, 101
Bijāya: 41, 66–67, 102, 142
Byzantium: 61

civil war: 13, 29, 55, 58–59, 61, 63–64
Cordoba: 10, 14, 20, 26, 29, 80, 170

dye: 3, 81, 114

exile: 12, 45, 47, 49, 54–56, 64, 70, 100, 113, 116, 126–28, 130, 137–39, 144, 146, 165
Elvira: 1, 4, 6, 11 n. 10, 12–39, 121, 134, 163, 166

fatigue: 3, 5–6, 70, 146, 151, 166, 171
Fierro, Maribel: 20, nn. 41–43, 24
fitna: 13–14, 25, 29, 32, 55–57, 62–66, 101, 141

garden(s): 104–105, 108–109, 111, 132–133
García Gómez, Emilio: 11 n. 10, 15–16 nn. 26–28, 34 n. 65
García Sanjuán, Alejandro: 13, n. 13, 34 nn. 65–66, 35 n. 73
Granara, William: 9, 11–12, 41 nn. 82–83, 42 n. 90, 48 n. 95, 50 n. 98, 51 n. 101, 67 n. 128, 68 n. 131, 94 n. 39, 100 n. 47, 113 n. 159, 114 n. 60, 116 n. 61
grief: 121, 123, 133, 139, 142–43, 145–46, 156
Gruendler, Beatrice: 49 n. 97, 87 n. 31, 93 n. 38, 154 n.10

heaven: 30, 44–45
hell: 64
hellfire: 64, 86, 147–48, 160, 165
Heinrichs, Wolfhart: 9, 93 n. 37

Ibn al-Athīr: 57 n. 109, 58, 59 nn. 110–11, 60 n. 112, 62 nn. 117–18, 63
Ibn Abī Zamanīn: 17–20, 29, 32, 172 n. 1
Ibn Jubayr: 9 n. 3, 70
Ibn Khaldūn: 60, n. 115
Ibn Rashīq: 6, 27, 74, 75 nn. 9–20, 76, 78, 103
Ibn Shuhayd: 26, 28
Ibn Tawba: 12, 20–24, 29–31, 40
impotence: 1, 86, 153
Italy: 66 n. 125, 129

Jawhara: 53, 128, 130–36
jihād: 69–70, 102, 151, 165–66

Kalbids: 58
khamriyya: 44–46, 68, 77, 98–111

Lewis, Bernard: 39 n. 80

madḥ: 49, 71–73, 103
Mahdiyya: 41, 55, 66, 94, 99, 100, 102–03, 137, 139, 142
Majorca: 41, 55, 67, 165
Mandalà, Giuseppe: 9 nn. 1 and 6
Metcalfe, Alexander: 66 n. 125
Monroe, James: 9, 34 nn. 70–71, 35 nn. 74 and 76, 37 n. 77, 38 n. 78, 105 n. 51
mourning: 11, 25–27, 50, 52, 56, 65, 119, 121, 128–30, 145–46

Naghrīla, Samuel ibn: 32
Naghrīla, Yūsuf ibn: 5, 34, 37–38
nasīb: 27, 67, 71–89, 98–134, 153–59
nostalgia: 1, 3, 11, 29, 44, 50, 70, 76, 98, 104, 113, 115, 118, 137, 151–52, 158, 162, 166–67

Orfali, Bilal: 3 n. 1

Palermo: 10, 41–42, 45, 55, 58, 61

raḥīl: 46, 68, 71–78, 99–122
rawḍiyya: 104–12
resurrection: 165
Roger II: 66, 102

Said, Edward: 98 n. 45
salvation: 89, 124, 148, 158–66, 173
Sells, Michael: 80 n. 27, 111 n. 56, 133 n. 7
Seville: 12, 41, 47–51, 53–55, 117, 128, 132, 140, 144, 164–65
sin: 11, 45, 64, 66, 84–106, 124, 150, 158–68
Sfax: 45, 47, 142
Shuraydi, Hasan: 3 n. 2, 4
Small, Helen: 119 n. 1
Spain: 1, 10–20, 52, 134
Stetkevych, Jaroslav: 106 n. 53
Stetkevych, Suzanne: 19 n. 38, 50 n. 99
Syracuse: 1, 41–42, 45, 47, 61, 68, 165

ṭayf al-khayāl: 68, 104, 123, 133
Tibyān, Kitāb al-: 13 nn. 15–17, 14 nn. 22 and 24, 15 n. 25, 21 nn. 45–46, 32 nn. 55–58, 33 nn. 59–64, 34 n. 66–68, 38, 39 n. 81, 40
Tunisia: 11

Umayyad(s): 10, 12–15, 19, 24–25, 29, 40, 121

white hair: 2–4, 43, 71–72, 77–78, 80–83, 88–91, 108, 112–13, 114, 118, 125, 143, 145, 147, 152–53, 160, 162, 166, 171
wine: 40, 44–45, 50, 71, 77, 92, 96–99, 104, 107–09, 112

Zāwī b. Zīrī: 12–14, 20–21, 24, 29, 32
Zirids: 5–6, 20, 55, 59, 66–70, 94, 101–02, 104, 138
zuhd: 4, 7, 16–17, 70–89, 147–66

TRANSCULTURAL MEDIEVAL STUDIES

All volumes in this series are evaluated by an Editorial Board, strictly on academic grounds, based on reports prepared by referees who have been commissioned by virtue of their specialism in the appropriate field. The Board ensures that the screening is done independently and without conflicts of interest. The definitive texts supplied by authors are also subject to review by the Board before being approved for publication. Further, the volumes are copyedited to conform to the publisher's stylebook and to the best international academic standards in the field.

Titles in Series

Transcultural Approaches to the Bible: Exegesis and Historical Writing in the Medieval Worlds, ed. by Matthias M. Tischler and Patrick S. Marschner (2021)

In Preparation

Maritime Exchange and the Making of Norman Worlds, ed. by Philippa Byrne and Caitlin Ellis